The Call to Teach

The Call to Teach

David T. Hansen

Teachers College, Columbia University
New York and London

Published by Teachers College Press, 1234 Amsterdam Avenue, New York, NY 10027

Library of Congress Cataloging-in-Publication Data

Hansen, David T., 1952–
    The call to teach / David T. Hansen.
      p.   cm.
    Includes bibliographical references and index.
    ISBN 0-8077-3469-1 (cloth : acid-free paper). — ISBN
0-8077-3468-3 (paper : acid-free paper)
     1. Teachers—Vocational guidance—United States. 2. Teaching—
United States. I. Title.
    LB1775.2.H35 1995
    371.1'00973—dc20   95-20148

ISBN 0-8077-3468-3 (paper)
ISBN 0-8077-3469-1 (cloth)

Printed on acid-free paper

Manufactured in the United States of America

02 01 00 99 98 97 96 95   8 7 6 5 4 3 2 1

To my mother, Anne, and to the
memory of my father, Lyle

Contents

Foreword

Over the last forty years as a scholar and practitioner, I have read many books about teachers and teaching. Some I have found so stimulating that they influenced what I thought, wrote, and did as a high school teacher, superintendent, and historian of education. I think of Seymour Sarason's *The Culture of the School and the Problem of Change*, Philip Jackson's *Life in Schools*, Dan Lortie's *Schoolteacher*, Willard Waller's *The Sociology of Teaching*, and David Tyack's *One Best System*. There are other books that I found provocative, wonderful experiences to read, but ultimately unconvincing and far less influential in my work.

Occasionally, however, I have come across a book that rediscovers in straightforward, clear prose an essential about teaching that I had either forgotten or so submerged in my experience and awareness that I no longer considered it. Moreover, in recovering a central feature of teaching, such a book asks seldom-explored questions. I recall that when I was teaching U.S. history at Roosevelt High School in Washington, DC, Jim Herndon's *The Way It Spozed to Be* and Herbert Kohl's *36 Children* directed my attention to how institutional values of the school and district worked against what I was trying to do with my classes and yet, even in the face of those organizational norms, these writers underscored that I still had the power to build a classroom community. Of course, I felt this in my gut but the power of each of these books, their anecdotes and revealing self-disclosure, helped me see it anew and it stuck.

David Hansen has written such a book—not a firsthand account such as Herndon's and Kohl's but a researcher's beautifully written, clear description and analysis of four teachers working with big-city children in public and private settings. Hansen sidesteps the familiar path trod by those who have written about teachers. He does not focus on teacher burnout in the face of dreadful working conditions and impossible expectations. He does not write about heroes or drudges, saints or incompetents. He captures ordinary teachers.

The teachers Hansen portrays for us belong to an invisible majority that gets no headlines and does not become the subject of television documentaries and films. He writes about teachers who have taught for years, enjoy what they do amid doubt and disappointment, receive the respect of their students and peers, and are looking forward to retiring. These teachers are the backbone of the nation's teaching corps; they stay in the profession because they find the work deeply satisfying. Hansen depicts teachers who serve the public well and find the work personally fulfilling. In doing so, he asks some puzzling questions about the nature of teaching in public and private institutions at a time when public officials worry about high drop-out rates among those entering the nation's classrooms.

I worry also about such attrition when I listen to my students who are preparing to be social studies teachers discuss their reactions to their more experienced colleagues in the public schools. These newcomers, who have come to teaching seeking the ideal of serving the young, watch veteran faculty in the lunchroom and listen to them at monthly staff meetings. Among these young student-teachers who think about their futures in the classroom unasked questions of their experienced peers hang in the air: How did she keep teaching five classes a day for fifteen years with so many rest-less and bored students? How did he keep grading those papers each week for twenty years? How did she keep her feelings under wraps all those years from the emotionally wearing lives of her students? Such questions ines-capably become condensed to one: How can I ever see myself as a teacher in five, ten, or more years if teaching is so hard and unforgiving?

Such questions also puzzle parents who know what it is like to deal with 2 or 3 children and wonder what it must be like to manage 30 or even 170 a day. When policymakers turn their attention to the workplace con-ditions that teachers face, they too must wonder how teachers can, year after year, deal with the uncertainty, the frustrations, and the sheer impossibility of meeting the conflicting expectations inherent to teaching.

While Hansen does not specifically ask these questions that puzzle new teachers, parents, and policymakers, I found his book addressing them in uncommon ways. What he does is recover from an earlier century words that have lost their original meaning in late-twentieth-century discussions of teaching. His rediscovery of the notion of "vocation" or "calling" as essential to the sustained practice of teaching—a combination of public service and personal fulfillment—becomes the central concept that explains why many competent teachers (neither heroes nor saints) not only stay in teaching but relish the challenge and treasure the personal freedom they have to shape what occurs in their classrooms.

Hansen watched these big-city public and private school teachers teach for two years; he listened to them as they struggled with their doubts; and he recorded their thoughts and feelings. He found that these four teachers somehow retained a vibrant hopefulness, knowing full well that they will again and again face disappointment over lapses in their performance and that of their students. This developing sense of vocation—it evolved over time—helped them manage the inexorable doubts that arose about what they did; it helped them grasp the wondrous thread of hope that makes teaching far more than just working in a school. His elegant language and the voices of these teachers ring true to my experience as a teacher and provide me with a deeper understanding of those veteran teachers with whom I have worked and whom I have admired over the last forty years in Cleveland, Washington, DC, and the Bay area.

Note, however, that Hansen does not offer this sense of vocation that he found in these four teachers as a cure for the wracking tensions and ills of big-city schools. Optimism vanishes in those who have come to know the daily struggles that children and teachers endure in these schools. Nor does he leap to policy recommendations for hiring or testing new teachers or some neatly packaged programs to instill this vocational impulse into flagging veteran teachers.

If optimism is a casualty of knowing more about urban schools, hope survives. What Hansen has found in these four teachers who entwine public service and personal fulfillment offers him hope in the very act of their teaching year after year. To teach is to be full of hope. The four teachers' spirit of vocation and how they voice it, enhanced by Hansen's graceful and vivid elaboration of their "calling," begins to offer us a language and a point of view that can make of teaching more than a "job," more than an "occupation," and even more than a "profession." After reading this book, I have come to share that hope also.

Larry Cuban

Preface

This book is about teaching as a vocation. I describe a vocation as a form of public service that yields enduring personal fulfillment to those who provide it. I make use of this idea to illuminate the working lives of four middle-school and high school teachers. I discuss the teachers' beliefs, their values, and their actions in the classroom. I show how the concept of vocation sheds light on why they continue to teach, and with conviction and success, despite the difficulties and challenges they and their colleagues everywhere face in today's schools.

I have framed the analysis that follows with a wide audience in mind. I intend it to serve as a mirror for teachers and for those preparing to teach. I hope that contemplating the idea of vocation will assist them in examining their self-understandings and their views of what the work entails. I hope to attract the attention of teachers who are dissatisfied and frustrated with their work. Adopting the perspective of vocation reveals productive and personally meaningful ways in which to renew oneself as teacher. It serves as a reminder of why many persons enter the ranks of teaching in the first place.

I have also written what follows for teacher educators, educational administrators and policymakers, researchers who study teaching, and parents and others who care about what is taking place in classrooms. To see teaching as a vocation invites reconsidering current assumptions about the nature of the practice and about how to understand what its practitioners do. I hope the book encourages rethinking methods of recruiting, preparing, and retaining good teachers.

I do not conceive this study as a contribution to the always expanding shelf of inspirational accounts of teaching. To speak of "calling" or "vocation" does necessitate the use of terms that are highly personalized, strongly normative, and even, at times, spiritual in their overtones. But this book is not a study of "exceptional" practitioners whose work should be viewed as an inspiration or as a model for others to follow. The teachers I describe do not consider themselves to be unusually effective, much less heroic or worthy of special recognition. They are dedicated to teaching and to their students' development, but perhaps in much the same way that serious-minded teachers everywhere are.

That being so, some immediate questions arise. Why feature their efforts in a book like this? Why attempt to understand what they do through the use of terms like "vocation" and "calling"? Aren't those terms too weighty for "ordinary" teachers, for those who strive to fulfill their obligations but not in ways that make news? Shouldn't such concepts be reserved for those who accomplish much and who do so in ways that capture the public's imagination— say, for example, the likes of Dr. Martin Luther King, Jr., or Mother Teresa?

The perhaps surprising answer to these last questions is no. I will argue throughout the book that the language of vocation brings us closer to what many "ordinary" teachers do, and why they do it, than do other current accounts of teaching such as those that emphasize occupational, political, and professional issues. Those issues are relevant to understanding the place of teaching in the educational system. For example, from an economic and organizational point of view teaching is an "occupation" rather than a vocation. In addition, teaching does have political aspects since teachers play a major role in the transmission of culture and knowledge; many also believe that teachers should play a central role in transforming knowledge and schooling, which, they imply, can lead to political change. Still others argue strongly in support of converting teaching into a profession on a par, say, with medicine and law. They claim that doing so will raise the prestige, the autonomy, and the dignity of teaching.

As important as those perspectives are, I will suggest that they remain conceptually and practically distant from what motivates and sustains teachers in their work. It is that motivation I will focus on in this book. Far from denoting something esoteric, restricted to an enlightened or heroic few, the idea of teaching as a vocation calls attention to the personal and service-oriented dimensions of the practice that draw people to it, and that enable them to find success despite adversity and difficulty. The notion of vocation highlights the quite recognizable convictions and faith that underlie many teachers' daily efforts.

*   *   *

I would like to be able to say that the idea for this book began with memories of teachers I had while growing up. But it has been the writing of the book itself that has brought to light for me what was distinctive and educational about being with Mrs. Abernethy in sixth-grade social studies, Mr. Utar in ninth-grade biology, Mrs. Rudski in sophomore English, and many others as well.

The actual motivation behind the book first took root in my work with an educational foundation that made available to teachers and schools a program intended to promote reading, reading comprehension, and critical thinking. For a number of years I traveled to more than thirty-five states. I met for several days at a time in seminars with groups of between twenty and forty teachers and adult volunteers. I taught seminars in small towns in Minnesota where it seemed that every adult within miles was in attendance (sometimes, along with their infants!). I taught public school teachers in urban Detroit, in rural Texas, in the industrial towns of Pennsylvania, in suburban Atlanta, and in Brooklyn. Over the course of those years I met several thousand teachers. I left almost every seminar I taught impressed with the number who cared deeply for their students and who sought to enrich their own knowledge and their ability to teach. I also met enough inadequately prepared and dispirited teachers to confirm just how demanding the practice of teaching is, and how vital are opportunities for continued learning and renewal.

The practical origins of this book reside in my work as a research assistant in a study called the Moral Life of Schools Project. That undertaking took place between January 1988 and June 1990, and was funded by the Spencer Foundation and directed by Philip W. Jackson at the University of Chicago. It included a third researcher, Robert Boostrom, who now teaches at the University of Southern Indiana. The project was an investigation of the moral influence that schools and teachers have on the students placed in their care. We published some results from the project in a book by the same name, *The Moral Life of Schools* (Jackson, Boostrom, & Hansen, 1993).

There were eighteen teachers involved in the project, including nine middle-school and high school teachers whose practices became the focus of my own research. Three teach in a public school, three in a Catholic school, and three in an independent school, all in a large urban setting. The subjects they teach include English, mathematics, physical education, religious studies, and social studies; one is in Special Education. The length of their experience varies from two years to nearly thirty. As that earlier study of the moral dimensions of schooling unfolded, I began more and more to think about the personal philosophies animating the teachers' work, and about what might account for their sense of satisfaction or of fulfillment as teachers. In the course of my research I began to note and to record anything that might prove to be of value in a study of this topic. As it turned out, there was a great deal to attend to: I observed over 400 classes taught by the teachers; I observed their interaction with students, peers, and others in their schools; and I conversed with them innumerable times in both formal and informal circumstances. When the project concluded, and after I had settled into my current position at the University of Illinois at Chicago,

I sought an opportunity to analyze from the perspective of vocation the extensive data I had collected. I am grateful to the National Academy of Education for a Spencer Post-Doctoral Fellowship, which between 1992 and 1994 provided the means for me to accomplish this task and to write this book.

Edward Buckbee, Janice Ozga, and Marybeth Peebles read the entire manuscript with care and raised many helpful questions. I thank them warmly for their frankness and thoroughness. Jonathan B. Imber of Wellesley College generously provided useful references. He also questioned my emphasis in the book on the "sense of vocation" rather than on "vocation" itself. He may not agree with my response to his question, but he should know how wise his criticism has been. Several audiences and individuals provided helpful reactions to earlier versions of my conception of teaching as a vocation: Joseph Kahne; Michelle Parker; Michelle Pierczynski-Ward; the John Dewey discussion group that Philip W. Jackson runs at the University of Chicago; Sophie Haroutunian-Gordon and her students at Northwestern University; the audience at the 50th annual meeting of the Philosophy of Education Society, which met in Charlotte, North Carolina, in March 1994; the audience at the National Academy of Education Spencer Fellows Forum held in New Orleans, Louisiana, in April 1994; and the doctoral students in my Fall 1994 Conceptions of Teaching and Schooling course. I remain responsible for the interpretations in the book and for any errors it contains.

Earlier versions of parts of Chapters 1 and 5 are published, respectively, in *Educational Theory* (Vol. 44, 1994) and *Curriculum Inquiry* (Vol. 22, 1992). They appear here in reworked form with the kind permission of both journals.

Brian Ellerbeck of Teachers College Press has been a strong supporter of this project from its inception. I deeply appreciate his sustained assistance, his timely encouragement, and his intellectual curiosity.

While I was writing the book, my wife, Elaine Fuchs, continued as ever to provide a remarkable example of what vocation means. In addition to supporting my own hopes and endeavors, she always shares with me her joys and her frustrations as a university teacher and researcher in molecular biology. Without knowing it, she reveals both the spirit of dedication and the often immense personal satisfaction that reside at the heart of vocation. Her presence in my life infuses whatever may prove useful to others in this study of teaching.

Finally, I am grateful to the four teachers whose practice I describe in the chapters to come. Although by prior agreement I employ pseudonyms, I want to record my appreciation for their willingness to permit me to become a more or less permanent visitor to their classrooms. I do not claim to have captured them as they "really" are as teachers, and this for at least two reasons. One is that the bulk of the data I present and analyze was collected during a two-and-a-half-year period that is now itself a number of years in the past. If the conception of vocation that underlies this book is sound, these teachers are today different practitioners—with respect to the contours of their beliefs and actions—than when I sat in the back of their rooms and conversed with them in hallways and school cafeterias. They will no longer be the same as they appear in the pages of this book. Second, like persons everywhere they are far too complicated and distinct for any one individual to come close to understanding. The philosopher Ludwig Wittgenstein once wrote a letter that helps explain this point. He was responding to his sister's dismay that he was going to "throw away" his academic career, as she put it, in order to teach elementary school in a remote Austrian village. His sister told him that, given his exceptional mind, he was acting like "somebody wanting to use a precision instrument to open crates." Wittgenstein told her how far she was from perceiving his thinking on the issue. "You remind me," he replied, "of somebody who is looking out through a closed window and cannot explain to himself the strange movements of a passer-by. He cannot tell what sort of storm is raging out there or that this person might only be managing with difficulty to stay on his feet" (Monk, 1990, p. 170).

Like every classroom researcher I, too, have been looking through something of a window. How open or closed it proved to be will be for readers to judge. However, I did have the opportunity to observe on average forty of each of the teachers' classes, and to talk with them in formal and informal circumstances many more times than that. This extended classroom observation, and the many conversations I held with the teachers, provided insight into their working worlds. Of course the window to which Wittgenstein refers can never be completely removed. One can never fully understand, much less adequately convey to others, another person's experience. But it is a good thing that such windows exist and can be opened, even if only part way. Otherwise we would truly remain strangers to one another, and teaching would be impossible.

1

Teaching as a Vocation

Sometimes it takes five words
of buoyant, tensile English
to explain one ancient leathery word.
—Diana Der-Hovanessian, "Translating"

"Teaching" and "vocation" are ancient and well-worn terms. The Old English root of teaching, *taecan*, means to show, to instruct, or, in more literal terms, to provide signs or outward expressions of something one knows. As typically understood, teaching means leading others to know what they did not know before—for example, algebra or the geography of a continent. It means leading others to know how to do things they could not do before—for example, how to prepare chemical solutions or how to play a sport. It means leading others to take on attitudes or orientations they did not embody before—for instance, to enjoy reading rather than just knowing how to read. And it means leading others to believe things they did not believe before—for example, that they can master certain skills and techniques and that doing so is worthwhile. Teaching comprises all these activities, and more. It can give rise to enduring and formative feelings, hopes, and understandings, in students and teachers alike.

The Latin root of vocation, *vocare*, means "to call." It denotes a summons or bidding to be of service. It has been used to describe both secular and religious commitments. For example, some persons have felt called or "inspired" by divine purposes to join a religious order and to serve faithfully a given community. They have become ministers, nuns, priests, rabbis, missionaries, or pastors. Others have felt impelled to serve not divine purposes but rather human ones. They have felt called to human society with its manifold needs and possibilities. Many nurses, doctors, politicians, lawyers, and teachers have felt the kind of magnetic pull toward a life of service exemplified in the idea of vocation. So have other persons engaged in activities not so readily associated with public service. For example, many artists, carpenters, laboratory scientists, parents, and athletes have felt inexorably drawn to what they do, deriving from it enduring fulfillment and meaning while also, in many cases, contributing something of social value.

In this introductory chapter, I draw together these old but still vivid terms. I sketch a conception of teaching as a vocation. I begin by examining the idea of vocation itself. I do so at some length, and this for two reasons. One is that the term connotes different meanings in some quarters today than what I have just ascribed to it. Before the onset of the Industrial Revolution two hundred years ago, vocation was understood to describe a life of service and devotion carried out under a religious impulse. That meaning continues to hold in some ecclesiastical institutions, although according to Gustafson (1982) its use there appears to be waning. To many people today, vocation is likely to call to mind purely economic considerations. For example, the familiar terms "vocational education" and "vocational guidance" describe efforts to prepare persons for specific forms of employment. In contrast, the notion of vocation I will elucidate centers neither on religious nor on economic motives per se.

A second reason why I spell out at length a conception of vocation here is that studies of teaching that employ the idea are rare. Works by Booth (1988), Gotz (1988), and Huebner (1987) are among the very few that come to mind. Booth (1988) illustrates his sense of calling by discussing his career as an English professor and by analyzing the value of English in the university curriculum. Gotz (1988) draws on the idea to criticize the notion of "profession" and to advance a view of teaching as an art. Huebner (1987) emphasizes an ideal of service to the young and strongly criticizes what he sees as institutional impediments to the enactment of a personal calling as teacher.

No study of which I am aware attempts to show, as I do in this book, how teaching as a vocation appears in actual practice in today's schools. No other inquiry that I know of argues in as systematic a manner as I will do that teaching as a vocation comprises a form of public service to others that at the same time provides the individual a sense of identity and personal fulfillment. In light of these aims, and to prepare the ground for the analysis to come, I first take the reader through a philosophical discussion of the idea of vocation. In the ensuing section of the chapter, I apply that analysis to the practice of teaching. This framework serves as a conceptual lens for the four chapters that form the center of the book. In each of those chapters I describe in detail the views and the work of one teacher. In the final two chapters of the book I take up questions raised in the discussion. I show how responding to them highlights the value of the idea of vocation to all who care about teaching and its impact on students.

A PERSPECTIVE ON VOCATION

The sense of vocation finds its expression at the crossroads of public obligation and personal fulfillment. It takes shape through involvement in work that has social meaning and value. This means that a great many occupations can have a vocational dimension. Medicine, law, and teaching come promptly to mind as examples. However, other activities such as athletics and gardening can be vocations, too, provided that practitioners have in view more than their own self-satisfaction. In many societies, athletics involve considerable teamwork and social loyalty and are often treated as helping to sustain a community's sense of identity. In Japanese culture, among others, gardening often embodies an important public meaning that takes it well beyond the realm of personal hobby. However, if a gardener's work was never shared with others, or never intended for others, then, according to the argument here, the activity would not be considered vocational (although it would still count as "gardening"). The activity must have more than a purely personal significance. For it to be a vocation, it must yield social value to others. It must be educative, edifying, helpful to others in some characteristic way.

However, vocation does not imply a one-way subordination of the person to the practice. Vocation describes work that is fulfilling and meaningful to the individual, such that it helps provide a sense of self, of personal identity. Again, this means that many activities can qualify as vocational, provided that they continue to meet the criterion of being of social value. However, being a teacher, a minister, a doctor, or a nurse would *not* be vocational if the individual kept the practice at arm's length, divorced from his or her sense of identity, and treated it simply as one among many interchangeable forms of employment. In such a case, the person would be merely an occupant of a role. This is not to say the person would conceive the activity as meaningless or would act in a mindless or mechanical fashion. He or she might regard it strictly as a job, as a necessary means to secure the time or the resources to do something else. Nonetheless, in addition to being of social value, an activity must yield a sense of personal fulfillment in its own right in order to be a vocation.

In short, a vocation describes work that results in service to others and personal satisfaction in the rendering of that service. However, this composite understanding must be clarified and extended.

Vocation Is Expressed Over Time

In principle, a person can serve the public and feel pleased in doing so by merely holding a door open for a few colleagues on the way into work.

Such an act may take five seconds. But a vocation emerges over a far longer period of time. As I outline below—and illustrate in subsequent chapters—a person with a vocational orientation toward teaching may wait and prepare for years before actually entering the ranks. Moreover, the person might engage in the practice for years before he or she genuinely begins to feel it to be a vocation and to treat it as such while working in the school and classroom. Many teachers, doctors, nurses, and ministers can attest to the fact that it takes considerable time to appreciate both what their work requires of them and how they can best fulfill it.

In brief, a person cannot "will" a sense of service into existence, nor wake up one day and "decide" to be of service. Those dispositions grow and take shape over time, through interaction with people and through the attempt to perform the work well.

Some Activities Cannot Be Vocations

Although many endeavors can qualify as vocational, some are ruled out of consideration entirely regardless of the personal meaning they may provide. Being a professional thief, for example, or a drug-dealer, are instances. Shakespeare's character Falstaff is off-base when he asserts, in *Henry IV, Part I*, "Why, Hal, 'tis my vocation, Hal; 'tis no sin for a man to labour in his vocation" (Act I, Scene 2, lines 104–105). As Falstaff well knows, it is a "sin" if the "vocation" is stealing from others. Such a practice characteristically has no social value.

Vocation Is Not Selfless Devotion

To some readers, the idea of vocation may call to mind the term's historical associations with Christian belief and practice. According to that perspective, the concept originally implied qualities such as selfless devotion, self-abnegation, an ascetic way of life, and a certain submission to the Divine. Later, in part through the Reformation that began in the sixteenth century, vocation came to denote a secular calling, but one into which one was born and which was to be carried out in a spirit of service to Christian religious and ethical aims (Emmet, 1958; Hardy, 1990; Holl, 1958). Hardy (1990) describes how the Puritans distinguished between a "general" and a "particular" calling. The former implied being called to a Christian way of life regardless of one's secular occupation. The "particular" vocation was the specific activity in which one labored, which would of course differ from those of many other Christians.

The understanding of vocation that guides this book is neither a Christian nor a religious one per se. However, valuable lessons for teaching can be drawn from the religious conception of vocation. For example, analogous to the Puritans' distinction between a general and a particular call, one can separate feeling called to teaching in a general sense—"I want to be a teacher"—from a desire to teach a particular subject or age level of students—"I want to teach high school biology." Furthermore, there will always be occasions when a teacher must be self-abnegating or even submissive to a higher end in working with students. A teacher may need in a very basic way to bracket his or her self-interest in order see what a child is struggling to say, to do, or even to become. Finally, some teachers may discover that strictly occupational or functional language is inadequate for describing why they teach. They may find themselves resorting to language with spiritual overtones, speaking, for example, of their hopes for and faith in their students.

In subsequent chapters I illustrate just how true is this last claim. However, I also argue that the idea of teaching as a vocation is best captured not through the idiom of ascetic self-denial, but much more through a family of words such as *active, creative, engaged, outward-looking*, and *imaginative*, which I return to in due course.

Vocation Has Social Rather Than Purely Psychological Origins

The idea of vocation denotes more than an inner or psychological state. It does presume on the part of the individual a hopeful, outward-looking sentiment, a feeling of wanting to engage the world in some substantive way. It presupposes an "inner urge," as Emmet (1958) puts it, to "venture and devote oneself in working in a first-hand kind of way" (p. 255). Those terms are carefully chosen. To "venture" forth raises the image of an adventure, a plunge into an activity whose outcome will be at least to some extent uncertain and unpredictable. To "devote" oneself in the doing of it recalls one of the original meanings of the term vocation—to commit oneself in an enduring way to a particular practice.

These internal motivations are important. However, they are only part of the story. A social practice is the other part, making it possible to *bring these motivations to life*, in the literal sense of those terms. Vocation cannot exist as a state of mind alone, disembodied or removed from a practice. As understood here, the sense of vocation is not something the person "possesses," and can "choose" to "apply" to a particular kind of work, or across many different kinds of work. Rather, it is a set of impulses that are outward-looking and outward-moving, focused on what is calling one to act. The idea of vocation presupposes a social practice in which to enact one's inner urge to contribute to the world.

Moreover, a "practice" is distinct from the institution in which one carries out its terms (MacIntyre, 1984). Practicing medicine is not identical to working in a hospital. Teaching is not the same thing as working in schools (Huebner, 1987; Jackson, 1986), even though the bulk of it takes place in those settings. The practice of teaching is much older than any particular school and, if history serves as a reliable guide, will outlast any particular institution in existence today. I make use of this historical perspective throughout the book and return to it at length in Chapter 6. However, I distinguish practice from institution here in order to reemphasize that the former has a certain priority over an individual's sense of being called to it. Put differently, the *vocation* proper precedes what I call the "sense" of vocation, that is, the sense of being drawn to the kind of work it represents.

Another way of making this point is to say that the inner motivation to serve that a person may feel is socially rooted. It is not manufactured by the person out of thin air. A person could hardly develop the desire to engage the world and to serve others *without* having been exposed, for a substantial period of time, to that world itself. Many are drawn to teaching because of teachers they have had, because of subjects they have studied and enjoyed, and because of young people they have known or with whom they have worked. In other words, the call to teach comes from what they have seen and experienced *in* the world, not solely from what they may have "heard" in their inner heart and mind. The sense of being impelled to act from within is coterminous with a sense of being called by something without.

Vocation Is Distinct from Other Activities

Vocation differs from other, familiar terms used to describe teaching, such as "job," "work," "career," "occupation," and "profession."

From the perspective of this book, a "job" is an activity that provides sustenance or survival. Jobs comprise highly repetitive tasks whose content is not defined by those performing them (say, working at a fast-food restaurant). The root meaning of job is *lump*, that is, an object or product—a meaning that leaves completely out of the picture the human being who performs the activity. Vocations are often sources of sustenance and survival, too, but they go well beyond jobs in terms of both personal autonomy and personal significance.

"Work" contrasts with job in that it describes an endeavor whose content the worker can define. The doing of it can yield genuine personal meaning. However, while work can contribute centrally to a person's sense of worth and self, it need not imply being of service to others. It need not involve participating in a practice, like teaching, that has its own built-in obligations and responsibilities toward others. As I understand the terms, one can speak of a hermit's "work," which could be deeply fulfilling to the individual, but not of a hermit's "vocation." As mentioned, the idea of vocation presupposes public service, in the sense, for example, that what the person does is conducted *publicly* and involves serving some particular *public*. An exception might be made of a person who lived a hermit's life praying for the well-being of others; but that life would still lack an overtly public dimension.

A "career" describes a long-term, sometimes lifelong involvement in a particular activity. Its original meaning is street or road—the Middle French term *carriere*—suggesting a route or direction. The term highlights the temporal dimension of work; for example, a person begins at a particular age and retires at a later one. The term has been applied to almost every conceivable type of job or work. A factory worker, a city employee, a professional athlete, an artist, a scholar, all can have a career. As many persons could attest, one's career can also coincide with one's vocation. However, from the perspective of this book career differs from vocation in similar ways that job and work do. For example, it need not imply pursuing an endeavor that provides personal fulfillment, a sense of identity, being of public service, and so forth. A person's career can provide lifelong economic support, obviously a central human value, but little more than that in terms of the meaning a life has had.

Moreover, the term is sometimes employed independently of particular activities. A person might say, "I have had a good career," and encompass in that phrase many different jobs. From this point of view career is too individualistic a concept for my purposes here. It can even imply manipulation, for example, changing from one job to another when the going gets tough rather than coming to grips with what a particular activity calls on one to do. As I have contended, vocation entails allegiance to a practice, not just to one's own personal preferences. (Incidentally, biologists have been known to speak of the "career" of a skin cell as it moves from the epidermis to the dermis; the "career" of a lion, as it grows from birth to taking its place in a pride; and more. As far as we know, however, cells and lions do not have vocations.)

An "occupation" is an endeavor harbored within an institution, which in turn is nested within a society's economic, social, and political system. From this perspective teaching is one occupation among several housed in schools, which, in turn, constitute one structural level in the educational establishment. However, persons can occupy positions without enacting a sense of calling. In contrast, the teachers I describe in subsequent chapters sometimes question whether they are "really" teachers. Their questions are not occupational—they certainly *are* teachers from an organizational point of view. Rather, they sometimes wonder about their effectiveness, their impact on students, and their reasons for taking on the role. As I will make plain, those questions are vocational rather than occupational in nature. The teachers also ask questions that can be seen as defining occupational rather than vocational boundaries, for example, to what extent they are expected to take on certain responsibilities hitherto left to others in the system.

Finally, the idea of a "profession" enlarges that of an occupation by emphasizing the expertise and the social contribution that persons in an occupation render to society. One original meaning of the term is "public declaration." Persons in an occupation—like medicine—can come to perceive themselves as fulfilling more than an institutionalized function. Rather, they can advertise the fact that they bring to bear specialized skill and knowledge acquired through careful, accredited training. They can publicize the codes of conduct to which they adhere regarding the use of that knowledge and skill. They can seek to increase their status, their prestige, and their autonomy from external guidance and control. They can try to augment the rewards their members earn, all of this in the face of other professions that compete for public respect and support (Abbott, 1988; Freidson, 1994; Kimball, 1992).

The notion that professionals owe allegiance to a code of conduct (whether formalized or not) and must be well prepared for their work reveals how the concept overlaps that of vocation. As mentioned previously, vocation presupposes a social practice with its built-in obligations and responsibilities. Moreover, feeling called to an endeavor does *not* imply that one will be good at it. The sense of vocation does not obviate the need for good preparation for the tasks one is called to perform.

However, at least two points distinguish a profession from a vocation as conceived here. First, as with the meaning of an occupation, persons can conduct themselves professionally but not regard the work as a calling. Professionals can fulfill their duties while deriving their sense of identity and personal fulfillment elsewhere (for example, in family or in hobbies, crafts, and arts). I return to this point in Chapter 7 when I respond to the question of whether teachers should see their work as a vocation. Second, the emphasis in the idea of profession on public recognition, greater autonomy, larger rewards, and the like takes one away from the everyday personal and moral dimensions of teaching. In contrast, vocation takes us "inward" into the core of the practice itself. The language of vocation brings us closer to what many teachers do, and why they do it, than does the language of job, work, occupation, or profession.

I am not aware of any previous studies that distinguish these terms in the way I have outlined here. (More extended discussions of the history and nature of work include Arendt, 1958; Bailey, 1976; Green, 1964; Jordan, 1949; Mintz, 1978; and Pieper, 1952.) I continue to clarify and illuminate the terms throughout the remainder of the book. As I do so, it should also become clear that my use of the idea of vocation differs from what is called "vocational education." As mentioned previously, that term describes programs in schools and in technical and training institutes to provide persons with the skills and capacities for specific forms of wage-based employment. This understanding of vocation is not what I am treating here.

VOCATION AND THE TEACHER

I have contended that the concept "vocation" describes work that has social value and that provides enduring personal meaning. In this section, I examine the relevance of that conception for teaching.

Teaching is a social practice whose importance is unquestioned, even if what makes it important remains the subject of continued debate. Teachers work in public environments, under the scrutiny of their students, their peers, their administrators, parents, and other concerned adults. Though much of their work may be conducted within the confines of the classroom, what goes on there is rarely left at the door. It becomes part of the lives of individual students, part of the life of the school, and often a central part of the life of the teacher. Teachers can play a significant role in what young people learn, in how they learn to learn, in how they come to view learning itself. They can influence young people's personal dispositions toward others, and toward their own futures. Their influence, for good or for ill, can extend well beyond the duration of schooling; anyone who remembers teachers they have had can readily attest to this.

In light of these understandings, what does it mean to suggest that a teacher, or a person who wants to teach, has a sense of vocation? What does it mean to say that a person has a strong and persistent inclination to teach? What difference does it make whether one describes that disposition with the language of vocation as contrasted with more familiar terms such as "occupational choice," "career decision," and the like?

For one thing, to do so suggests that the person regards teaching as more than simply a choice among the array of jobs available in society. It may even mean for such a person that there is something false about describing the desire to teach as a choice at all. An individual who is strongly inclined toward teaching seems to be a person who is not debating *whether* to teach but rather is contemplating *how* or *under what circumstances* to do so. The person may be considering teaching in schools, in institutions of higher education, or in one of many other settings—from military bases to visitors' centers—in which teaching can occur. But it may be years before such a person actually takes action. He or she may work for a long time in other lines of endeavor—business, law, parenting, the medical field—before the right conditions materialize. Those conditions can encompass both practical issues and psychological concerns such as whether the person finally feels "ready" to give teaching a try. The posture outlined here in fact describes many persons who are entering teaching today (Crow, Levine, & Nager, 1990). In addition, many such persons appear to develop their interest in teaching independently of the advice of an employment counselor (cf. Hardy, 1990). (There is a substantial literature on vocation in which the term is conceived purely as a job choice; see, e.g., Carpenter & Foster, 1979; Holland, 1973; Mitchell, Ortiz, & Mitchell, 1987; Pavalko, 1970.)

To describe the inclination to teach as a budding vocation also calls attention to the individual's sense of agency. It implies that the person knows something about him- or herself, something important, valuable, worth acting on. One may have been drawn to teaching because of one's own teachers or as a result of other outside influences. Still, the fact remains that now one has taken on that interest oneself. The idea of teaching "occupies" the person's thoughts and imagination. Again, this suggests that one conceives of teaching as more than a job, as more than a way to earn an income, although this consideration is obviously relevant. Rather, one believes teaching to be potentially meaningful, as the way to instantiate one's desire to contribute to and engage with the world.

That stance presupposes, in turn, that one assumes human striving itself to be worthwhile. It takes for granted that the person presumes (whether consciously so or not) that he or she has something to offer—something, perhaps, that no one else can provide. Writing about religious novices, Lesage (1966) contends that each should behave "as if he felt that he was selected for a task that no one else could perform" (p. 104). Only by assuming this attitude, Lesage claims, can novices throw themselves into the work of service and devotion and, thereby, experience the fullness of their calling. According to Emmet (1958), who discusses secular as well as religious practices, vocation describes activities that

> individuals can only undertake because they have certain personal qualities. One person cannot fulfil the vocation of another, as one might step in and perform another's function, or instruct someone else to carry out a purposive action which he had planned. Vocation does not admit of interchangeability. The office of prophet may be an institutionalized role within certain societies. Yet if the mantle of Elijah falls upon Elisha, it may also be because Elisha is himself a certain kind of person. (pp. 6–7)

Emmet means that individuals who conduct their work as a vocation will perform it in a unique way, in part because of their distinctive qualities and character as persons. (Emmet does not treat teachers or education in her book, which is a sociological and philosophical study of the relation of individuals to their society and the roles it contains. However, her ideas about vocation are provocative and I cite and make use of several throughout this book.)

Teachers are not prophets, but neither are they interchangeable, at least if one grants that teachers do more than mechanically transmit a mandated body of knowledge. I discuss this viewpoint in detail in Chapter 7, after I have had the opportunity to present to readers the views and practices of several teachers. However, one of my reasons for seeking in this book to revitalize the idea of vocation in teaching is to underscore the centrality of the *person* who occupies the role. Despite a host of common obligations and practices, no two teachers have the same personal and moral impact on students (Jackson et al., 1993). For better or for worse, every teacher has a distinct and varying influence on students' orientations toward learning, toward knowledge, toward other people. Moreover, those differences have to do with a lot more than overt dissimilarities in personality and teaching style (Hansen, 1993a). They have to do with the ethos of the person, his or her characteristic conduct when in the presence of students, his or her reputation, expectations, hopes, fears, worries. The relationship between a teacher and students is invariably a moral one, even if that relationship is cold or impersonal or aloof—for those qualities themselves constitute messages about how to interact with others and how to regard and treat what people accomplish. These claims support the notion that an individual thinking about becoming a teacher may indeed have something to offer that nobody else can provide—even if the person may not appreciate (as yet) what that "something" might turn out to be.

This last caveat calls attention to the fact that while a person may have a strong inclination to teach, he or she may have equally strong questions about it and about his or her fitness for the work. One can conceive teaching as a vocation and still harbor real doubts about how successful one might be (or is) in the classroom. Doubt and commitment can go hand in hand, as the lives of many well-known figures show. For example, Emmet (1958) recalls how some of the Hebrew prophets questioned themselves and their suitability to meet the "call" they heard: "'I am only a dresser of sycamores' . . . 'a child' . . . 'a herdsman.' 'Why *me* to go and talk to these people?'" (p. 254). The uncertainties and doubts that accompany teaching have been well documented, as have the depths of self-questioning those states can trigger (Floden & Clark, 1988; Huberman, Grounauer, & Marti, 1993; Jackson, 1986; Rose, 1989; Sikes, Measor, & Woods, 1985). Teachers often cannot know for sure whether their students have learned the material, much less whether their efforts have contributed to students' intellectual and moral well-being. Yet such doubts need not lead to paralysis—nor to abandoning teaching or its prospect altogether. On the contrary, some have argued that the unknown and the unmeasurable in the practice invite creativity and an individualized response on the part of the teacher, and render teaching the compelling work it is to so many (Huebner, 1987; McDonald, 1992; van Manen, 1991).

Moreover, commitment to a practice *without* entertaining doubts about it can border on ideology or close-mindedness. Brann (1979) describes an ideology as a system of ideas, beliefs, and thoughts that is closed to further questioning. The idea of teaching as a vocation does not, in this sense, imply holding to an ideology. It describes an inclination to teach that can coexist with lifelong questions and doubts—about how teaching really "happens," about its impact on students and teachers alike, and about whether one is truly suited to the work. Vocation connotes a disposition to be of service in a form that can evolve as one responds to one's circumstances—to the changing needs of students, to the changing shape of knowledge. This orientation is not so much ideological as it is temperamental. Keats touched on it in his praise for Shakespeare. He attributed Shakespeare's successful art to what Keats calls his "negative capability," that is, his capacity to accept uncertainty and doubt and to refuse to reach for easy answers or intellectual crutches (Forman, 1935, p. 72).

Teaching seems to require something of this capability—if not to the depths of a Shakespeare—if a person is to remain meaningfully engaged in it. It is a truism that the work is full of surprises: classroom lessons that lead to unexpected questions and insights; lessons that fail despite elaborate planning; spur-of-the-moment activities that work beautifully and that may change the direction of a course; students who grow and learn; students who seem to regress or grow distant. The wonder is how a person could willingly accept and also learn from this barrage of joy, disappointment, surprise, sadness, and delight without being borne by a sense of vocation. However, the point here is that that sense does not presume a form of social zealotry. Persons with vocational orientations are not necessarily "heroic," a point I return to below. The sense of vocation implies a measure of determination, courage, and flexibility, qualities that are in turn buoyed by the disposition to regard teaching as something more than a job, to which one has something significant to offer.

To regard teaching as vocational further presumes a sense of it (however inchoate) as an activity whose meaning is larger than the sum of its parts. It is larger than carrying out a finite number of prespecified duties and responsibilities, with a preordained set of rewards as compensation. Emmet (1958) argues that a person with a sense of vocation will often not know

> just where it is going to take him. This is because he will not merely be carrying out a specified function according to recognized norms, but will be feel-

ing out after new possibilities in ways of thinking and working. So one stage may open up further possibilities to another, and he will find that he has to go on and on. He cannot set himself a limited objective and then call it a day, as he could if he were just doing a job according to established norms. . . . There will be an inner incentive which prevents [the] person from treating his work as a routine job with limited objectives. (pp. 254–255)

In metaphorical terms, teaching is felt by a person with vocational dispositions as constituting more than carrying brick, mortar, and shovel. Rather, it implies being the architect of one's classroom world. A person who wants to teach doubtless hopes, at some level of thought or feeling, to have a say in what aims and purposes will guide the classroom, as well as in how those goals might be realized. This means supplementing and possibly extending the functional requirements of the job. It may mean questioning some of those requirements. For example, rather than just "delivering the goods," a teacher may find himself or herself paying increased attention to what students say, think, and feel about what they are learning. This posture also implies that the person with a sense of vocation will be his or her own final critic, a stance that seems to accompany any work perceived as more than routine.

An additional test of a vocation, according to Smith (1934), "is the love of the drudgery it involves" (p. 182). Smith's pithy formulation is hyperbolic. Still, every vocation embodies its share of mundane chores, and teaching is no exception. Teachers have to straighten up their classrooms, keep their materials organized, listen to innumerable questions and concerns, and much more. Some might say that it is precisely those everyday doings that, knit together over time, can undergird a sense of meaning and fulfillment in the work. Just as an enduring memory of a journey comes from having attended to specific events and obstacles along the way, so part of the satisfaction that can derive from vocation comes from paying attention to its details. This is not to say that a person with a vocational orientation toward teaching must bring to the practice a refined sense of perception. Rather, it means the person is disposed to be attentive to detail and nuance; he or she has the initial sensibility to develop alertness to what is going on in the classroom. Nor is it to romanticize the "drudgery" — the *need* to address details. Rather, it is to emphasize that the repetitive obligations of teaching are not a distraction from the vocation but constitute part of the main event itself, the locus where all the individual steps one takes add up to both the teacher one becomes and the influence one has on one's students.

The metaphor of architect highlights the elements of agency and autonomy embodied in the idea of vocation. Other things being equal, a person with a sense of service comes to inhabit the role more fully than does a person who sees it as only a job. This does not imply that the former will necessarily be better at discharging the responsibilities of the role. A vocational disposition toward one's work brings no guarantee of results. A feeling that one has something to offer does not translate by itself into qualities that actually make a difference. However, a vocational orientation does imply that the person will be more likely to try to shape the role of teacher, to give it an original and creative stamp. At first glance, that distinctive touch may be hard to perceive. A casual or short-term visitor to a classroom may feel there is nothing new or at least nothing noteworthy about what the teacher is doing. But that impression may change the more one witnesses classroom proceedings, at least if one presumes that a teacher who is engaged in the work tends, as argued earlier, to leave a personalized imprint on what takes place there. The fact that that imprint may come to the surface slowly rather than immediately says nothing about the strength of the teacher's sense of vocation or about his or her possible effectiveness. It attests more to the nature of teaching itself, a practice whose impact and consequences tend to emerge over time, often in uneven and unpredictable ways. Emmet (1958) is right that enacting vocation requires "creativeness within [one's] role" (p. 242). With respect to teaching, however, that creativeness may take subtle forms. It may require time to perceive and to understand. Moreover, it may continue to take new forms, because of changing social and cultural conditions—leading, for example, to new views of what students ought to know—and because of changes in the teacher—resulting, for example, in a deeper appreciation of what the young can do.

For these reasons the idea of teaching as a vocation should not be associated solely with persons of unusual stature or energy, whose doings sometimes end up being widely publicized within a particular school or beyond. Such individuals often dramatize qualities that others simply enact more quietly. As mentioned, the fact that a teacher's creativity and originality may express itself subtly does not by itself call into question the possible impact that teacher may have on students. A teacher's intellectual and moral influence on others can derive as much from a kind of everyday continuity in his or her practice as from heroic efforts.

Furthermore, the idea of vocation does not imply the redemptive motive of "saving" others that is associated with some religious and secular practices. Albert Schweitzer used to advise would-be medical helpers who came out to Africa in order to "do something special," as they put it, to go back home unless they understood that the work they could do there was not, as he put it, "something out of the ordinary." Schweitzer would recommend that they turn around unless they had "no thought of heroism" but rather appreciated the sense of a "duty undertaken with sober enthusiasm" (quoted in Emmet, 1958, p. 254). Schweitzer's counsel implies that along with a desire to engage the world, the sense of vocation presumes a certain mixture of realism and humility, at least in incipient form. Those qualities would seem to make possible a more respectful appraisal of oneself and one's setting.

In summary, what I have said in this section about teaching as a vocation reduces to several points. One is that the person regards teaching as more than a job, although income and other practical considerations remain important. The person brings a sense of agency and commitment to the work that, in turn, embodies the belief that he or she has something to contribute to it. However, the notion of being "called," of having something distinctive to offer teaching, does not imply a kind of blind faith in one's capabilities or desires. Rather, teaching as a vocation goes hand in hand with questions, doubts, and uncertainties, some generated by the nature of the work, some by the sheer fact that the person treats the work as more than a routine task (any endeavor that is not routine seems to involve unpredictability). In addition, one regards the work as larger than fulfilling its discrete requirements, although the details of practice are also seen as worthy of attention.

I also argued that the sense of vocation can come to life only in a social practice. Moreover, social practices like teaching, nursing, ministering, have their own integrity. They have their own identities that must be balanced with the individual's uniqueness or sense of service. To argue that teachers are not interchangeable is not to imply that they "own" teaching. The weight is as much on the other side of the coin: Without the practice of teaching, would-be teachers would have no context in which to act. Teaching presupposes a social medium that provides many of the meanings associated with it. Persons do not simply invent those meanings out of whole cloth. They are meanings characteristically associated with helping others learn and improve themselves intellectually and morally. In brief, would-be teachers step into a practice with traditions undergirding it, with layers of public significance built up over generations. The sense of teaching as a vocation presumes a willingness to engage with the public obligations that go with the task, to recognize that one is part of an evolving tradition.

This framework constitutes a way of looking at and thinking about teaching. It is the point of view that guides the next four chapters, each of which focuses on the work of a single practitioner. I turn to a brief preview of those chapters now.

PROSPECTIVE

The four teachers readers will meet work in an urban setting in a large midwestern city. Ms. Payton teaches in a public school that serves nearly

2,000 students in grades seven through twelve; 75% of the students are black, 20% white, and 5% Asian and Hispanic. Ms. Payton, who was in her late thirties at the time of my research, teaches physical science to high-achieving seventh graders, and to classes composed of high school students of varying grades who have done poorly in science up to that point. Mr. Peters, who was in his mid-twenties, works in a Catholic high school that serves 300 boys, all of whom are black, in grades nine through twelve. Mr. Peters teaches Introduction to Religion to ninth graders and Comparative Religion and New Testament to upperclassmen. Mr. James, in his late thirties, works in the same public school as Ms. Payton. He is a Special Education teacher, working with small groups of students with particular physical and behaviorial difficulties and needs. Ms. Smith, also in her late thirties, teaches sixth-grade social studies in an independent school that serves 1,450 students from preschool through twelfth grade; 63% of the student body are white, 25% black, and 12% Asian and Hispanic. Ms. Payton is black, the other three teachers white. Their teaching experience varies from three years to fifteen.

To judge from informal testimony from peers, administrators, and students, all four teachers are highly regarded in their respective schools. All four have continued to teach to this day. I focus on them in this book because of the ways in which their settings and their personal perspectives contrast, yet also reveal a shared understanding of the meaning of being a teacher.

Over the course of a two-and-a-half-year period, I observed on average forty of each of the teacher's classes. I also conversed with each teacher many more times than that—in their classrooms, while walking with them through the school halls, over lunch or coffee in the cafeteria, at special assemblies and other school events, and more. We also interacted more formally at bi-weekly meetings held as part of the project touched on in the preface (Boostrom, Hansen, & Jackson, 1993; Jackson et al., 1993). In addition, some four hours of one-on-one conversation with each teacher were recorded, during which time they described at length their beliefs about teaching and their conceptions of themselves as teachers.

The teachers' remarks and everyday practices reveal them to be strongly dedicated to teaching. However, they enact their sense of service in strikingly distinct ways. That fact suggests that it may be more useful to speak of the "senses" of a vocation than it is to reach for a single, unified definition of the term. It implies that the idea of vocation cannot yield a formula or blueprint for the conduct of teaching. For this reason, in the chapters to follow I will in fact rarely employ the term "vocation." Rather than promoting a list of dos and don'ts in teaching, the concept provides a way of thinking about what animates teachers in carrying out their role. This way of thinking bears little resemblance to images of heroism or self-sacrifice; the teachers themselves would quickly repudiate such tags. However, taking a close look at their work will allow readers to "see" the working out of vocation in practice.

The idea of vocation also underscores just how central the person is who occupies the position of teacher. It highlights the fact that the role or occupation itself does not teach students. It is the person *within* the role and who *shapes* it who teaches students, and who has an impact on them for better or for worse. The four chapters that follow illustrate what it means to shape the role of teacher. At the same time, the analysis illuminates the ways in which teachers are themselves influenced by the structure of their role in today's schools. No teacher can dodge the forces in school and in society that bear down on his or her conduct and decisions. No teacher is an island unto himself or herself, notwithstanding the stereotypical image of teachers working behind closed classroom doors. However, the pressures and influences in schools need not determine what teachers do. Those forces condition their work, and limit the range of action available. But within those rough and shifting boundaries teachers have remarkable autonomy and discretion—typically, a good deal more than any individual teacher is aware of.

The accounts that follow also document how complex classroom teaching is and how ambiguous its outcomes can be, even for the most serious-minded and energetic practitioners. To consider teaching a vocation does not discount those complexities. Far from it. The idea calls attention to how persons can confront them, understand them, and continue to teach regardless of the doubts and anxieties those complexities engender. The perspective of vocation spotlights qualities such as perseverance, courage, and imagination. It illustrates the place that faith plays in teaching, with the latter understood as the ability to believe without having much, or any, evidence to support that belief. For instance, all four teachers discuss their faith in students who have done poorly in academic terms, but whom they believe can do better. The discussion will also bring into view how the teachers fall short of their own standards of practice. I address those imperfections not with an eye to judging the teachers as good or bad per se, but rather to shed further light on how vocation appears in practice.

Emmet (1958) argues persuasively that it is natural for persons who bring a vocational orientation to their work to describe it in poetic, even spiritual-sounding terms. The idiom of "occupation" or "job" alone cannot capture their feelings, their beliefs, and their convictions about what they do. The teachers' self-descriptions in the next four chapters bear out this point. To interpret their testimony, and to draw from it the lessons it contains for thinking about teaching, will lead me into normative waters of my own. I will move beyond the descriptive and analytical and will provide a considered interpretation of much that we will see and hear. I invite readers to do the same, perhaps with an eye on either their own views of teaching or on those of teachers, or would-be teachers, whom they may wish to understand.

2

Shaping a Classroom World

Ms. Payton's afternoon Physical Science class has twenty-four seventh graders. Reflecting the demographics of their public high school, half the class is girls, the other half boys; fourteen are black, four Hispanic, four white, and two Asian. Ms. Payton has taught for fifteen years, all in the public school system including the last four in her present site. I will introduce her teaching by describing how she and her students responded one afternoon to a potential interruption of their routine. Their response, including both what they did and did not do, reveals much about the ethos of Ms. Payton's classroom and about her orientation toward her work.

Formed into pairs, the seventh graders are busily conducting an experiment on transforming solids into gases. Ms. Payton walks up and down between the benches, answering questions and ensuring that everyone is following correct procedures. The students are busy and focused. Most do not even notice their teacher passing by.

In the midst of the experiment an upperclassman appears at the door, escorting a prospective student (a sixth-grade boy) and his mother on a visit to the school. (This is a "magnet" school, accepting a limited number of students with good records from around the city, as well as all students in the immediate geographic area.) Ms. Payton welcomes the visitors and invites them to observe the class from some empty seats at the benches. The boy's mother sits down, her son following suit by taking a place at the bench in front of her.

The young visitor has kept his jacket on and zipped up to his neck. He looks cautiously around the room, starting with some posters on the cabinets above the sink to his right. The posters declaim the importance of handling materials carefully and cleaning up work areas properly. Just then Ms. Payton walks by, and, turning to one of her nearby students, says: "Paul, since your partner isn't here today, can you work with our visitor and show him how we do things?" Paul nods affirmatively, and the boy's mother motions her son to go on over. As she and Ms. Payton converse, the boy gingerly takes the empty place beside Paul. Paul gives him a quick glance, then instructs him to go to the teacher's front bench and bring back the small amount of copper that is to be heated. Paul resumes setting up his burner.

But the prospective student doesn't appear to have taken in Paul's request. He stands near the table, and, save for a darting look or two around him, stares at the ground. Paul glances at him once more, then leaves his station to get the copper himself. He takes it to a side counter where students weigh and mass objects. Noticing the visitor still dawdling where Paul left him, another student setting up a burner nearby catches the young fellow's eye and jerks with his thumb over to where Paul is now working. The boy walks over and watches Paul's doings, now and then looking around the room at the others. For the next few minutes he follows Paul around obligingly, until his mother comes to take him away.

One obvious aspect of this episode is the young visitor's tentativeness. Certainly, Ms. Payton's remark, "show him how *we* do things" (emphasis supplied), did not encompass the boy. Ms. Payton's unselfconscious directions attest to the fact that her classroom, like classrooms everywhere, embodies a world unto itself. It features its own unique version of the roles, the obligations, and the duties of teacher and student. Presumably, the sixth-grade visitor had had at least six years experience with such roles. But his hesitancy reveals that the content of those roles varies from class to class as widely as do the individuals who occupy them.

I begin with this typical lesson—"typical" of Ms. Payton and her students, that is—because both her response and that of her class to the visitors discloses the habits and attitudes at work in her classroom. Although Ms. Payton attended politely to the visitors, she continued to go about her business. Her students were so involved in the experiment that many hardly noticed her making her rounds. Most paid little attention to the visitors as well (Ms. Payton did not announce their arrival nor introduce them to her class). At first, a few glanced over at them, test tube or stirrer in one hand, paper towel or stand in the other. But then they continued with their assignment. Paul, the student called on to chaperon the visiting student, fulfilled his teacher's unspoken confidence in him. He attended to the visitor discreetly. At first he treated him as a "regular" partner with shared duties. Perceiving that the young fellow was not ready for this, he calmly did everything himself.

These subtle actions reveal the beliefs and understandings that have transformed Ms. Payton and her students from a group of strangers—which they were on the first day of the school year—into a community. Their conduct reveals their acceptance of certain responsibilities, such as working independently and respecting their time and materials as well as those of others, all of which display purposeful attitudes of industriousness and accomplishment. Their response to the potential interruption—or, better, their lack of response—stands in marked contrast to classrooms where any distraction that comes along is seized by students, and sometimes by teachers as well, as an occasion to squander time (see, for example, classrooms described in Page, 1987, 1991).

Ms. Payton plays the central role in shaping her classroom into a work environment. She guides her class with a firm and consistent hand. As we will see, she is well prepared, well organized, and confident about the value of her subject matter. At the same time, there are costs that accompany her resoluteness, both for Ms. Payton and for her students. At times, she advocates proper procedures and behavior so strongly that that in itself becomes an aim rather than what it is intended to create, namely conditions for learning. At other times, she can be impervious to students' self-doubts and concerns. Ms. Payton recognizes these uneven features of her work, and others as well that I will touch on.

These tensions in her work reflect the fact that the enactment of a sense of vocation in teaching is always problematic. As I argued in Chapter 1, a vocational orientation does not provide an automatic "guide" for what one should do. It does not in itself dissolve the ambiguities and complexities that inevitably accompany working with students. Nor does it confer sudden powers to influence students at will. Unless one wants to indoctrinate students, one cannot force them to absorb particular knowledge and attitudes. Teaching always entails patience and compromise. It requires reflection on what one does. It necessitates a willingness to change. As we will see, Ms. Payton confronts these and other challenges in ways that enable her to continue to teach with interest and conviction.

ARCHITECT OF A STRUCTURED SETTING

Many of the urban, minority students Ms. Payton has taught for fifteen years have had to endure economic and social inequities. Many have experienced less than adequate home and educational provision. Some have considerable difficulty in school, while others have become disenchanted with formal education. Ms. Payton says she appreciates that making the transition from home and neighborhood to school can be hard for students. Those worlds can feel utterly remote from one another. Some educational critics have argued that the blame for that gap lies with schools. They contend that schools are inherently artificial, bureaucratized institutions that dampen rather than kindle curiosity and genuine learning. Such critics argue that schools should be radically restructured: for example, to become more diversified from one another in what they offer and also open to parental choice (e.g., Chubb & Moe, 1990); or to become sites for curricular experimentation including through regular input from students (e.g., Nicholls & Hazzard, 1993); or to become institutions where moral considerations are paramount, for instance through identifying the uniqueness of each learner and what he or she should be taught (e.g., Noddings, 1992). Some critics have gone one step further and averred that schools should simply be abolished (Illich, 1970).

Ms. Payton strongly values what she regards as the distinctiveness of school. She believes that school can provide students with genuine opportunities to grow. "I tell students," she explains,

> that school should be a place where you can leave your problems behind, where you can find good, regular activity, a structured place. . . . I would like them to really become interested in their grade, in their work, what they can do. . . . They shouldn't have to dwell on their problems all the time. I like to give them a place where they can *work*. Kids need rules and structure or else they jump all over me and each other.

For Ms. Payton, "work" applies both to academic learning and to moral learning, with the latter understood to mean developing positive attitudes toward oneself, toward others, and toward education. Her entire approach to teaching reflects her desire to distinguish school from other environments and to render the former into its own special and valued place.

Her values find expression even in the physical arrangement of her classroom. The setting has the businesslike feel of a laboratory, of a place in which to work and to do nothing but work. It is large and square, with two doorways at opposite ends of one wall, and large windows facing west on the opposite side. The room is clean and well lit. Ms. Payton sometimes sweeps up during the day rather than waiting for the custodians to do so at the close of school. Her office, which she shares with other colleagues, can be reached through a side door. Ms. Payton's long front desk includes cabinets, a sink, and a gas outlet. Behind it are sliding blackboards, these along the same wall as the entrances to the classroom. In front of her desk are fourteen solidly built tables, each intended for two students. The tables are usually arrayed in four rows facing Ms. Payton's desk, separated by a gap down the middle so that she can walk in and around them with ease during quizzes and experiments. Along the north and south walls are numerous counters, washbasins, and cabinets, the latter crammed with lab equipment (some purchased by the school, some with students' lab fees, and some by Ms. Payton herself). Each pair of students shares a cabinet.

Unlike neighboring classrooms, the room features virtually no decoration of any kind. There are a half-dozen dog-eared posters affixed to the cabinets announcing the importance of safety and cleanliness (e.g., "Read All Labels Carefully"). There are also a few commercially prepared posters with inspirational messages intended for students. For example, above a picture of a girl running the high hurdles are the words "Effort works in the classroom, too." Another poster portrays a girl dressed in bright red leaping into the air, this below the words "Enthusiasm really picks up your grades." In light of Ms. Payton's no-frills approach to education, the inclusion of these posters was probably not her idea (she shares this classroom with other teachers). Moreover, the actions they portray—running and leaping—are quite out of place in her classroom if not in most classrooms everywhere, evidently a fact lost on the designers of the posters or on whoever put them up in the room.

As the vignette that opened the chapter illustrated, Ms. Payton strives to keep her students focused on the tasks she sets for them. These routinely include group review of homework, in-class reading, lectures and note-taking, individual student presentations, quizzes, and, most time-consuming of all, scientific experiments. Over the course of a two-year period, I observed forty-six of her classes, each forty minutes in length. During that time Ms. Payton taught four classes, each of which met seven times a week including two double periods intended for experiments. She taught two classes of Physical Science to seventh graders, some of them high-achieving students bussed from around the city. She also taught two upper-grade Physical Science classes composed mostly of eleventh and twelfth graders, many of whom had failed their one previous high school science course (typically biology). The contrast between the comparatively high academic interest and energy of many of her seventh graders and the lassitude of her high schoolers was a constant source of tension and worry for Ms. Payton, a point to which I return below.

With her seventh graders, Ms. Payton is all business. She attends diligently to the details of their work and conduct. For example, she routinely interrupts students early in the school year whenever they employ pronouns in describing their work. She insists that students use nouns and appropriate scientific names and that they identify their understanding of any technical terms they employ. "Technical" encompasses a wide domain in her classroom; for instance, it includes terms such as "dissolve," "evaporate," "heat," "solid," "gas." If a student remarks, for example, "We saw the same thing [on the experiment everyone had just finished]," Ms. Payton responds, "Put it in your *own* words! You didn't write down 'same thing' in your write-up!" To a student who blurts out, for example, "What's the answer to number 5?" Ms. Payton invariably replies, "You're not going to just ask me for the answer! You're going to ask it in such a way that we can explain to you how you answer this kind of question!" She regularly reminds her classes, "I only accept complete sentences in written work." She refuses to discuss vocabulary that students had the opportunity to look up at home or in the library but failed to—hoping thereby, she explains, to teach them some self-sufficiency. Nor will she spell words that the class has already studied and that, consequently, they should know. But she reminds students that they are responsible for knowing the terms.

As a matter of habit, Ms. Payton redirects student questions to their peers: "Who can explain that to Mary?" Moreover, after a student answers a question, Ms. Payton turns to others to ask them if they understand. In one instance a boy replies uncertainly, "Yeah, sort of." "'Sort of'?" responds Ms. Payton. "Well, kind of, yeah, I—" "'Kind of'? Ask another student to explain it to you!" "Excuse me," she interrupts her buzzing class one afternoon, "why do you all talk when Robert is speaking?" She waits for silence to descend, which does not take long. "Maybe, Robert, they think you're just speaking to me. Talk to *all* of us." While giving directives such as these, which she does frequently, Ms. Payton acts in effect as a teacher of public speaking. She also reinforces the sense that the classroom is a community in which students should develop a cooperative and educational relationship with one another, rather than solely with her. Toward that end, she routinely has students evaluate some of each other's homework, in-class exercises, and oral reports. She coaches students to offer comments that are helpful and academic (rather than personal) in nature. On occasion, she provides them written evaluation forms to employ. She believes these activities promote learning and shared responsibility. "It keeps the work in *their* hands as much as possible," she says, "so they learn more and do better."

Her attention to academic detail is complemented by her attention to conduct. One afternoon in October Michael admits he does not have his homework. When asked why not, the boy replies, "You only told us once what it was." Ms. Payton seems taken aback by this explanation. Recovering herself, she turns to the whole class: "Is that true?" "Yes!" interjects Michael, "you told us in the beginning!" "Yeah," affirms Marcus, another boy who did not do the work, "you told us only once!" "IS ONCE ENOUGH?" declaims Ms. Payton in a riled voice that carries its own answer, while surveying the entire class. "Yes!—Yeah!—Yeah, it is!" echo various students. "I think so, too," concludes Ms. Payton, eyeing Michael and Marcus in a way that says "Case closed." Michael's excuse was never heard again in the classroom—nor were others, for that matter, at least not in such public circumstances.

THE LOOK AND SOUND OF ENGAGEMENT

The homework episode illustrates the fact that Ms. Payton rarely leaves unquestioned any conduct she finds objectionable. This is also the case during experiments, when she hovers around the room checking on students' progress and making sure they are not endangering themselves or their classmates. In the midst of these open-ended activities her seventh graders' natural exuberance comes to the surface. They enjoy the experiments a great deal. They watch attentively as she demonstrates steps at the front of the room. Many shift in their seats or stretch their necks to get a good view. Then one student from each team of two comes up to the front to obtain necessary supplies.

One afternoon in February they queued to receive the small amount of hydrochloric acid they would need to separate copper out of copper oxide. The first step in that process was for each team to break apart chunks of copper material in their crucibles. Staccato hammering filled the classroom, as if a horde of woodpeckers were at work. Patricia, ever an impatient pupil, smashed her crucible to bits by banging away at the copper too hard. Her partner shook her head as if to say "not again!" and admonished her to ask Ms. Payton for another crucible. Ten minutes later the room filled with the sound of a tree full of cicadas, in this case a crescendo of plastic stirrers wisking around inside test tubes. As one student in each team busily stirred—sometimes with tongue out in concentration—their partners hovered around them, bobbing their heads to catch a look at the test tubes from different angles, some offering an endless stream of advice: "Careful!"—"C'mon, man, not so fast!"—"Okay, okay! It's goin'!"—"Let me see!"—"Okay, I'll take a turn now!"—"No! You were the one who got the copper!"

Meanwhile Ms. Payton continued to make her rounds. "Don't just stand there and wait," she said to one pair, "go on to the next step!" "Whose coat is this on the floor? It's a hazard, move it." "Whose bag is this? Stick it under your desk." "Don't run, please!" she suddenly called out, and a boy abruptly slowed to a walk. "Latitia! You can stay at your desk with your partner, you don't need to go over and play with them!" One pair of students dropped a glass beaker, which shattered on the floor. The class started buzzing. "You all gonna be nosy now?" Ms. Payton interrupted. "You know what broken glass sounds like! You're not supposed to stop what you're doing!" Meanwhile, she helped the two students clean up the debris.

A short time later, students started lighting their burners in order to heat materials in their test tubes. Ms. Payton's alertness picked up a notch. She reminded students to put their safety goggles on, or to pull them down from their foreheads over their eyes. Soon, a waft of sulphur floated above the room, mixing with the incessant and eager chatter of the students.

In their absorption during such experiments, students often shout to obtain Ms. Payton's attention. "MS. PAYTON!" She immediately shouts right back: "I DON'T APPRECIATE BEING YELLED AT ACROSS THE ROOM, SCOTT! . . . EXCUSE ME! I'M TALKING TO SOMEONE

ELSE NOW! . . . WHY ARE YOU USING SUCH A LOUD VOICE IN SPEAKING TO ME?" Her booming replies often startle students, even well into the school year. She explains that she deliberately uses her voice to obtain students' attention and cooperation. She does so, in part, to compensate for what she regards as her short physical stature: "I've never really felt that the students gave me a hard time because of my stature. They generally can see past that, especially when they hear my big voice that just resounds in the room and they don't know what to do about it. . . . When I get really loud with students, it's a shock to them."

In sum, Ms. Payton is attentive to both academic work and to what she regards as good conduct. She routinely fuses comments about the one with directives about the other. For instance, while making her rounds one morning in October she said to a student, without breaking stride, "Roberta, you don't ever sit like that in this class!" The girl immediately unfurled her legs out from under her, putting her feet on the floor (Ms. Payton had in mind both courteous demeanor and safety). Another student, play-acting at basketball, tossed a crumpled paper into the garbage can by Ms. Payton's desk. "Excuse me!" Ms. Payton called out. The boy whipped his head around. "THAT IS NOT DONE HERE!" she emphasized, striding over toward the cowed young fellow. "You are to hold that wad in a vertical position over the garbage can and release it!" She repeats these instructions, if less often in such parade-ground terms, whenever a student forgets the rule. For example, a week after this incident another boy shot a basket. "Hey!" Ms. Payton snapped. "Oh! I forgot!" responded the boy. "No!" admonished Ms. Payton. "No forgetting, no *anything*! You pull that out and go back to your seat!" For the remaining few moments of the period the boy sat still, practicing holding the paper wad out in the proper fashion.

In addition to enforcing her own rules, Ms. Payton closely observes those of the school. That fact further reflects her habitual attention to details, and it reaffirms her belief in schooling in general. "My colleagues know," she explains, "that I'm a serious person in regard to respecting the rules of the school. If there's a procedure to be followed, I'm going to follow it. I don't think I'm above the rules at school. . . . [So] if there is a rule, a procedure, I'm going to hear it." She is not a "stickler for the rules," she insists, but she does believe they help provide a supportive setting in which to work. As mentioned previously, she believes that a safe and structured school environment is valuable for her students. She applauds the principal's policy of having all students wear photo identification (supplied by the school), this in order to eliminate the danger of unsavory outsiders prowling the halls looking for trouble. "But some students tell me," Ms. Payton says in dismay, "that I'm one of the few that keeps enforcing this. I can't believe it!" She wishes that first-period teachers would enforce the regulation, thereby freeing everyone else to take it for granted the remainder of the day. She also complains that some students are so fashion-conscious that they keep taking their ID's off. In her own first-period classes, she diligently implements the rule, reminding students of what she perceives as the valid reasons underlying it.

That Ms. Payton explains to students *why* she endorses the rule softens the impression she sometimes creates of being heavy-handed and nitpicky. She is aware of her reputation for running a tight ship. She need only listen to colleagues and others in the school on an everyday basis to be reminded of that fact. For example, one morning in December while Ms. Payton was walking down the hall with her students, a teacher serving as hall monitor said in a genuinely admiring voice, "Ah! Here comes Ms. Payton's class, we won't have to worry about them! Ms. Payton's students are always in good control!" Ms. Payton could not help but smile at this, as did many of her students, pleased to hear their teacher complimented and perhaps pleased to see her reaction as well.

At the same time, such remarks from colleagues raise doubts in her mind. Ms. Payton's orientation to teaching exacts its price, one that spurs her to reconsider her practices. As we will see in the next section, that reflective process breeds further questions and doubts. On occasion, it even leads to humorous results. Referring to what her peers say about her well-controlled students, she explains:

> I used to be like a little mother hen. If I ever had to take my [homeroom] someplace, they all had to walk in one straight line, not saying a word. I would tell them, "How long do you think it will take us to walk from this room to our destination?" The students would tell me, "Two to three minutes." "I'm sure that you can remain silent for three minutes, right?" "Of course we can." And they'd do it.
>
> Now I feel awful if my students are in a straight line. At the beginning of the school year, the little seventh graders would always line up in a straight line because their teachers had taught them that. I said, "Please don't walk in a straight line. Let's just all walk together and we'll remain quiet." . . . And they'd look at me so strange, "she doesn't want us to walk in a straight line!"

Ms. Payton's seventh graders may find her directive baffling because so much of her conduct seems predicated on the belief that teachers should exercise fully the authority invested in their role. I have suggested that her everyday practice expresses that belief symbolically, often in powerful ways. Yet she also enunciates this conviction directly to her students. One afternoon in

November, she called on a student who had volunteered to explain a diagram she had drawn on the board of a balanced lever. The boy walked confidently to the front, but then hesitated. "Well, maybe," he sputtered, "uh, I think—" "Come on, Eric," cried Ms. Payton, "what do you mean 'I think'? You *tell* us. You're the authority when you're up here!"

Ms. Payton's remark illustrates her unqualified belief in her own authority in the classroom. She wants her students to understand unambiguously how to conduct themselves so that they can concentrate on their academic work. In practice, that aim implies that she must herself act, when in the presence of her students, in a clear, consistent, and confident manner. Yet she distinguishes being an authority from being an authoritarian (cf. Nyberg & Farber, 1986; Sennett, 1980). "I can't act like a bully," she argues.

> I can't stand over some kid and say, "Just sit down because I said so." I would have to say: "If you can get into your seats as quickly as possible, so that we can get organized and settled, I can give you the directions for the experiment and you can have more time to perform it. That's a good reason for sitting down and being quiet, not just because *I* want you to, or because I want my class to look like it's orderly." I always play off their intelligence, you know, like "don't you agree this is the wiser thing to do?"

As we have seen, Ms. Payton does not in fact always provide a rationale for her directives. Nonetheless her approach appears to pay dividends. In time, her classroom becomes a focused and work-oriented environment. Judging from extensive observation and from informal comments from her seventh graders, many respect and like their teacher and genuinely enjoy her classes, particularly the experiments and the often elaborate science projects in which they engage. Many appear to treat her watchfulness and her commentary on their conduct as if they were natural and justified.

Ms. Payton's alertness to what takes place in her classroom recalls a dimension of vocation outlined in Chapter 1. I argued that enacting vocation—whether it be in nursing, doctoring, teaching—requires accepting responsibility for the often mundane chores that so often accompany the work. Like an artist who must patiently organize and arrange his or her materials, a teacher must patiently ensure that his or her "studio" is ready for use. Ms. Payton has no difficulty meeting this obligation. She appears to regard her daily academic and organizational tasks as neither busywork nor drudgery. Rather, from her point of view the mass of details that fill her everyday practice seem to constitute a *wealth* of details. Taken together, they provide occasions for concretizing her values as teacher. They become the materials for creating what feels to an observer like a *substantial* class-room, one whose ethos comprises a palpable solidity.

In part, that felt quality derives from the fact that some students take on her businesslike demeanor. For example, as the school year advances it is not unusual to observe the first students who arrive in class react to how students from the previous period have treated their classroom. "They have such a messy [homeroom] before this class!" complained a student one morning. She and a classmate promptly began clearing away crumpled papers and other debris. During regular cleanup time after their experiments, students often chastise one another for not putting materials away prop-erly. At the bell they routinely push their chairs in rather than bolting from the room (as is the norm in the school), a habit they may have learned from witnessing Ms. Payton perform this task herself early in the school year.

These and similar actions appear, at first glance, to be utterly hum-drum and quite irrelevant to education. However, within the crowded con-texts of schools and classrooms, they take on significance because without them it can be difficult for participants to concentrate on academic work. Some might argue that their significance is even broader in that learning to take care of details fuels the disposition to learn to take care of larger mat-ters as well. Of course there is a thin line here between caring for details and being obsessed with them. However, the point remains that the atten-tion Ms. Payton and her students are willing to give to apparently minor and mundane doings carries more significance than firsts meet the eye. As the vignette that opened this chapter reveals, those doings reveal a purposeful orientation toward learning itself.

Moreover, Ms. Payton's seventh graders reveal in numerous ways their engagement with the academic material. I already mentioned how exuber-ant many are in conducting experiments. Their involvement also surfaces in the subtle ways they resist the pressures embodied in the student culture of the school to make fun of, if not actively disdain, academic prowess. (Such pressures appear to be widespread in American schooling [Cusick, 1973; Henry, 1963; Peebles, 1994].) Consider Charles, a boy who transferred into the class halfway through the fall term. He is a tall, good-natured fellow with a guileless face and a deep laugh. It took him a few weeks to accustom himself to the setting— to learn how "we" do things, to recall Ms. Payton's terms. However, Charles soon became an active member of the class. During one of their double-period sessions in February he performed almost all the work intended for him and his lab-mate. His partner, Girard, goofed off— except when Ms. Payton came near—and made one crack after another about his classmates, including Charles. Charles laughed along obligingly, but meantime carried on with the experiment. He almost seemed to take pains to disguise how much enjoyment he was obviously deriving from completing each step of the process. His engagement became further apparent in his reaction to Joe and Zhou, a neighboring pair who at one point during the experiment invited him to examine their results. Charles immediately ignored Girard, as if the boy weren't even there, and looked intently at what his neighbors had done. The fact that Joe and Zhou assumed Charles would be interested attests to his attitude toward what the class undertakes. These kinds of subtle acts, which one can witness nearly every period in Ms. Payton's classroom, symbolize what students may be deriving from the working environment she has helped bring into being.

The everyday actions of Ms. Payton and of many of her seventh-grade students suggest that the roles of teacher and student are not "emptied out" in their classroom, as McNeil (1986) and others have shown sometimes takes place in schools. According to these studies, administrators and teachers sometimes abandon—unselfconsciously, as often as not—serious attempts to stress academic work in exchange for good behavior from students. McNeil (1986) dubbed this a "contradiction of control." That contradiction can be witnessed in the high school in which Ms. Payton works. However, in her classroom the roles of student and teacher are *filled out*, given substance through their focused, everyday doings. An observer can see, hear, and even smell (recall the matches lit during experiments) the ways in which her seventh-grade classes feature a culture of involvement.

CHALLENGES TO A TEACHER'S VOCATIONAL IDENTITY

Matters are different in her two classes for upper-grade students, many of them with poor academic records, and many with little or no academic ambition. Ms. Payton struggles to reconcile her belief in high standards of performance with the apparent inability of these students to motivate themselves for schoolwork. She has worked with students of this age for three years. She describes how much she has had to learn in that time:

> You see, they have not developed self-motivation. And the older they get, if they still need to develop that, the more difficult it's going to be for them to make any kind of accomplishment. . . .
> They cannot reach inside themselves and find reasons to want that A grade. And some of them don't have parents who will encourage them. Some've actually given up on these kids, actually given up on them.

Ms. Payton explains that she learned these facts the hard way. In part, she says, the students themselves "fooled her." They had learned over the years how to feign interest and to bluff their way through. "The first year I taught high school physical science," she says,

> I assumed that because the students all were alert-looking, they all had paid their fees [for lab materials], most of them turned their work in the first month, that Wow! I got a real good group of high school students! So, I start piling it on. I'm thinking they're moving right along. Then I started grading their papers. And most of these students had learned defensive maneuvers. They had learned how to look attentive in class. They had learned that, a lot of times, you turn your paper in and the teacher is gonna just put a check on it, that means a perfect grade just because you did it. . . . The students would take the homework questions and would not have anything as an answer to them. They would just write down the questions, then rephrase each as an "answer."

Ms. Payton said that their actions resulted in her losing respect for them. She began to find it hard to *be* with them. In part, as she explained, this was simply a matter of experience. "I've had fifteen years of teaching," she says, and "twelve of those were exclusively with seventh graders. So it would take a long time for high school students to win my heart completely over."

Moreover, she lost patience with them because in her view the upper-grade Physical Science curriculum had already been simplified. It centered on the basic laws of physics, mechanics, and chemistry, and employed the same textbook used with her seventh graders. But it did not include the same range of in-class experiments as the seventh graders were assigned. Such facts alone make it almost inevitable that Ms. Payton would hold a strike against these students, even before meeting them for the very first time. According to the students' informal testimony, they harbored resentments themselves, deriving in part from their awareness that their curriculum is less sophisticated than that of younger students—even though they are also mindful of their own poor academic records.

Ms. Payton chafed at what she perceived as her students' listlessness, their lack of interest, and their preoccupation with fashion and social life. Waxing sarcastic, she describes why they have such a "difficult time" arriving at class punctually. "Think about all the temptations that they encounter along the way [through the halls of the large school building]. There's a Bobbie Joe, a Sally, a Sue they haven't seen for that day or for that week, or they've got to go ahead and spend a little extra time getting themselves pretty after gym. So you see these are valid reasons for them to come a little late for your class!" Although Ms. Payton reports tardiness on her attendance sheets (employed systemwide), she does not punish students for this infraction. Rather, she encourages them to come even if late because she believes at least some contact time with them is valuable. Moreover, unless a student is present she refuses—save in the case of excused absences—to give him or her the homework or handouts for the day.

Ms. Payton also reports that she is both amazed and put off by what she regards as her high schoolers' highly sensitive and easily bruised egos. In comparison, she regards her seventh graders as much more hardy and mature. "With my seventh graders," she explains, "I am very firm, and I expect them to absorb material faster. I know they like to play so I don't allow too much playing; they don't know that they're doing this, coming in and bothering someone's books or taking someone's hat or purse." She says she can comfortably challenge her seventh graders intellectually, and can point out forcefully errors of fact and of interpretation. In contrast, she avers, with high school students

> I have to give them more plain old love and understanding. If I tried the same approach with high school students, they first of all may not know what I'm talking about. And secondly, they will pick up the tone in your voice and be really upset about it. They can get a negative attitude if you correct them in a very firm way. . . .
> They're gonna be embarrassed in front of their peers, and will not easily forgive and go on from it. They may hold it as a grudge for the rest of their year.

She explains that she knows much more about the home lives of her high school students than those of her seventh graders simply because so many have problems of one sort or another. She recognizes that many have after-school jobs, that some are helping their parents manage younger siblings, and that, as she grants, adolescents in general desire independence. But she appears to resent having to play the role of nurturer and caregiver to them.

To an outside observer, her upper-grade students appear decidedly unenthusiastic about schoolwork. They act passively in class. They do poorly on quizzes. They complain about having to do homework, admitting frankly that they place their after-school jobs and social activities above academics. They do not listen well. For example, while Ms. Payton's seventh graders tend to leap into their experiments as soon as she finishes reviewing procedures, "with the high school students," as she says, "you give them all the directions and you say 'OK, you may start,' and they are still looking at you. And they'll get up and they'll start asking each other, 'Well, what do we do first? Ms. Payton, is this what we do?' As if I hadn't said a thing!" Students repeatedly try to cajole Ms. Payton into giving them simple fill-in-the-blank worksheets, the kind of time-filling activities educators deplore but that have evidently been customary fare for these students. Even as late as April of the school year, Ms. Payton finds herself having to say, "Put your name on your work, you may forget when you turn it in."

Ms. Payton does not disguise her feelings about what she regards as the laziness and, worse, shiftiness of some individuals. Describing one fellow who keeps copying others' work, she complains:

> He doesn't notice that I'm watching him. See, I'm over on this side but I've got an eye on Greg and I've got an eye on Burton who is a senior who has found ways—I don't know *how* he got to be a *senior*! He is the most dependent person I have ever seen! I don't think he writes his name down on a paper till his partner does!

Ms. Payton feels so negatively about some students that in criticizing one boy, Greg, she cannot complete her objection but turns instead to her even stronger feelings about another. In addition, in part because of the daily contrast with her more energetic and cooperative seventh graders—"who like knowledge for knowledge's sake," says Ms. Payton—she occasionally loses her temper with her upper-grade students.

For example, one afternoon in April a girl confessed that she had not done her homework. When Ms. Payton asked why, the girl replied that she had had a poetry test to study for. "What's that got to do with it?" snapped Ms. Payton. "That *really* relates, doesn't it! Fine! I'll remember that when your parents ask about your grade in science, I'll just tell them that!" The girl stared at her lap while the rest of the class sat hushed. Ms. Payton proceeded with the lesson. In another class, she asked students what they thought of the design and content of the quiz they had just taken (I return below to her habit of seeking student feedback on their assignments). One boy replied, with ill-advised candor, that he didn't know the steps to solving some of the problems. Ms. Payton swooped in. "Oh? Now, why wouldn't you know? Have you been in class recently?" "No," the boy admitted (as Ms. Payton knew full well). "If you don't come," she barked, "you won't know. Did you call a classmate to get the notes?"—"No."—"Did you try to call me?"—"I don't know your number."—"Not my home number, I don't give that out. I mean call the school next time!"

Ms. Payton does not relish such confrontations. Far from it. Her high school classes make her tense and agitated. "For me, the hardest thing to accept is that I can teach physical science to seventh graders and we can learn together and we can have fun and enjoy science. [But] there's an added burden with the high school student. I feel a level of seriousness that's uncomfortable for them and it's uncomfortable for me." She knows that her temperament, governed as it is by her high expectations, grates on her upper-grade students. On a midterm course evaluation that she had them complete, a number of students wrote that she was "mean." "I know what [they're saying]," she sighed. "I need to work on that." More than once, I observed her apologize to a student for losing her temper.

At the time of these events, however, Ms. Payton had not yet fashioned a way to communicate with her high school students that satisfied her (and them). Her troubles attest to a problem that confronts teachers everywhere. What does one do when one must teach students whom one has trouble liking or respecting? How should a teacher handle negative feelings about students who do not commit themselves to academic learning? What does one do about students whom one regards as passive, bored, resistant, indifferent, or worse? It goes against the grain of common sense and basic human capability to expect teachers to feel the same positive way about all students. Unless one is a saint, one can hardly help having critical views of some individuals. Nor can one simply switch off those gut-level feelings. One cannot *make* oneself feel a certain way about another person. Most teachers, like most other people, cannot help but have their reactions and act on them. It is also quite natural that regardless of the level of education, a teacher will tend to incline favorably toward those students who listen, who try, or who, especially, like what the teacher gives them to do— who like the books the teacher likes, who like the academic activities the teacher likes, who like the very subject itself the teacher may have dedicated a life to teaching.

On top of these all-too-human proclivities, it seems problematic to expect teachers to treat all students in the same way. Such an expectation would contradict the widely accepted notion that teachers should recognize each student's uniqueness, a recognition that by definition means treating students differently: for example, being more patient and providing extra attention to those who are struggling, or being more challenging with those who are moving effortlessly through the curriculum.

The lesson to draw from Ms. Payton's differential treatment and attitudes toward her students is not that teachers should try to deny their feelings or seek to alter them through sheer will power. Rather, one lesson that emerges from Ms. Payton's predicament is that teachers might strive to be mindful that they are regarding and treating students differently. They might seek to acknowledge their feelings and beliefs. Taking this step makes it possible to reflect on their sentiments, which in turn can lead either to a reasoned affirmation of what they are doing or to a change in conduct (Buchmann, 1989; Murdoch, 1970/1985). In addition, such reflection can help one resist first impressions, to keep at arm's length the kinds of quick and easy conclusions about some students to which all who teach seem prone. On the face of it, this advice is obvious. Everyone should try to be open-minded about other people and what they can do. Yet teachers have an obligation to be especially conscious of this moral imperative. Their practice is centered around the idea of helping learners grow and flourish, and one cannot appreciate how students may be changing unless one is open to revising one's opinions of them.

Perhaps the hardest lesson of all embodied in Ms. Payton's predicament is to learn to teach *as if* students might undergo change at any moment. I call this the hardest task because it encompasses change the teacher may never actually see and may never even hear about. That fact makes adopting such a posture no easy matter, particularly if one is disappointed in one's students, or, worse, dislikes some of them. Teaching is an uncertain enough endeavor without having to add the burden of accepting the fact that one may never know if one has made a genuine difference. Such a stance requires considerable faith in the integrity of one's efforts, and equally strong faith in human nature. Henry Adams wrote that "A teacher affects eternity. He can never tell where his influence stops" (Adams, 1918, p. 300, quoted in Jackson, 1986, p. 53). Adams's statement suggests that teachers might conduct themselves as if something beneficial may be rubbing off on even the most recalcitrant student. (Of course one can only go so far. As another familiar saying has it, no teacher can teach everyone, and no teacher can fail to teach someone. One may have colleagues who are better able to reach a particular student.)

Ms. Payton was struggling to improve her working relationship with her upper-grade students when I first began to visit her classroom. She continued to do so during the subsequent two years. She began to alter her curriculum for them, not to "water it down," she insisted, but to "slow it down" so that students might attain some success. She introduced less material and assigned less homework; she provided additional opportunities for earning credit; she allowed students to repeat certain exercises they performed poorly on. She undertook this curricular reform cautiously and nervously. According to her testimony, she was moving from the known and the well-proven to what was for her new territory (Hawthorne, 1992; Paris, 1993). She *felt* the experiment to be a direct challenge to her typical expectations and standards. "I don't want to overburden them," she said about her upper-grade students. "But I always question myself, how much should I reduce my standards? When is, where is that point at which you shouldn't reduce it anymore? I always question the validity of what I'm teaching about what we are covering."

She knit together her attempts at curricular reform with her efforts to be less "mean" with these students. Here is how she described her evolving perception of herself and of her students:

It covers the feeling of accepting people. I mean that I think it's
morally wrong to demand of someone that which they cannot
accomplish. It is wrong to frustrate a student. It is wrong to put
them down. It is wrong for them to never find success in your
classroom all year long. I think that's morally wrong. Therefore, I
will change my curriculum, and keep changing my curriculum so
that some of my students will find some success.

I think we have to do more than just say, "We think the
curriculum that we're offering students is the right curriculum."
Who could ever be sure of that? No matter how much you try, and
how much reading you do to stay on top of it. In fact what's right
for one kid may not be right for another kid. . . . Besides the
academics, I'm dealing with a real human being. And, I don't feel
comfortable with kids who have that high frustration level.

Rather than simply plowing ahead and letting the chips fall where they may,
Ms. Payton invested considerable time in reflection, and considerable energy
in the classroom, in order to perceive her students' capabilities in a more
understanding light. She struggled to ensure that the "change" in her curriculum did not mean lessening its academic rigor. (As mentioned previously, the course was already somewhat geared down in comparison to what
seventh graders experience.) According to my observations, Ms. Payton did
slow down proceedings; she focused in greater depth on selected topics;
and she did interact more amiably with students.

However, at the close of my observational sojourn she was realizing
uneven gains in terms of student interest, effort, and success. That outcome
should come as no surprise. She was working against years of habit on her
students' part, habit that for many appeared to have hardened into nearly
complete disengagement with school. She was also up against years of habit
on her part, habits of wholehearted belief in the value of schooling that in
themselves made it continuously difficult for her to develop a new approach.
She also had barely begun her self-designed project to change her style of
working with the high schoolers. For a fifteen-year veteran, that process
invariably takes time and steadfastness, both of which she was willing to
invest.

PERSON AND PRACTICE

I suggested in Chapter 1 that the practice of teaching will itself "teach"
persons what the work entails. Engaging oneself in the task can lead one,
through time and experience, to appreciate one's obligations as teacher,
and this in a way that no amount of prior exhortation from others can

do. Ms. Payton came face-to-face with a central responsibility built into teaching: that one should not give up on students one may dislike or find disappointing, but rather should persist in seeking ways to reach them.

In accepting that challenge, Ms. Payton also learned something about the limits of her capacity and willingness to change. As she often said, she is an experienced teacher who has found successful ways of performing the job, and well-formed routines are hard to break. Though she sought to be more cordial with her upper-grade students, neither with them nor with her seventh graders did she seek to become personal friends. She maintains her distance, and, moreover, regards that distance as essential to the fulfillment of her role as teacher. According to her testimony, she developed this attitude almost despite herself.

> When I was a younger teacher, and a lot thinner, I was easily
> confused with the students. And a lot of the boys would literally flirt
> with me, walk up and put their arms around me. And I said: "No,
> I'm going to do something that will make them not wanna come up
> and do that." So I had some tactics, things to help them realize that
> "you're the student, I'm the teacher, there's a big difference
> between them. I'm here to teach you, I'm not here to be your
> buddy, your friend. We have to have that respectable distance
> between us." I had all kinds of rules in the classroom. In fact the
> school where I came from, I was known as a tyrant!

Over the years, she says, she has become "pleasanter," "smiles more," and has fewer "restraining rules." Nonetheless, she continues to believe that a certain formality and role distance are prerequisites to successful teaching.

This is not to say that she avoids becoming involved in her students' personal lives. Whenever students act out in unusually poor ways or fail to do their work, she promptly devotes time and energy to talking with them, their parents, her colleagues, and counselors in the school. She moves quickly to get to the root of any problem. For example, one day in April a student in her class poured acid on the coat and belongings of another student that were stored in a hall locker. Ms. Payton swiftly confronted all the parties involved and drew in adult support. The affair became a complicated story of learning how the offender had obtained the acid, why he had used it so harmfully, and what kind of punishment the school should mete out (the boy was suspended, as it turned out). In the course of these discussions it surfaced that the twelve-year-old boy was living alone, with both parents divorced and currently away. Ms. Payton took the lead in resolving the matter and in trying to ensure that the boy would have adult supervision during his suspension.

She also attends routinely to the more day-to-day conundrums students fall into: bickering with peers, arguing over who did what during an experiment, forgetting to bring in materials, losing things, and much more. Moreover, she has a reputation as a teacher who fearlessly interrupts fights and squabbling in the halls. On several occasions while I was observing, a student ran into the classroom between periods to ask Ms. Payton to come break up a dispute. Ms. Payton also regularly talks to parents about students' work and behavior. For example, she describes what she did about three upper-grade students who were repeatedly tardy to her first-period class. "They seem very sorry when they come in," she said. "And I've talked to all three parents and all the parents have given up on getting the child up, they won't. I think two of the parents are gone to work anyway by the time the child is supposed to get up so the kid has a bad habit and there's nobody else at home to help push them on out the door."

The point remains that Ms. Payton will not "talk to kids like I'm talking to one of my friends." As mentioned previously, she values a certain distance between herself and her students. When asked about the fact that becoming familiar with a student's problems can create a personal bond and can also lead one to like the student, Ms. Payton replies: "If it's true, I try to keep myself from thinking about it, because I know it would really affect how I would treat them." She fears that dwelling on such matters might lead her to become "easier" on her students—that is, it might lead her to *fail* to be the educator she feels she ought to be. She says she strongly dislikes bumping into her students in the neighborhood or in its shops and restaurants. "I don't want a student coming up to me in the video store or something," she emphasizes.

In short, with the exception of individual crises, Ms. Payton will familiarize herself with students' personal contexts only to the extent that that knowledge can help her craft a better learning environment for them in her classroom. Almost every contact she has with students is oriented toward that aim. She calls parents and talks individually with students about their problems only outside of class time. As mentioned previously, her response to their problems at home or in the urban setting at large is to provide them with that much more structured a world in school. She endeavors to contruct in the classroom what she feels will be a new world for many students, with new kinds of experience, with genuine opportunities to learn. She does not shy away from the tensions and conflicts her approach to teaching sparks. As we have seen, students sometimes chafe under her firm hand. This is no surprise, in that much of her effort constitutes a direct assault on the miseducative habits some manifest of not concentrating, not trying, not coming to grips with the material under consideration. Ms. Payton reflects on her students' capabilities and wants to understand their potential and capacity. However, once she walks through the classroom door, she conducts herself as if she had no doubts whatsoever about the value of her teaching.

The idea of rendering school into a "special" and "different" place is as old as schools themselves. The rhetoric it triggers can become a rationale for teachers and administrators to ignore students' problems and travails, which are often acute in today's urban settings. Does Ms. Payton "hide" behind her desire to create a special world in the classroom for students? Is her self-understanding a convenient way to avoid dealing with certain problems and challenges her students face? There may be some truth to that possibility. But then to grant it is to say nothing particular about Ms. Payton. Every teacher the world over steers clear of many legitimate problems students confront. It would be impossible to teach if one did not do so. There would simply be too many issues to attend to, and one would devote so much time to learning about them and understanding them that teaching would fall by the wayside. Moreover, to presume that one can actually learn about and deal with all such matters would be hubris. It would promote a version of what Finkel and Monk (1983) call the "Atlas complex," the feeling that one has to be an all-knowing, all-wise resolver of every problem and dilemma. It would be equally misguided for those outside the classroom to argue that teachers should take on this superhuman level of responsibility.

The question for a teacher becomes how to bring into awareness personal judgments and "blind spots," so that one can be mindful of them and seek to correct them, presuming they turn out to be pertinent to the act of teaching. Moreover, the other side of the coin is that, as Ms. Payton has learned over the years, urging students to leave their personal problems at the door can in fact open them to entirely new and helpful experiences. In effect, Ms. Payton does not *ignore* students' personal contexts as much as she *presumes* that students are not determined by them. She does not treat students as if their futures were already set in advance. She acts as if students can and do appreciate new educational opportunities.

Ms. Payton is neither a surrogate caregiver nor utterly impersonal. If those two states are taken as endpoints, she falls somewhere to the right of center, in the direction away from surrogate caregiving. How far off center is impossible to say, and, moreover, to establish that is not the point. Rather, to judge from her testimony and my own observations, Ms. Payton is a teacher who strives to remain open to new perspectives. She routinely elicits feedback on her work. For example, every term she asks her students to fill out evaluation forms of her own design in order to assess their academic progress and to identify obstacles to success that they perceive. Ms. Payton also asks for evaluations informally. For example, after completing a quiz or a new kind of exercise, she often asks students if the activity was fair, helpful, in need of improvement, and the like.

She seeks advice, counsel, and criticism from her colleagues. Some feedback comes her way without her asking, and usually much to her delight. "Teachers ask the students [who have had her as teacher]," she says,

> —like in chemistry—"how did you know to do that that way," or "how did you reason that out like that." "Well, Ms. Payton had us do things like that, she had us practice things like that." And, that makes me feel good, you know, because it says that they didn't just take a body of knowledge that they may forget. They took a process, and I think a process is more deep-rooted in you than the facts.

As we have seen, that "process" ideally involves attention to detail, thoroughness in execution, sound preparation, and more. To judge from her colleagues' testimony, Ms. Payton is providing her seventh graders with a foundation not just in science but in how to be successful students.

CONCLUSION: SOURCES OF VOCATION

Ms. Payton suggests that her accomplishments as teacher derive from her intellectual restlessness and her desire for new challenges. She recalls vividly the origins of that drive. In seventh grade, she says, she "discovered" learning. She remembers how "thrilled" she was to have so many different teachers, each responsible for a single subject—this after having either one or only a few practitioners handle everything in elementary school. She dates her lifelong commitment to education to her "awakening" as a seventh grader.

Ms. Payton becomes animated in describing her desire to keep growing and changing. "I do think that there's room for me to grow, and I have to feel that way. I have to feel that I'm not at the end, because if you're at the end, or if you're at the top, the only place you can go is back." She describes why she enrolled some years before in a graduate program to earn a library science endorsement (she already had state certification to teach biology and physical education). "I was working with my students on science fair projects," she says.

> We wasted too much time in the library—I didn't know where the right resources were. So, I discovered there was a class called Library Resources for Math and Science. And, after taking that

class, I was hooked. I said, well, when I get to be real old, and I don't have time to run around and collect all the equipment [routinely needed in her classroom], and I can't keep up with reading the mass of information coming out in science—which even now I can't keep up with—I could see myself as a little old lady helping other people find information. And whenever I'm not helping someone, I can read!

When asked if she feels more comfortable or confident in the classroom than in previous years, she refers again to her desire to continue to grow:

If you mean comfort level in terms of feeling that you are satisfied with what you're doing, totally in control, and there are less things to worry about now than there were in previous years, if that's what you mean by comfort, then I'd have to say no because I am never satisfied with what I'm teaching or how I'm teaching. I am always open for improvement.

She has enrolled in university science courses nearly every year since beginning her career as a teacher. She has undertaken some of that course work in order to earn state certification, some to make up for what she did not study in college, and some purely out of a desire to educate herself further:

I always took a class in science to better myself. I realized that when I first started teaching, the gap between what students knew and what I knew was maybe this far apart, let's say that it was just inches [she holds thumb and forefinger up]. But the gap now, we can say like, I don't know, it's yards apart relatively speaking.

Ms. Payton begins each academic year with a thick file of lessons and activities ready to implement. She explains that prior planning is essential because then she "can focus during classtime on the students, on where they are." She appears to go the extra mile—often, quite literally. For example, to prepare for a field trip to a well-known amusement park in the metropolitan area, she drove the sixty-mile roundtrip in advance of the appointed day in order to scout the park for activities that would provide lessons in physics. She also regularly spends large sums of her own salary on equipment for her classroom laboratories. One year, according to her account, she spent nearly $5,000. She quickly added, as if embarrassed to admit this sum, that she could take a tax deduction for donating the equipment to her school. Nonetheless, that kind of personal expenditure is unusual, as is the extensive time she must invest buying and setting up the equipment. Finally, much of the public recognition she earns may be due to the fact that she is regularly asked to serve as a judge on local and state science fair competitions. She carries out that charge with enthusiasm and leadership.

Ms. Payton is delighted to have colleagues whom she regards as more knowledgeable than she. Some have specialized in biology, chemistry, or physics, while she continues to teach general physical science. The strength of her faculty makes it easier, she says, "to explain to my husband that I could never stop going to school. He could never understand after I got my master's why I wasn't satisfied, why I didn't stop going to school." More significantly, from her point of view,

> I don't feel threatened by the kind of challenge [strong colleagues] present. I feel that's where I want to be. I think my colleagues respect me because I'm very serious about my subject, and I am very open and honest about what I don't know. I am very willing to serve on committees where we have to decide on curriculum or materials. I'm willing to put some blood, sweat, and tears into it. And I have come to realize that when your colleagues know that you're not just getting by, and they know you're not fronting and you're honest, and that your efforts are for education and you are for students, but you are for rules and regulations also, you get the respect.

The comprehensiveness of Ms. Payton's self-description complements what she describes as her competitive, inner drive to succeed. "If you don't have a competitive edge," she claims,

> or if you didn't have a competitive aspect, then it means you don't evaluate. I like to evaluate myself against other teachers. They're the only standard that I have to try to better myself. And when I see other teachers doing something better than I'm doing, then that's just a model for me to follow. And I've *got* to have models, I've got to. I left my other school because I thought that there was no one there and, I hate to admit this, I didn't think there was a person there I could model from and that was an awful feeling, you know, because you start thinking you're too good and you say "I'm not good."

She adds that it was troubling to her

when everybody is coming to you to solve the problems and you think, you say [to yourself], "what a lousy solution I had," you know, but it is the better of the choices. That's why I left the other school. . . . I felt, if I went to a school that was more challenging than my school, then I could really find out how good I was. And, if I found out that I wasn't that good, I had people to model myself after. I would have a better standard.

She speaks with admiration of colleagues who achieve recognition beyond the school walls, and who strive to improve themselves by attending summer institutes and the like. "There are teachers [here]," she concludes, "who don't do that, who just seem to be there for the money, and for the summers [off] and for the fringe benefits. I'm not saying they're poor teachers. I'm just saying that they're not the standard by which I would want to be measured."

Ms. Payton wants to work in an educational medium characterized by high expectations. As we have witnessed, that desire fuels her efforts to craft a productive learning environment for her students. At the same time, it creates tensions for her when it comes to working with students who have lost interest in schooling. As a consequence of her interacting with such distinct groups of students, every school day involves a balancing act. However, that challenge appears to motivate Ms. Payton to self-criticism, to ponder alternative curricula and instructional methods. Her sense of vocation finds expression in her attempt to remain true to two sets of obligations, which I revisit in subsequent chapters: those embodied in the practice of teaching, which require her to try to teach all her students, and those that comprise her own desire to be a person who believes in and enacts high standards of accomplishment.

3

Entering the Practice

Mr. Peters was in his second year as a teacher when I began the research on which this book is based. He taught religious studies at St. Timothy's, a Catholic high school for boys located in the same urban setting as Ms. Payton's public high school. According to Mr. Peters, he was learning about teaching by trial and error. As he put it, he was undergoing the cost of not having had any formal teacher education before he accepted his position. "I figured I could teach with no certification," he said. "There weren't many people in the school who had it, and I'd been told it doesn't really mean that much. And we have certified teachers that, one wonders what the effect of certification really is!" However, by his second year he appreciated that "you're in a classroom with teachers your whole life, but teaching doesn't just 'rub off.' Teaching is a very different activity than being a student." He sought to become better organized and more systematic in his work. He sought "a methodology," as he put it, "certain approaches to questions and ways of using literature. I want to practice at that, and develop some philosophy [behind it]."

Over the course of two years I observed thirty-seven of Mr. Peters's classes, each fifty minutes in length. I witnessed events that support his view that he had much to learn about teaching. His second year as teacher was a bumpy, often difficult time for him in the classroom. He struggled to connect with the boys—to gain their respect, to interest them in the material, and to present and teach his subject in a coherent, pedagogically sound manner. Those goals sometimes eluded him, although never entirely. Through sheer energy, persistence, and consistent preparation for class, he attained a modicum of success. Moreover, according to his testimony and my own observations, he crafted good working relations with many individual students (and colleagues as well). Nonetheless, he admitted that he had more days than he would have preferred when he went home troubled and doubtful about himself.

Mr. Peters did not abandon teaching. On the contrary, his third year in the school could not have been more different from his second. His lessons were better organized and sequenced; he had a clearer rationale behind his curriculum; and he taught with considerably more confidence and enjoyment. He also exerted leadership in the school. For example, he was selected to serve as a member of the important Disciplinary Committee, which recommends courses of action for all students having problems in school and is composed of the vice-principal and four faculty members. "Transformation" may be too strong a term to describe the change between Mr. Peters's second and third years as a teacher, but it comes close because the conditions in which he worked had for all intents and purposes remained the same: his students with their varying needs and capacities, his colleagues with their differing views and personalities, his administrators with their set of concerns, and so forth. However, as we will see, Mr. Peters was not the same.

I center this chapter on Mr. Peters's turnabout as teacher. The fact that he was able to rebound from a difficult second year attests to his sense of vocation and to what he learned about himself and about the obligations built into teaching. I describe the extent to which his religious faith buoyed him, how and why he was able to teach with newly minted confidence, and the role that his colleagues and other circumstances played in his success. Mr. Peters's odyssey from being a teacher who felt somewhat lost to one who felt in command of himself and his teaching responsibilities merits attention for what it reveals about the place of vocation in the conduct of teaching.

JUGGLING BELIEFS AND VALUES IN TEACHING

As a glance at a university department of comparative religion shows, persons do not need to belong to a particular religion in order to study and discuss its doctrines and practices. Mr. Peters sought to teach in that spirit: not, as he pointed out, to "indoctrinate" his students into the Christian faith, but rather to push them to think about what they did believe in and to juxtapose those beliefs with the perspective of Catholicism. His difficulties in his initial two years reflected, in part, his uncertainty about how to balance the obligation to teach Christian religion with his own desire not to preach or catechize.

One of the courses he taught was Introduction to Religion, required of all freshmen. According to the school's curriculum guide, the course is intended "to introduce students to a range of religious topics—including personal growth, faith, God, Christ, love, sexuality, service, and prayer. Through weekly reflection papers and assignments, students are asked to come to a more mature understanding of the Christian faith through an exploration of their own questioning and through their own personal experience." How to define and accomplish these multiple aims was left up to Mr. Peters. The task presented him with both considerable flexibility and vexing ambiguity. For example, how ought he to interpret that key word "understanding"? How ought he to address everything from sexuality to prayer in a coherent fashion? What assignments should he use, and what are "reflection papers"?

These questions, or versions thereof, can be asked about any subject: English, history, art, mathematics. For example, they can be asked about Ms. Payton's Physical Science curriculum. As mentioned in the previous chapter, Ms. Payton wants to teach more than just facts. She seeks to teach her students a process that combines thinking, reasoning, and disciplined procedures in the laboratory. But every teacher in her place would need to ponder what exactly a "process" is, as well as what the best way to teach "it" might be. Can or should one learn it through mimicking others? Can or should one learn it by moving from theory to practice, or by moving from practice to theory? What is the difference between a "process" and a "fact"? As soon as such questions are posed, the ambiguities and complexities in any curriculum come to the surface. The curricular challenges Mr. Peters faced are encountered by every teacher who takes the trouble to reflect on his or her subject matter.

To establish his curriculum and his instructional approach, Mr. Peters consulted with colleagues and with outsiders whom he knew. He took many of their suggestions, while also developing his own activities. These included regular journal writing (a version of the stipulated reflection papers), in which the boys wrote in response to questions such as "If I could change one thing about myself I would . . . , " "Friendship to me means . . . ," "Do you believe in or experience a 'higher power' in your life?" and "Is my God alive?" He engaged students in systematic reading aloud in class of the Bible, particularly the Gospels, accompanied by discussion of the text's meanings. He assigned readings and conducted discussion on individuals who had overcome various problems—drug abuse, crime, racism—in making their lives a success. Talk of character and values, some of it built into the lessons, much of it spontaneous, laced all of these classroom activities.

However, Mr. Peters's balancing act in his first two years between preaching and teaching sometimes succeeded neither in getting the boys to come to grips with the lessons of the Bible nor to reason out their own points of view. For example, one afternoon in April of his second year Mr. Peters asked his ninth graders to write down their "values," defined simply as "any values that you hold, that come to your mind." The boys plunged into the activity with considerable chatter and joking. Mr. Peters exhorted them to "put down as many values as you can, fill up that whole page."

Ten minutes later, he instructed the boys to stop, and called on volunteers to share their responses, which he wrote on the board. The first offerings included family, parents, school, education, and work. As the list grew, so did the boys' bantering. Soon, they were calling out items such as video games, girls, rap music, various sports, Nike shoes, and more. Mr. Peters dutifully wrote them all down. Meantime, the class was becoming more and more boisterous. In the midst of his comments on the boys' "values"— "Good! You guys have lots of good ideas!"—he also called out "Sh!" and "Raise your hands to speak, give others the respect you want!" and "Hey, these other conversations have to cease!" His commands created brief lulls in the boys' playfulness, much like the sudden moments of calm one encounters while walking on a windy day yet knowing that the gusts will soon blow in again. "Make sure we're listening, c'mon guys!"

After filling most of the blackboard, Mr. Peters instructed the boys to prioritize the "values." Walking over to an unused portion of the board, with chalk poised in hand, he asked, "Which do you see as the best, or the highest?" Predictably, the boys called out family, parents, and the like, although some irrepressible fellows shouted out sports and games—which had still not been distinguished from values. Before Mr. Peters could ask further questions, the period came to an end. He returned to the theme the next day, and in fact did so throughout the remainder of the year. But it was unclear, as he indicated himself in conversation outside of class, whether he successfully drew the boys either into thinking for themselves about how to distinguish values from tastes and preferences, or into appreciating critically the Catholic conception and justification of moral values. The lesson featured considerable student participation, but it is unclear whether it yielded an educative experience. Mr. Peters seemed to harbor doubts about the proper content of the lesson and about the timing of his activities (the period ended before he could explicate the core term, "value"). His uncertainty seemed to invite the levity with which some students treated the task.

Consider another episode, also drawn from his second year in the school. In addition to teaching two sections of Introduction to Religion, Mr. Peters taught three sections of an elective course for eleventh and twelfth graders entitled New Testament. (Each of his five courses enrolled between twenty and thirty boys.) The course focused on the life and preachings of Jesus and the Apostles, and examined the text of the New Testament. I will present in some detail a typical class with his upper-grade students. It illustrates how prepared and hard-working Mr. Peters was, but also the difficulties he had at the time in keeping students focused and engaged with their work. It reveals the ambiguities and tensions that had emerged between him and his students regarding how they should conduct themselves in the course.

One morning in April the boys took their seats, as always talking and laughing loudly. Mr. Peters stood at his desk up front sorting through a few papers. He turned to the board and wrote "Matthew 25." One student rose from his desk and handed a sheet of paper to him. Looking up from it, Mr. Peters said to the retreating youth, "Thank you, James, for the homework. I'm looking forward to it." He turned to a student sitting in the front row. "Where's *your* journal entry, Stephen?" The fellow shrugged his shoulders and sat forward clasping his hands. Surveying the entire class, Mr. Peters remarked in a more formal tone, "That's the third time in a row! You're going to fail this course if you don't keep a journal. Now here," he added testily while turning to his desk, "here is a notebook of a student who was recently expelled. He won't need this anymore." Students seated nearby chuckled. "I've torn out the pages he had written on, and I'm going to give it to you. This can be *your* journal book. I expect you to use it."

"Okay," Mr. Peters continued, "you'll need your Bibles for this." Most boys already had their books out. However, one fellow in the front row sat there watching Mr. Peters as if waiting for something to happen, which shortly did. Mr. Peters asked, "Where's your book, Anthony?"

"I don't have it," the latter responded matter-of-factly.

In an earnest voice, Mr. Peters urged—while again looking around the whole class—"Look, your father was in here the other day. I had to tell him you were in danger of falling through the cracks. And now you've come to class without your book!" Several students laughed while Mr. Peters held his arms out, looking at Anthony. Resignedly, he went over to a stack of Bibles on a small bookshelf in the corner and brought one to the boy.

Before Mr. Peters could officially signal the start of the day's lesson, a student blurted out from the back row: "Do we have to write our paper *tonight?*"

Another boy echoed, "Yeah! I still don't get what we're supposed to do!"

Mr. Peters looked from one to the other. "Today's Thursday and you've had since Monday to think about it. I think that's a lot of time, a sufficient amount of time, Mr. Smith. We went over this in detail, it should be pretty straightforward. You can always come talk to me about it if you're having trouble."

The theme of the paper was "inclusiveness" versus "exclusiveness" in the formation of a church. The boys were to write three-page essays.

Mr. Smith said, "Yeah, but I just don't see what 'inclusiveness' is supposed to be all about." A third student chimed in, "You always make it sound so simple!" Meanwhile Mr. Smith muttered under his breath, "Man, this is *stupid*."

"Look, we have a lot of work to do today, let's get going," decided Mr. Peters. "Come and see me if you have problems. Now," he continued, turning to the whole class, "I want you to take a few minutes or so to review the reading, then we'll break into small groups and address some questions."

Most of the boys began to review the Gospel chapter, while others poked around in bookbags or talked with neighbors. A few minutes later Mr. Peters interrupted them. "Now, take down these three questions. I want you to work through answers to them together. When we're done, we'll compare and discuss what each of your groups has come up with." The questions concerned the "Kingdom of God."

"I want you to really think freely on this, talk to each other, see where you really stand on these issues. In the other period, for example, one student said that to him the Kingdom of God was like McDonald's, you can 'fill up' there."

This analogy sparked a few guffaws from the class.

Apparently caught short by their laughter, Mr. Peters said, "Now this is kind of an off-the-wall answer, and I wasn't too pleased with it, but this is how I want you to answer the questions. It's not what you think Matthew 25 says, but what you yourselves think or believe. Now, you can use the book, you can use the text, to go there for support for your opinions, you can manipulate Matthew to fit your answer. But come up with your honest thoughts about this. Any questions, then, about this?"

There appeared to be none. Mr. Peters divided the class into groups of six or seven, for a total of four groups. As the students began to turn their chairs in order to face one another, their teacher called out, "*Lift* your chairs when you move them! Remember the library is just below us!"

For the next twenty minutes or so, Mr. Peters went from group to group, prompting the boys to stay with the task. He urged them to think about how they might formulate responses to the questions. He made references to the Gospel. However, in his absence the boys drifted into joking, examined books or assignments related to other classes, chattered about sports and other outside interests, and only sporadically attended to a question as a group. One tall boy leaned his seat way back, legs spread wide in front of him, bouncing a pencil (eraser tip down) on his desk. Up and down, up and down, until the pencil sprang awkwardly out of his grasp to the floor. He bent over reluctantly to retrieve it. In another group it appeared that one fellow single-handedly wrote answers to all three questions. In still another, most of the work was in the hands of two students.

After making the rounds several times, Mr. Peters announced: "Okay, let's stop our small-group work now. I want us to hear what each group came up with." Some students continued to chatter among themselves. Mr. Peters raised his voice as he pivoted around at the front of the room.

In words that reflected his hopes more than what actually took place, he said: "I SAT IN ON SOME EXCELLENT DISCUSSIONS, a lot of *good* thinking going on. Now let's hear from each group, from the person who recorded his group's thoughts." (He had instructed each small group to appoint a recorder.)

In response to the first question—What is the Kingdom of God?—one group (or rather, two or three in the group) came up with the idea of "a stable relationship."

"Good, I like that," said Mr. Peters. "It's like the kind of relationship we've talked about building with God. What did this group come up with?"

"We said the Kingdom of God was like a place prepared for us, it's, like, there for us."

"Good, your answer suggests the Kingdom is not something in the *future*, it's there *now* for us. That's an interesting idea, good. What about this group?"

A student nudged his neighbor, "Okay, man, read it!" The boy read: "The Kingdom of God is our original home. It is where Adam and Eve first lived. It is a home for all of us to return to."

"Okay, good, that's another good image. It suggests that the Kingdom is all around us, it used to be where we lived, but it's still really *here*." Mr. Peters walked over toward each group as its report was delivered.

"We said that the Kingdom is a reuniting of us with God, and—"

"—Hold it, Jamaal." Turning to another student, Mr. Peters said, "Keith, c'mon," two short words that signaled an appeal to the boy to stop distracting the class. Keith shrugged and grinned at the group he interrupted. Almost everyone else in class, however, seemed to pay close attention as each spokesman read an answer, this in contrast with their lax demeanor while in the small groups.

"Okay, Jamaal," prompted Mr. Peters. The boy repeated his answer. "Yes," replied Mr. Peters, "'reunion' is a theme we've talked about, remember it was the theme of the film we saw last week. Anybody want to add anything to these answers? I think they're good, they reflect some good thought, this is what you can do together. Remember what we've been saying about a church: We're individuals but we still live together, we work out faith and problems as a group, as a community, as a church. Okay, let's hear from the groups about the second question."

This concerned when the Kingdom of God will come. The third question addressed what it takes to become a part of the Kingdom. The lesson continued as before, Mr. Peters punctuating his responses with an occasional turn to an individual, "Give his answer the respect you want for yours when you speak." The groups articulated answers such as "The Kingdom will come when we go to meet God," "It will come when we don't expect it," "To become a part of the Kingdom, we have to show faith, and we have to show repentance." Mr. Peters commented substantively on every answer.

"What if there's still doubt about the Kingdom?" interjected one student as they heard answers to the third question. "Like when we talked about Thomas and his doubts. What if you can't *give* an answer to one of these questions?"

The class watched Mr. Peters as he replied, "Okay, that's a good question. And you recall we have talked about doubt before, how often we sometimes want proof, how we've talked about faith not requiring proof. But this is good. Maybe you can ask yourself, think of something you believe in even if you haven't seen it."

"Evolution," declared the student. "That we're descended from apes."

"Well, okay," said Mr. Peters, hand on chin and looking at the floor. The class was silent. After a moment, he averred "Actually, you can do scientific studies to prove that we are descended from apes, you can find evidence for that idea. But look," his voice suddenly rising, "what about your *future*? You can't see it yet, right? But do you believe in it?"

"Yeah, sure," said the student. A few others chimed in, "Yeah, you bet!" "Yeah, it looks good to me!" Chuckles and quick jokes filled the air.

"If you had never heard of God," another student called out, "who would you give credit for your strength to?" The class swiftly quieted down, again with no apparent signal from Mr. Peters to do so.

Once more Mr. Peters hesitated, looking down at the floor. He replied, "You can still respond to God even if you've never heard of Him. Think of the very first people who responded a long time ago. They had never heard of Him. They just responded to their experience, that there is more to the world than what we see." For a moment, the entire class regarded him closely.

However, the period was almost at an end. "Okay," said Mr. Peters in a tone that announced the close of discussion, "let me put the journal entry up on the board." He wrote: "What do I feel about the Kingdom of God?" Turning back to the class, he said, "I think we had some good discussion. You know, I don't know if I'm always very clear about these issues, I'm always juggling a lot of things at once. It's not surprising that you should be doing so, too."

The boys began to pack up bookbags. "Remember," added Mr. Peters, "your papers are due tomorrow. If you have questions about them you can see me today during lunch or after school. We went over the outline and we—" The bell smothered the rest of his sentence, and the boys crowded their way out the door.

As Mr. Peters's closing remarks suggest, this class period reveals many of the difficulties that troubled his second year of teaching. While he sought to have the students learn to reason for themselves, his comments on their small-group work embodied more his own understandings than the boys'. He did not ask the boys follow-up questions for evidence or for illustration or support from their text. He had no mechanism in place to ensure that all the boys, or at least most of them, actually contributed to their small-group efforts. That fact, combined with other clues such as the students' complaints about the paper assignment, attests to the tenuousness of his connection with the class. Some boys appeared restless, testy, unresponsive to his pleas and exhortations. Although Mr. Peters gamely tried to field all their questions, his uncertainty about his posture as teacher—including whether he should conduct himself as an "ambassador" of Catholic doctrine—showed through in the brevity of some of his replies.

Mr. Peters's uncertainty about his role as teacher was further symbolized in his remarks about the nature of a church. "We're individuals," he declared to his students, "but we still live together, we work out faith and problems as a group, as a community, as a church." To describe a class as a "church" is to lend it a normative meaning rarely associated with the more familiar term "classroom community." Many teachers and educators applaud the latter idea, with its connotations of students and teachers cooperating and interacting reciprocally. In contrast, a church denotes a community that not only acknowledges these relational orientations but also shares comparable beliefs and practices. Mr. Peters seemed unsure about what his classroom ought to be: a community in which individuals can question ideas and hold substantively different beliefs and values, or a church in which all are guided to embrace the same views. As mentioned, the mandate from the school's curriculum guide was ambiguous on this score.

To highlight the distinction between community and church is not to spotlight a dilemma unique to Mr. Peters. Every teacher doubtless struggles from time to time with the question of how much of himself or herself to inject intentionally into the classroom—how much one ought to make plain to students one's own values, stances, and "answers" to life's questions. Every teacher must find his or her place along the continuum between preaching and teaching: between telling or exhorting students *what* to think and helping them learn *how* to think for themselves. There are no blueprints for resolving this challenge, even if, as Mr. Peters explained, a good teacher preparation program can provide useful frameworks for pondering it.

Mr. Peters's actions during the lesson underscore his dedication to teaching. Clearly, he had thought a good deal about the three questions he selected as the mainspring of the discussion. He was able to respond substantively to almost every comment and interpretation offered by students. He also remained consistently involved in his teaching, attempting time and again to draw students into the work and to monitor their conduct. He was aware of the boys' academic progress, or lack of it, and called these matters to their attention. As Mr. Peters admitted in the remarks that began this chapter, he needed some useful pedagogical tools. But he did not lack the will or the desire to teach.

Moreover, that visible disposition itself may have had a larger impact on his students than first meets the eye. The fact that students asked such pertinent questions—"What if there's still doubt about the Kingdom?" and "Who would you give credit to if you had never heard of God?"—coupled with the fact that virtually the entire class listened attentively to Mr. Peters's responses to them—suggests that the course material was affecting the boys more than they were willing to let on. Indeed, one lesson Mr. Peters was learning the hard way, as he pointed out, was *not* to take his students' actions at immediate face value. Students who appear to joke and horse around may not in fact be ignoring the proceedings. They may be affecting adolescent pride and disdain for "school" in order to disguise interest in the material (Cusick, 1973; Henry, 1963; Peebles, 1994). Or, their conduct may reflect aspects of a distinctive cultural style imported from outside the school, so that what might be taken from one point of view as disengagement actually represents something other than that (Gilmore, 1983; Heath, 1983; Peshkin, 1990). The point is that first impressions of student conduct may be misleading, to teachers and outsiders alike.

In addition, some of Mr. Peters's difficulties were more contextual than personal in origin. For instance, he was in his mid-twenties at the time, making him one of the youngest adults in the school and one of the few who did not have a prior reputation with the boys to make use of as a "resource" to command attention and respect. (I heard more than one of his colleagues begin a new course with words such as "If you've had me before, you know what I expect. . . .") Of course a reputation can also be a hindrance. It can precede a teacher to the classroom and become a stereotype he or she must overcome in order to reach students. Such in fact was the case with Mr. Peters, who in his otherwise successful third year in the school had some trouble with older students who had had him in his first year and who, he said, were finding it hard to "see" him in a new light. In brief, Mr. Peters's youth alone required him to work that much harder than older hands to develop working relations with the boys.

Cultural differences also came into play, in two respects worth mentioning. Mr. Peters is white and middle-class in background, while all of his students are black and, in some cases, from low-income families. Mr. Peters grew up in an environment almost entirely white, while all of these boys have lived in communities almost entirely black. From the start of his work, Mr. Peters appreciated these differences. He sought to enlighten himself on ways to work well with the boys, a task that he says was difficult at the beginning simply because of their mutual ignorance regarding each other's expectations and presumptions. To resolve his own doubts and to rectify his lack of knowledge, Mr. Peters talked regularly with black colleagues about the students. Based on my observations and on informal testimony, his colleagues took to Mr. Peters and offered him considerable support. As one teacher put it, they thought highly of his energy and his dedication. Mr. Peters also spent considerable time with the boys' parents, guardians, other relatives, and friends (some of whom were frequent visitors to the school). He embarked on his own search for cultural knowledge. He had all along read and talked with others about black Americans' experience. However, in the summer before his third year he read more systematically a number of novels and books about black culture authored by black Americans. These and other efforts paid off, as the next section will show.

A second cultural factor relevant to Mr. Peters's problems was the culture of the school. Unlike some of his eighteen colleagues (black and white alike), Mr. Peters sought as a matter of pedagogical form to hold back on lecturing and to resist proffering his own ideas to students as if they were the obvious things to believe. He encouraged students to develop their own opinions. In many instances in his second year, it seemed apparent that his approach was confusing to some individuals. They were simply not used to having interpretive questions tossed in their laps, whether about specific subject-matter issues or about the question of what is worth believing and knowing. The official posture of the school, congruent with the atmosphere in the homes of many of the boys, is unambiguous and unquestioning about what values the students should hold. In the midst of this didactic moral environment, Mr. Peters's attempts to get his students to think independently could hardly be expected to unfold smoothly. He needed time and experience to develop procedures that would engage students without also confusing or alienating them.

Far from having to worry about "converting" his students, Mr. Peters complained that some students enroll in his classes with their minds already made up about religious questions. As he put it,

> My problem is that the kids *already* come to the school kind of indoctrinated with Baptist Christian and even Catholic Christian doctrine. I mean, it's amazing: At the end of my final exam this quarter I said, "Just write one concise statement on what you think you've learned. As few words as possible, what you think you learned in the third quarter." And I had a kid saying, "We learned that Jesus Christ is the Son of God and died for our sins and for the

sins of all." We never talked about that! Never talked about it. The kids in a sense have been indoctrinated with that, and they walk into religion class, you know, they just kinda turn that tape on. I have to deal with that a lot. I'm trying to *un*doctrinate them in a sense so that they can start thinking about who they are.

In short, students' expectations and assumptions about religion presented their own challenges to Mr. Peters.

As Mr. Peters grew in awareness of the cultural circumstances in which he worked, he became more confident in his teaching and in his relations with students. He worked to develop more finely tuned approaches in his teaching. He provided more careful and nuanced directions, so that, for example, he could complete lessons in a timely manner. He employed additional tactics to spark his students' thinking, for example building follow-up questions into the discussion. He was both more self-controlled and more assertive in his disciplinary posture, while at the same time more clear about his rationale for the work he called on the boys to perform. He appeared more aware of individual students' academic strengths and weaknesses, while also more aware that he could (and should) be frank with them about what they need to do in order to learn. He still encountered difficult and challenging moments, but these seemed not to throw him off his stride as they had done before.

More and more, Mr. Peters counseled boys individually whenever he detected emerging problems or concerns. He did so before and after class, in the hallways, in the cafeteria, during individual reading and writing sessions in class, and during the time he spent with boys in his capacity as soccer coach. He placed a chair next to his desk at the front of his room, often calling boys up for conferences. One morning in December, for example, he called up a student who seemed visibly distressed. It turned out there had been a death in the boy's family. After a quiet discussion, Mr. Peters wrote the boy a note and sent him to the vice-principal's office to see about being sent home. That same period, a student said he had forgotten to bring a pencil. Mr. Peters took one from his desk and handed it to the boy, saying "I'll give you this pencil to use, but it has a cost. Write a sentence of your choice ten times clearly on the back of your exercise sheet, in your best penmanship." Toward the close of the period, he called the boy up to the conference (and sometimes confessional) chair and spoke with him about his writing and penmanship and how to improve them. He also called up a student who had written a short paragraph on a recent assignment while everyone else had submitted the required full page. "This is not going to do it, Steven," he said to the boy. "You know, I want to be able to use you as a good example to others."

As another instance of change, in his third year Mr. Peters made use of reading he had recently done to recast his lesson on values reported on earlier in this section. Once again, he elicited from students their sense of what they valued. However, this time he engaged them in more systematic discussion of what principles and criteria people might employ to define and prioritize values. He had students write essays on core values such as friendship, love, respect, loyalty, compassion, and more, which he posted prominently on bulletin boards in his classroom for all to see—a public way of valuing their work in thinking carefully about values.

Mr. Peters said he felt like a "new man" his third year in the classroom. He sought to explain this turn of affairs by comparing the experience with his third year as a high school student. He recounted how he suddenly grew in confidence that year, finding genuine satisfaction in both academic and social life. He began to feel "at home" in school, he said—just as he was now feeling "at home" as a teacher. From the very beginning of his third year as teacher, he explained, he established "a different kind of atmosphere" in the classroom. He believed he had a more confident and more command-ing presence. He appreciated the fact that his students seemed at times "a little afraid" of him, a wariness he says he capitalizes on to draw them into their studies and to have faith in his counsel as their teacher and in some cases their mentor. He discovered what he called a "moral stance" toward his work: that it *is* worthwhile to promote learning and thinking in his class-room, as challenging as that task can be. In the next section, I spell out in greater detail some of the elements of this change as well as what accounts for them. I discuss what might be called Mr. Peters's discovery of vocation and what it involved.

FEELING AT HOME IN ONE'S VOCATION

Before becoming a teacher, Mr. Peters had felt drawn to the idea of serving others. That idea emerged from his religious background, just as it has for many persons the world over.

> My personal beliefs, like compassion and care and love and seeing the worth of the downtrodden, have been symbolized in my reli-gion. . . . I know a lot of non-Christians who feel the same way about suffering in the world, and service, and the disempowered. It might just be a human feeling. . . . [But] they have been brought forth to me and impacted into my heart and soul and all that through people—Christians—who have modeled their lives on Jesus and on Christian tradition. I mean definitely, that is important. An idea of service to others.

That idea led Mr. Peters to enroll in divinity school on completion of college, with the possible aim of becoming a priest. However, by his second year in the program he felt "removed" from the world and sought a way to contribute to it tangibly (and immediately). When he learned about the position at St. Timothy's, he applied for it even though he had never taught before or prepared himself to be a teacher, and even though he had little experience living or working in a cultural environment that differed from his own.

According to his testimony, from the very beginning Mr. Peters's pedagogical aim has been to teach his students not what to believe but rather what belief itself involves or entails. He explains that he tries to steer a middle way between what he calls "dogmatism" and its relativistic opposite of "anything goes." He tells students often—and says this often in discussion outside the classroom—that his purpose is to engage them with questions of belief, faith, hope, and personal identity. He does admit to being "pretty Catholic" in what he talks about. "I treat the Bible differently than a Protestant minister," he explains in referring to how he phrases his questions. "And I treat human experience and our relationship [with] God differently than another religion would. So in that sense I'm not just leaving it open to whatever you think. . . . I tell them, 'I'm just asking you the question. I'm not telling you what to believe.' But you know, in the framing of the question you've already set one on a certain path." Although Mr. Peters will allow a line of discussion to take its own course, he continually weaves in comparisons and contrasts with Catholic doctrine and practice.

Mr. Peters endeavors to take seriously his students' questions, and their skepticism as well. "I can be a religion teacher," he says, "but if someone decides not to believe in God, I don't take that personally. [Or,] if someone [does] decide to believe in God, I don't say, you know, 'I've saved another soul.' . . . That's between God and that person." "I don't make people into Christians," he argues. "I don't make people into any religion. I don't make people believe." He distinguishes his work from proselytizing, which he contends does not belong in the classroom.

Mr. Peters's religious faith matters a great deal to him. He underscores how important a role that faith played in transforming his third year in St. Timothy's into a much more fulfilling and successful one than the previous two. His account emerged when he was asked if he would teach differently if he did not hold his religious beliefs. At first, he was unable to respond to the question, as if finding it hard to imagine himself *without* his deepest beliefs. One reason for his silence, Mr. Peters explained, was that he wanted "to do justice" to the centrality of his religious faith in his life. "The reason I can't answer your question," he said, "is not because I don't have an answer. I'm too afraid of minimizing the answer by saying something, so that's why I shy away."

In any event, Mr. Peters replied by talking about how being a teacher has challenged his convictions, and yet ultimately regrounded them. To cite his own terms, he believes that his work has "rekindled" and "reconstructed" his religious sensibility. It has renewed his beliefs, "nourished" and "awakened" him. He adds that the process has been reciprocal: Just as teaching has revitalized his beliefs, so that confidence itself has, in turn, enhanced his practice. Before taking his post at St. Timothy's, he had held what he calls a "Christian humanist faith" in the inevitability of moral and social progress. Now, he says, "My vision is not simply to come in here and to care for people and spread love and goodwill, and then the world will be a better place. I don't see that we're just gonna overcome some of the problems that these kids have through compassion or whatever." He strives to avoid what he calls "accommodationist" and "meliorist" strategies—the former referring to the act of enduring things as they are and abandoning hope, and the latter to the belief that the world is moving inexorably toward the Good. Perhaps thinking of his own struggles as teacher as well as of broader social issues, Mr. Peters claims that it is important to acknowledge human limitations. He regards this acknowledgement as an opportunity to grow in wisdom. It is at this point, he claims, with "the recognition of all that incapableness on our part, where religion really begins to happen. . . . One begins to say 'We are in need.' . . . That's the point where grace occurs and where religious communities, and someone like myself, come strengthened in our commitment to bring about things like justice, and to educate, and to bring about compassion for those who are uncared for."

Some of Mr. Peters's difficulties in his initial two years, he suggests, derived from his doubts about the efficacy of his efforts and about his understanding of the nature of teaching. Others derived from the troubled lives some of his students led (see below). During that period he admits to having gone home at times "in despair." He roots his ability to rebound from those moments directly in his faith. Having to respond to such predicaments "rejuvenates" him, he says. "It's [in] the moment of despair [that] grace occurs. I mean at least for me, when one is really down. I've gone home from classes and burst into tears just from what's happened and from students and from a feeling of hopelessness. [But] I always find myself out of those experiences gaining a sense of what the Christians call grace, of renewal, of hope." When asked about the characteristics of that despair, he insists that one must really "feel" it. "It can't be false despair," he explains. "If you don't really feel the depths . . . you don't really need the whole, you don't need the grace. To use another Christian image, if you don't really experience crucifixion you can't have resurrection."

Mr. Peters's use of such strong and dramatic symbols attests to both how seriously he takes his work and how deeply he feels its successes and failures. While the language he employs may strike someone outside his faith as exaggerated, another look at his experiences as teacher offers a glimpse of its source. Mr. Peters must deal with the troubles and fears his students bring with them from their often violence-scarred urban neighborhoods and, in some cases, unsettled home lives. Their school is located in an economically depressed setting that is not immune to the violence so often associated with such environments. A school counselor, popular with students and colleagues alike, was murdered only a block away. During my nearly three years as a visitor, two students were killed in their neighborhoods, a loss felt acutely in the small and tightly knit educational community of St. Timothy's (Hansen, 1994). Time and again, Mr. Peters had to respond in some way to students' personal needs.

He also had to deal with students who aggressively rejected him and other authority figures. For example, one morning in December in his upper-grade Comparative Religion course a tall, well-built boy who was doing poorly in all his courses arrived a few minutes late to class. Normal procedure in the school calls for tardy students to obtain a late slip from the front office to give to their teacher. However, in this case the boy walked nonchalantly into the classroom, stopped, took out a piece of toilet paper on which he had written something, spat on it, and handed it to Mr. Peters. Taken utterly aback, Mr. Peters held up his hands and refused to accept it. As the class watched hushed, Mr. Peters gathered his strength and said, as the boy settled in his seat, "Not very funny." Then, in an angry tone he added, "It's not a good idea to spit on notes if you want to play in the game Saturday night!" This triggered a mock chorus of awe from the class, "OOOO!" The student completely ignored Mr. Peters the entire period. In addition to bruising encounters such as this—which, while not an everyday occurrence, do take place often enough to weigh on Mr. Peters—there are as mentioned other more serious dilemmas and losses that challenge the faith and commitment of all in the school.

Mr. Peters's metaphoric language of having to "experience crucifixion" calls attention to the kinds of predicaments that teachers everywhere confront. All teachers have their own images and symbols to capture their feelings of loss, hurt, anguish, and frustration, as well as those of joy and success. Every teacher enters the classroom with a body of knowledge and with a set of values (not necessarily set in stone) in which he or she believes. When students are not ready to appreciate that knowledge and those values, or especially when they resist or reject them, one can approach one's emotional and psychological limits as teacher. Despite one's very best efforts—or, indeed, because of them—one can begin to lose heart. For what is at issue is not uncertainty about one instructional method as contrasted with another, or about one curriculum versus another, all of which could be studied systematically to decide which is most appropriate. Rather, what is potentially in question is one's entire constitution as a teacher and person. In the face of perceived failure, one can feel that one is "wrong," "missing something," a "bad fit" with students and with teaching itself. One can feel that one's circumstances are unfair, that one is giving but not receiving. One can feel helpless, not knowing what to do, not even knowing how to get the frustration out of mind let alone how to resolve it in practice. As many teachers could attest, these troubling sentiments can dominate one's consciousness, even one's dreams. "Stop it!" one cries to oneself, "stop dwelling on it!" However, just as one cannot *make* belief or *make* conviction, so one cannot simply *unmake* frustration. Altering one's feelings and beliefs takes time.

Mr. Peters's response to the challenges in teaching is to plumb his interior depths to find his religious belief and faith. He regards such a process as quite unlike grasping at straws or easy answers. He is sensitive to the impression that his religious posture may appear, as he put it, "foolish." "'You know Peters,'" he said in jest one day, "'he works at St. Timothy's and is kind of, you know, he's been there a little too long and he's a little despairing and now he's developing this philosophy.'" Mr. Peters's faith appears to enable him to anticipate a better future, including for himself as teacher. His struggles to teach during his initial years triggered memories of those who had taught him and who had helped him flourish as a young person. Despite his problems, he says that he "knew there was a way of reaching these students because I [had seen] it happen. I knew it was possible; not in my room, at that point, but it was possible." He contends that teachers need to harbor such images of the possible, to have the conviction that their own work can improve, that they can in time learn how to reach students. Without such hope, he opines, "I can see that [teaching high school] could become very difficult, tedious, personally frustrating. Because kids often don't learn the way you want them to learn. They don't take that bank of knowledge en masse and just stick it into their heads the way you would like them to. If you're just looking for that, I can see all kinds of room for frustration."

A SENSE OF ACCOMPLISHMENT

"'Why do we need to learn religion?'" Mr. Peters says his students sometimes ask. "'It's not gonna help me in life. It's not gonna get me anywhere. It's not gonna get me a job.'" As teachers would be the first to affirm, students ask such questions about every school subject. They do not always take for granted what educators assume about the value of curricula. Many first-year teachers report finding this state of affairs unsettling, if not intimidating

(Bullough, Jr., Knowles, & Crow, 1991; Dollase, 1992). That sense of disquiet will be greater to the extent that a teacher candidate has not pondered questions such as what his or her subject contributes to human development, why one has elected to teach it rather than others, and so forth.

By the time Mr. Peters reached his third year in the classroom, he had thought a good deal about his rationale for teaching religious studies. "I kind of like this question [of worthwhileness]. It helps me articulate [what I'm doing]. I really feel strongly that there is a reason for religion [courses] and there's a real strong reason why we don't teach a curriculum that *doesn't* include it." He argues that religion classes expose students to fundamental questions about self and human purpose. He believes the issues that arise in his courses—for example, "What if you have doubts about the Kingdom of God?"—provoke independent thinking. Moreover, Mr. Peters suggests that in taking such matters seriously, he convinces students that he is not trying to lure them into what to believe. It makes it easier for him to persuade students that he is not trying to convert them into "social workers," as he put it, or into persons with missionary zeal. Rather, placing such topics on the table enables him to ask students to reflect on the persons they are becoming.

As mentioned previously, almost all high school teachers confront at one point or another students who regard school learning as irrelevant, as an imposition, as "uncool," even as a potential threat to their sense of identity (Arcilla, 1994). In some respects, Mr. Peters faces a greater challenge than do teachers of more mainstream subjects because of the powerful normative connotations of religion, and, in his specific context, because of the often intense exposure to religion many of his students have received their entire lives. On the one hand, as Mr. Peters explained previously, some students come so steeped in religious doctrine that he feels compelled to try to call that learning into question. On the other, some students come to his classroom put off and alienated by the incessant religious talk they have grown up hearing. Sometimes, they turn that resentment toward his curriculum. Mr. Peters explains that Richard Wright's *Black Boy*, which is part of the school curriculum, is

> an encapsulation of what I hear from kids—[Wright's] real rebellious feeling about religion and the fact that it was stuffed down his throat, and how he just kind of turned it off. I'm aware of that. . . . [Students] don't want to have it stuffed down their throat, they don't want to "turn the mind off" [as they sometimes put it to him]: "Well, if I just have faith, you know, it's kind of like believing the earth is flat, isn't it, until someone tells me different. I don't wanna be *stupid*!"

Mr. Peters tries to avoid such preachiness, while nonetheless striving to engage the boys in thinking about religious questions. He also seeks to respect the faith and religious belief some students do espouse. "I've never been one to go out and shout, you know, 'Jesus Christ is Lord,'" he explains.

> [And] kids who are religious or who want to be religious or who do experience that life is more than just what it seems, they don't want to go around shouting "Jesus Christ is Lord." A lot of reasons they reject Christianity is because they see [some] people going crazy like that. "Why do I have to act like a fool?" Part of my communication is, "Well, you don't have to act like a fool."

Mr. Peters endeavors to model for the boys a way of conducting themselves in which they can honor both their beliefs and their need for dignity and self-respect. "I kind of always wanted to be a person," he offers, "that says *in* his life that you can be very religious and be just a normal person." Mr. Peters's aim recalls the argument in Chapter 1, that the idea of vocation in teaching does not imply preaching, missionary zeal, or heroic actions. Rather, according to Mr. Peters's testimony, it comes closer to a biblical lesson that he and his students study, the Sermon on the Mount. One of several themes they consider is the remark at Matthew 6:1–2: "Beware of practicing your piety before men in order to be seen by them. . . . When you give alms, sound no trumpet before you . . . that [you] may be praised by men."

The longer he taught, the more mindful Mr. Peters became of the tensions between the content of the subject he teaches and the realities of the boys' world outside the school. He explained:

> When you're teaching kids who come from upper-class or middle- or upper-middle-class backgrounds, I kind of feel comfortable saying "Look, what's money gonna get you? What's gonna make you happy? What do you need?" Because they come from a "have" background, they're "have's." . . . But with these kids you can't say, you know, "you should strive to be a little more poor." . . . I'm not sure these kids need to hear it and I need to kind of work with that. Like we hold up St. Francis at this school. . . . Well, St. Francis gave up all his stuff to be poor. And that's okay, I think that's okay if you start out rich or if you're hearing that and you've got a lot. But if you don't have anything and you hear that message you're like, "Why would someone be giving up his stuff?"

By his third year, Mr. Peters had begun not only to recognize students' concerns and even suspicions about the subject matter, but also how to turn those reactions around. He encouraged students who doubted the curriculum to articulate in class and in their journal writing what they did believe in—what constituted their ground of action. At the same time, he endeavored to fulfill his curricular obligations to the school. He accepted the charge that his ninth graders should leave their Introduction to Religion course knowledgeable about the Bible as interpreted through a Catholic lens. He believed that his eleventh and twelfth graders should leave their Comparative Religion course cognizant of both the content of and the distinctions between Christianity, Islam, Buddhism, Hinduism, and other religions they touch on more briefly. But he also sought through his questions to assist students in identifying their own beliefs.

Sometimes, his questions took students by surprise. "When you make that stand," Mr. Peters explains—referring to his commitment to ask such questions—"you're always going to find someone who says, 'Well, I don't want to talk about God,' or maybe 'I don't believe in God.' And you know, it's easier [for the teacher] to sit back and say 'Oh, we're just talking *about* the question of God.'" But Mr. Peters seeks to tap into students' actual beliefs. According to his testimony, what he interpreted as recalcitrance in his initial year or two, he now perceives as embodying potentially valuable questions about the subject matter itself. As a consequence, he seeks to pay greater attention to the "messages" and "signals" boys may be sending him through their remarks and behavior.

One way he does that—which differs from his first two years—is to be more patient. He says that when he first began to teach he had a quick fuse and would send students out of his classroom to the front office. "My feeling was," he explains, "[that] if you're irritating the class, you obviously don't want to be educated. Why don't you go across the street and go to the playground. It was like 'I don't want to take care of you, I want to teach.'" Now, however, he seems to see "teaching" as a bit more encompassing, as embodying an obligation to try a bit harder to establish an educational connection with students. "I've simply abandoned that [previous] approach. . . . If a student is having a problem learning, you don't say 'Hey, you have a free will. If you wanted to learn, you'd learn. If you don't, fine, I'm going to send you out.' No, I'm there to kind of show the kid the light. And so, if you're having a problem, I'm not going to send you out. You're gonna be right next to me." His remarks recall Ms. Payton's efforts to work more effectively and respectfully with her upper-grade science students.

Still another reason that Mr. Peters turned a corner in his third year was that he learned to recognize and reflect on signs of his possible influence as teacher. This is not to say he had overcome all his earlier doubts. Rather, he appears to have understood something about the unavoidable uncertainties of teaching. As he said about students who visibly improve,

"I'm not really sure if it's exactly what I design or not. Just to be honest about that, I'm not sure. It's not as easy as giving a kid an algebra problem; 'now he can do it, okay, I taught him.'" He appreciates how complex it can be to distinguish his influence on students from the many other events and people in their lives. "It may not be what I'm teaching, ostensibly, in the class. You know, I may be going for some cognitive understanding of a concept, and it triggers some kind of affective responses. And they happen. I can't really gauge them, I can't predict them, I can't plan them. But when they happen I say, 'Right on, it's great.'"

However, Mr. Peters does pay attention to whether *and* how students participate in class discussions (Hansen, 1993b). He keeps close tabs on how they perform on quizzes and tests, most of which he designs and almost all of which require written responses rather than multiple-choice or fill-in-the-blank answers. He monitors their writing in their journals. He ponders what colleagues tell him about students. And he heeds what students tell him directly. In the middle of his third year, for example, Mr. Peters described what a student had written in his journal.

> He said—I'll have to paraphrase, although at one point I had memorized his words—he said, "This religion class means a lot to me. You have been teaching me a lot about myself and about God. To this point, I have been really confused about that." And he finished it by saying, "Mr. Peters is the bridge between me and God." . . . And I said, wait a minute! No I'm not! But, I understood what he was trying to say, and that kind of feedback makes me feel that some kind of success is going on.

As was true with Ms. Payton, I witnessed signs of such success that Mr. Peters may never have learned about. For example, one morning in April the school was preparing for a memorial service for a student named Robert Williams who had been shot and killed several days before in a public park. During the homeroom period just before the service, in one of Mr. Peters's colleague's classes, the teacher asked her students if they wanted to talk about their feelings. A boy raised his hand. "In my journal here," offered Michael, holding up his notebook from religion class, "I wrote about how depressed I was to hear of Robert's being murdered. I was afraid. So I just stayed inside, I didn't want to go out, I was afraid what happened to him would happen to me. But then Mr. Peters, he said once that 'Goodness rules the world.' I asked him if he still believed that now and he says he still sees Good overall, and I feel I have to come outside, I want to see that Goodness, because there must *be* something Good if Mr. Peters sees it and believes it."

CONCLUSION: THE ENACTMENT OF VOCATION

One day in November of his third year of teaching, Mr. Peters drew on the blackboard nine dots, spaced as shown in Figure 3.1A, while also instructing his ninth graders to copy them on a sheet of paper: He issued the class a challenge: Connect all nine dots with no more than four straight lines, without ever removing pen or pencil from the page.

The boys dived eagerly into the task. Shouts of fun and frustration quickly filled the classroom. "C'mon!"—"Mr. Peters! you cain't do it!"—"Man!" The boys checked their neighbors' efforts, straining out of their seats to look across the aisles, or getting up on one knee to do so. They needled each other gleefully: "Fool, that ain't gonna do it!"—"Man, look at you!"—"C'mon, boy, you ain't done it neither!" Mr. Peters watched calmly. He refused to provide any hints. Instead, he offered a word of advice: "Don't impose rules on yourself aside from the ones I mentioned. Don't put on yourself rules that don't exist."

After fifteen minutes Mr. Peters dramatically announced the solution. He recalled the rules of the challenge: Connect all nine dots with no more than four straight lines without raising one's writing instrument from the page. He went to the board and drew the solution shown in Figure 3.1B. As he completed the puzzle the class exploded with cries of delight, wonder, and mock outrage. "Man!"—"That's cool!"—"Mr. Peters! How're we supposed to get that?" Mr. Peters replied, while turning to the board, "Most of us impose this reality." He quickly made nine dots and drew four lines to make a box, leaving the center dot unconnected. Pointing to the four sides of the square, he explained: "We make this boundary around life, and say 'This is all there is.' This is like imposing on yourself the rule: God doesn't exist because we can't see him. But *you* decided the rule that only what we *see* is real. We put in this boundary." The boys listened intently. Mr. Peters subsequently returned to this example and others whenever he urged the boys to reconsider their assumptions and beliefs.

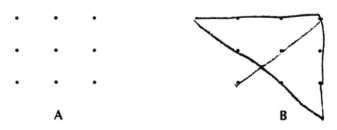

A   **B**

FIGURE 3.1: Mr. Peters's Challenge

Mr. Peters did not fully resolve the tensions between his hope that students learn to think for themselves and his equally strong hope that they take seriously Christian religion. That recurring dilemma aside, however, he did extend his own imagination as teacher to a point where he felt, as he put it, "at home" in the role. He did so despite the fact that his working conditions had not changed. Students still had many needs. His school still presented him and his colleagues with difficult challenges. Working for considerably less salary than his public school counterparts, Mr. Peters was pressured simultaneously to be a good role model, to be firm with students, to educate them, and to inspire them. His lesson about setting self-imposed boundaries applies to his own practice. His experience suggests that the sense of vocation in teaching leads not to a cloistered classroom world, but rather to an adventure beyond the walls of the familiar (Nicholls & Hazzard, 1993). At one point, Mr. Peters said in reference to his classroom presence: "I think students know by the way you teach, and the way you are, that 'this person believes this, but he's not forcing me to believe in it, he's giving me the opportunity. He's asking me to take the risk.'" Perhaps Mr. Peters attained some success with students because of the risks he himself undertook.

4

Staying the Course Through Difficulty

Mr. James works in the Special Education department in the same public high school as Ms. Payton. Mr. James has taught for fourteen years, all in the public school system. He works with students with physical disabilities and with those who are the least academically successful, many of whose problems stem from their antagonistic posture toward teachers, administrators, and school in general. All of Mr. James's students have at one time or another been pulled from regular-track classrooms in order to receive services from his department. Many are routinely absent from school or tardy to class. Many do not graduate.

Mr. James composed the following statement in order to capture his sense of teaching in today's society:

> Teachers and students work together on a battleground of values. While delivering subject matter and striving to inspire thought, teachers promote equally important notions of behavior and attitude, of right and wrong. Students observe, "This is how he acts. He's on the ball." Or, "He's lost; he hasn't got a clue." Qualities such as strength, honesty, compassion, and tolerance are advanced by the teacher's example, or a ceaseless scrutiny will observe them to be lacking.
>
> Teachers are always responding to problems and crises with young people. It is a teacher's duty to bring order to chaos, to answer violence with peace, to replace confusion with clarity. These adverse conditions are not defeated by swift strokes, but students focus on the teacher's handling of a crisis. Her choice of a position is crucial; it establishes which values are preferred. While operating as a rational and humane model of values and decorum, however, the teacher is still an emotional, visceral creature. Blatant injustice, for example, calls for outrage, an affective response that must be felt and expressed.

Over time, students will discover what is embraced, what is despised, and what is considered insignificant by their teachers. If we are perceived to be doing our jobs well, our values will seem more credible to our people.

Mr. James's talk of a "battleground of values," to which I will return throughout this chapter, mirrors how he described himself one day in conversation. "I'm a plague-fighter," he declared, referring to Albert Camus's *The Plague*. Readers of that novel will recall its gripping account of how a group of citizens battled an infestation of bubonic plague in their city, with the "plague" symbolizing the fascism that had plunged France into its convulsions of the 1930s and 1940s. Mr. James appreciates the Camus story in part because he perceives himself to be working on a moral frontline. He sees himself as a rival to the complex circumstances and forces that lead his often troubled students astray. He seeks to bring to their lives what he calls "order," "peace," and "clarity." He conducts himself as a moral agent—as a person, that is, who *can* have a positive influence on students—and as a moral educator—a person whose pedagogical obligation is to steer students toward the Good.

However, Mr. James's personal manner and his style of working with students are anything but battling or strident. Both within and outside of the classroom, his customary demeanor is calm and poised. He rarely raises his voice, even when he is confronting students for bullying their peers or teachers, for not doing their work, for taking advantage of him. These often unpredictable clashes punctuate virtually every period of the school day for Mr. James. But his dealings with the unruly or learning-disabled students placed in his charge are not marked by loud appeals to conscience or by heroic efforts to inspire (nor, for that matter, by attempts to frighten or intimidate them). Instead, he enacts what to an observer appears to be a patient, unswerving commitment to reasoning with students. He acts as if *his* model of respectful conduct can eventually become more appealing to students than *their* often disagreeable, if not downright hostile, one. Moreover, as we will see, Mr. James's posture reveals the underlying sympathy he bears toward his students' predicaments and troubles. It reveals his insight into the source of their resentments and their fears. Ironically, as we will also observe, that very awareness hinders his academic effectiveness. He concentrates so intently on his personal rapport with students that he sometimes treats that as an end in itself, rather than as an aspect of helping his students grow intellectually and succeed scholastically.

I will illustrate in this chapter just how difficult Mr. James's working environment can be. At times, the circumstances in which he labors border on the impossible. They raise many pressing questions—for example, about student motivation, about the structure and governance of today's schools, and about the public's commitment to providing an education for all young people. As important as those questions are, however, of more immediate interest—given the focus in this book on vocation—is why a person would continue to teach in the face of such obstacles. Mr. James's actions and testimony reveal that to do so requires neither heroism nor even a notion of combating "the plague," as he puts it. It depends more on an inner resilience and a firm conviction in the value and purpose of service as a teacher. Mr. James's work shows that the sense of vocation can be actualized in even the most unpromising conditions.

AN EDUCATIONAL BACKWATER

Mr. James's low-key and poised style of working takes on added significance when juxtaposed with how marginalized he, his students, and his Special Education colleagues are in their high school. Teachers from academic departments are often reluctant to work with students in the program, either because of their learning disabilities or, more often, because of their unusually poor behavior. Some of these students repeatedly badmouth teachers, other adults, and peers, often severely disrupting lessons. Based on my observations as well as on Mr. James's testimony, it is not that subject-matter teachers simply dislike these students—although a good number do not disguise their feelings on that score. Rather, their collective cry of "Get them out of my classroom!" mirrors their obligation to teach five or more classes per day, each composed of thirty or more students. Moreover, at the time of my research in the school, academic periods were but forty minutes in length. Understandably, teachers would like to distribute their limited time as fairly as possible among all their students, without having to devote extra time continually to particular individuals. Whether they *should* devote such time and how they might do so are questions that have been taken up in recent debates about whether and how students with special needs should be included in regular classes (see, e.g., Gartner & Lipsky, 1987; Howe & Miramontes, 1992; Stainback & Stainback, 1992). Teachers would also like to focus as much as possible on the academic subjects that constitute the main reason why they and their students are in school in the first place.

Nonetheless, the fact remains that Mr. James works in a department regarded by many of the school's constituencies as its backwater. Judging in part from informal testimony from teachers, administrators, and students, many of the young people dealt to him are viewed as the flotsam and jetsam of the school, perennial losers who need to be kept under control until they can be eased out of the system. Some of Mr. James's own Special Education colleagues appear to have given up on the students as well. For example, one morning in February a staff member strolled into the classroom and said to a student, in an incredulous voice, "Oh! you're *working*?! When everyone else is—" "—having fun?" completed the boy, whose classmates were bantering and wandering around the room. Signs of apathy and of demoralization, some subtle, some stark, are not hard to detect in the ethos of the department.

In light of these circumstances, it may not be surprising that Mr. James wondered aloud more than once what an observer could possibly find of interest in the work he did. His poignant query expresses not a lack of interest on his part in the work, but rather a recognition of just how forlorn his occupational niche can appear to others. Much of Mr. James's teaching takes place in Special Education "Resource Rooms." However, that term does not apply to material resources. The room in which Mr. James most often works is a windowless, featureless place located just off a hallway on the third and top floor of the school. It has fluorescent lights overhead. It contains his desk, that of a colleague, two round tables with four or five chairs of varied sizes at each, a bulletin board, a blackboard on a display stand, and some file cabinets crammed with well-worn and mostly outdated textbooks. The fact that the chairs are of different dimensions suggests that they have been scavenged from elsewhere. The used-up look of most of the books contributes to the atmosphere of neglect and abandonment. There are also board games on the shelves, many intended for young children. For example, the game Read Around states on the box that it is for children ages 5–8. The sheer presence of such games in a setting ostensibly designed to help high school students academically gives one pause. So does the cutout sign placed one year at the top of the bulletin board: "Resource Room Whiz Kids." A critic might suggest that that display, however well-intentioned it may have been, subtly mocks the students, and teachers, assigned duty in this out-of-the-way room.

In a typical Resource Room period, Mr. James works individually with from three to eight students, the number depending on the particular period and on attendance that day. Mr. James assists them with their homework, especially mathematics, and with other regular classroom-based assignments such as preparing term papers or oral presentations. These periods are also used to administer to students any of a number of standardized psychological, motor, and academic tests. Among other purposes, these tests are employed to determine whether a student requires Special Education services.

During the two-year period I observed and spoke with Mr. James, he carried three Resource Room assignments daily, each forty minutes in length, as are regular academic classes in the nine-period school day. Mr. James also taught three mathematics classes that he designed for Special Education students and for which he obtained approval from both the school administration and the Mathematics Department. Each class had a comparable number of students as his Resource Room periods. Mr. James's purpose in creating the classes, he explained, was to provide his students an opportunity to attain something rare for them: academic success in a formal classroom setting. Toward that end, he managed to schedule the classes in regular classrooms rather than in the cramped Special Education offices. He also endeavored in the classes to interact with students as a group rather than individually, as is customary during Resource Room periods.

In addition to these six instructional periods, Mr. James had one period for lunch and two periods intended for planning, formal consultation with staff and students, and filling out the extensive paperwork notoriously associated with Special Education. In practice, these periods became occasions for trouble-shooting. Individual students and faculty alike often solicited his advice on various problems. He was routinely called on to adjudicate disputes and to resolve disagreements concerning students in the program. He obligingly substituted for other teachers, sometimes on short notice—for example, at the very beginning of a period when someone is suddenly needed. In brief, his daily life in the school comprises a whirlwind of public mediation, personal counseling, and academic advising and teaching.

In his Resource Room periods and in his more formal mathematics classes, Mr. James continually urges students to focus on their work. His pleas are necessary because most of the students display short attention spans and fall into incessant teasing and banter with one another. Many exhibit a short emotional fuse. Mr. James promptly resolves petty disputes that break out, this before they escalate into angry exchanges and, on occasion, blows. He typically realizes limited success in his math classes in getting students to work as a group, in part because of his inexperience as a "regular" classroom teacher, and in part because both he and his students seem habituated to the individualized instructional style characteristic of the more familiar Resource Room periods.

As a rule, Mr. James's students reveal little capacity or taste for systematic academic effort. In some cases, their performance is a consequence of learning disabilities. In others, it derives from a long record of rejecting school authority, of "getting by," or of being shunted along in the school system without having much attention paid to them. As the vignettes that follow make plain, their often volatile, confrontational behavior reduces Mr. James to the role of shepherd, running hither and thither to attend to their interruptions and individual demands. The vignettes have been chosen because they typify Mr. James's working day:

Rick walks in late to a math class and LaShondra says mockingly, "Speak of the devil!" Rick belligerently retorts that she looks "real fat" today. LaShondra is outraged and hollers back at the boy. Mr. James interjects that "devil" is only a figure of speech. Rick apparently interprets this to mean that his teacher is taking sides with LaShondra, and he storms angrily from the room. Mr. James follows in pursuit, in part, as he explained, to keep the boy from falling into trouble with other teachers or with the hall monitors (students are not permitted in the hallways during classtime without a pass).

Chris strolls idly into the Resource Room after being thrown out of a class by a substitute teacher. "Chris," says Mr. James wearily, "you've got to learn not to stand out so much. You did real well last week, but you need to control yourself even with a substitute."

Mr. James attempts to resolve a dispute between Andrew and another student. "You don't have to be *hostile* about it, Andrew. You *don't* have to be hostile about it." Andrew replies that Mr. James is always against him. "Now that's below the belt," Mr. James replies, reminding the boy of how much time and attention he gives him. Andrew pouts, then snatches a book away from the student he had been quarreling with. Mr. James asks: "You think it's right to just snatch someone else's property?" Mr. James and the boy continue to spar the remainder of the period, Andrew aggressively, Mr. James with as much patience as he can muster.

"Okay, let's turn to number 3," announces Mr. James, math worksheet in hand. It has already taken him nearly fifteen minutes of the forty-minute period to round up his half-dozen students. Terrell responds to his instructions with a grin: "You want to go ahead and do number 3, Mr. James, you go ahead!" With a wry look, Mr. James shakes his head at Terrell. The boy turns to a neighbor. "Mr. James, okay, he want to do number 3!" A while later, Mr. James says the class should now address number 4. A student blurts out, "I don't want to do number 4! I want a million dollars! All you want [from us] is paper!"

During a Resource Room period, Mr. James asks Jackie, a latecomer, to move to another table so he can continue working with two students already there. Jackie barks back, "You just goin' to *move* me? I *was* goin' to do my work, but not now!" "Okay, okay," Mr. James quickly replies, "stay where you are!" Jackie then adds, to nobody in particular, "I don't know what's the matter with me, I felt like doin' work today. I even answered questions in [first period] class today!" She turns back to Mr. James and demands some paper to write on. "Hurry up, Mr. James, I'm losing the urge to work!"

Two boys in a math class continue jabbering even after Mr. James has asked them several times to stop. Finally, he halts his lesson and walks over to them. "Excuse me!" he announces. The boys neither look up nor cease their chatter. "*What* are you doing?" says Mr. James, exasperated. "I said 'excuse me!'" Chris looks up and says matter-of-factly, "You're excused, Mr. James," and resumes his talk. "Okay, Chris," reasons Mr. James, "you've been around long enough to know when I'm being sarcastic." Chris retorts with another snide remark, at which point Mr. James marches out to call the boy's mother. Hearing Mr. James's intention, Chris leaps out of his seat and follows him to try to talk him out of it. Meanwhile, the other students in the class complete their worksheets in a desultory fashion.

Terrell interjects in the midst of a class, "You know, I have a lot of trouble with the ladies, Mr. James!" Mr. James ignores him and starts to work with several other students. Terrell turns to a peer, "Me and Mr. James are having a man-to-man talk about women!" The two boys laugh and banter. At the end of the period Terrell says, almost proudly, "So long, Mr. James. If you see a girl beatin' on me in the hallway you know what I've been talkin' about!" Mr. James grins back while shaking his head.

Mr. James writes a problem on the board, which prompts Andrew to shout: "We're not doin' that, Mr. James, it's got *fractions* in it. I ain't gonna do that one!" "Okay," replies the teacher, "we'll do this at the end if we have time." The class never got to it.

"Okay, let's get started. Sean, what about the first one?" "What about it, Mr. James?" Sean bursts out laughing while looking around at the others, who are all ignoring him. Suddenly he waves to someone passing by in the hallway. Mr. James repeats calmly, "How would you handle this one, Sean?" Sean looks down at his worksheet and falls silent. Mr. James turns to another student (although he will come back to Sean several times). For the remainder of the period Sean gazes out to the hallway, jokes with his classmates, and talks aloud to himself. "Mr. James says 'what do you do next,' 'what do you do next.' Man, you do nothin'! . . . [Referring to a girl passing by in the hallway] That girl helped me cheat on my quiz! . . . Yeah, that class is so dull you can watch the dust fall!"

The impression quickly forces itself on an observer that these Special Education periods often constitute little more than formalized babysitting, Mr. James's efforts to teach notwithstanding. This is not to place blame directly on Mr. James or on his students, despite the latters' rough-and-ready behavior. There are institutionalized limits to what they can accomplish. For one thing, Mr. James and his colleagues are not subject-matter specialists. They understand that the academic assistance they provide can rarely match that of fully prepared subject-matter teachers. "They never let me teach regular kids," Mr. James said in reply to the question whether he had ever taught a class outside his department. When asked if that fact implies that "they" don't believe he's qualified to do so, Mr. James replied:

> Maybe. Okay. Sure. Special Ed is probably not the highest ranking department in the hierarchy [of the school]. In fact, some people probably think it's the lowest. . . . Once in a while it pops into your head that you're not [a teacher]. "You don't have a full class. You're not—" because I don't have as large a class. I don't have as many students as a regular teacher. . . . There's always a bit of a stigma. We function in many ways kind of as a cross between a teacher and a counselor. . . . [But] we're marginally teachers and marginally counselors.

Mr. James adds that his students are perfectly aware of these perceptions. He reported that one student said to him once, "They picked you out right away! They didn't want you! They sent you to us!"

The burden of working with students whom other adults appear to have abandoned wears on Mr. James and his colleagues. A sense of holding on, of keeping a finger in the dike, pervades the constrained environment in which they work. Some faculty treat the students—justifiably so, it often appears—as if they have no sense of responsibility, no pride of accomplishment, no future prospects. But those expectations only exacerbate the problem. Students and some teachers alike exhibit little respect for their time or effort. Sometimes, not a single student is present in the Resource Room at the start of a period; sometimes, no teachers are present. In those cases, students joke and tease or wander out to the halls, there to disrupt the life of the school.

Mr. James must devote considerable time and energy to persuading students to adopt a learning posture. As the vignettes above attest, "commanding" them to cooperate would work about as well as King Canute's demand that the tide stop coming in. "I used to shout at them," Mr. James says, "but that just didn't work. They're used to shouting and being shouted at everywhere they go. And if that doesn't work, then what have you got left?" But Mr. James's use of persuasion rather than bluster also derives from his ambiguous role. As he underscores, his role is neither teaching nor counseling in the full sense of those terms. That fact places the students' role in question as well. Are they to seek personal advice and counseling from Mr. James, or are they to regard him as an academic instructor? Perhaps because they are unsure how to answer the question, the ambiguity that their doubts generate goes unspoken and unacknowledged, which only fuels their uncertainty and confusion. In turn, these conditions undermine Mr. James's authority. Because the locus of his authority is not immediately apparent, as it is for his counterparts in regular classrooms as well as for counselors and administrators, he often finds himself relying on personal rapport and appeal alone (Page, 1987, 1991).

Jackson and colleagues (1993) argue that an "assumption of worthwhileness" undergirds the willingness of teachers and students to engage in academic work. Focusing on subject matter presupposes the idea that doing so is in fact worthwhile. In the absence of this assumption, meaningful teaching and learning are difficult to conceive. Such appears to be the case in Mr. James's department. Students and some teachers do not bring to the table the expectations for work and learning implicit in many regular classrooms. Instead, they either do not know what to expect, or, as the vignettes suggest, they expect very little. To suggest that their conduct reveals an "assumption of worthlessness" would be too strong. But witnessing what takes place in the department occasionally brings the notion to mind.

Mr. James unwittingly hampers his own efforts to teach and to influence his students' conduct. For example, he undercuts initiative by unquestioningly supplying students with paper and pens or pencils. He hands out his office key so that students can help themselves to materials. His department does have a budget for these and other items (such as bus tokens). However, the practice of handing them out willy-nilly to students—many of whom do not, incidentally, come from poverty-stricken homes—discourages their coming equipped, their planning ahead, and their learning to care for tools and other resources of learning. Indirectly, the handouts may contribute to the incessant, often petty demands students make on Mr. James.

Mr. James repeatedly tells students that education is important. But he sometimes tries to secure their cooperation by offering such counsel as "Work-study would get you out of school early, Rick, and that's a good deal." Furthermore, his habitual responsiveness to students causes him, unintentionally, to waste instructional time. When in the presence of his students, Mr. James often acts like a baseball catcher behind the plate. He takes in whatever the students throw his way behaviorally. He has to scoop some of their actions "out of the dirt," while many others are "high and wild." As we will see, Mr. James has his reasons for conducting himself this way. Still, to complete the metaphor, unlike many regular classroom teachers Mr. James often cannot even call his own pitches. Time and again, students simply run around the academic agenda of the period.

SIGNS OF INFLUENCE

Readers may wonder whether this troubling account of Mr. James's teaching environment is exaggerated. If conditions are really as unfortunate as depicted thus far, why would any reasonable person accept working in them? What, if anything, can be redeemed from them? Why include Mr. James's efforts in a book centered on the idea of vocation in teaching, when it is hard to perceive in his situation the possibilities for meaningful service and for personal fulfillment that that idea represents? Moreover, might it not be unfair to Mr. James to do so, given the fact that he is not in a position to have the academic impact that Ms. Payton and Mr. Peters have?

Every description of a school environment is partial. It can never encompass all points of view, nor can it exhaust all the meanings derivable from the setting. If taken as the only possible interpretation, it can scarcely avoid distorting the picture. Mr. James does face a difficult task, every day. However, he also realizes his share of successes, at least if one grants that "success" can be defined relative to one's circumstances and relative to the expectations one can reasonably fulfill. Given Mr. James's context, it would be questionable at best to expect him to accomplish what Ms. Payton, for example, is equipped to do with her motivated seventh graders.

Some of Mr. James's students do improve their behavior and performance sufficiently to be accepted back into regular classes. Others improve in math under his tutelage and are able to move back into the academic mainstream. At times, his students become quite absorbed in what he is teaching. One afternoon in February, for example, Mr. James was demonstrating a geometrical proof on the blackboard. As his enthusiasm grew, he uncharacteristically took off his sports coat and threw it over a chair. All of the students were closely attuned, so much so that Jackie offered a running commentary: "Mr. James is really getting into it, he's really hot! He's taking off his jacket! He's doin' it!" The point is that all the students were "doin' it" as well.

For some of Mr. James's students, the academic assistance he renders is all they have available aside from what their regular teachers provide. Some do not have parents, guardians, or other adults in the home who will take an interest in their schooling. Perhaps as a consequence, it is not unusual to hear a student tell Mr. James about a successful academic experience in a classroom and then thank him for his help in making it possible. One morning in May, Diana said to a classmate, "Even though I'm actually for euthanasia [in special circumstances], in the debate I'll be against it." Her peer sputtered "Why? if you're *for* it?" "Because that way," said Diana, "I can learn why some people are against it." She smiled at Mr. James, who had been devoting considerable time to helping her think through her position. At the bell ending the period he called out, "Let me know how it goes!"

When Mr. James's schedule permits, he attends his students' regular classes to listen to their oral reports, speeches, demonstrations, and the like. One morning in November, for example, he visited Valerie's English class to listen to her poetry reading that he had assisted her with the week before. On another occasion in May, he sat in on Donald's judo demonstration. Several weeks earlier, in April, Mr. James attended an English class where Leonard gave a speech on social discrimination in the school—a topic that Mr. James's students bring up regularly in conversations with him. The boy complained about his classmates' "fixation" on dress, shoes, and overall appeareance, which he claimed led them to tease students like him who are overweight or who suffer from various disabilities. "I have dyslexia," said Leonard, "and I'm still in Special Education. I have no problems with that. Jesus, the Hunchback of Notre Dame, the Elephant Man, the Catcher in the Rye, Lenny in *Of Mice and Men*, all faced social discrimination." In words that recall Mr. James's own urging with his students, Leonard concluded: "Try not to be a cause of discrimination. Everyone is snobbish about something, but you don't have to act so to others." Leonard received praise for the content and structure of his speech from the English teacher and class. These and other occurrences reveal that while Mr. James's occupational conditions remain problematic, they are not as hopeless as might first meet the eye. Some individuals respond well to his personalized attention. They visibly appreciate his efforts on their behalf.

Mr. James's conduct and his views of students contrast with reported accounts of "teacher burnout," a term coined to describe practitioners who have either lost or never developed the ability to interact productively with adolescents—and who, in some cases, have come to dislike them (Ashton & Webb, 1986; Cedoline, 1982; Dworkin, 1987). Despite working in trying circumstances, Mr. James shows no signs of becoming either emotionally unstrung or morally drained. He does not fight verbally with students, or shout at them, or intimidate or humiliate them. He maintains his self-control and reasons patiently with students, however aggressive or recalcitrant they might be, and however slow and uncertain their progress. He has been working with such students for fourteen years.

I had the opportunity to observe thirty of Mr. James's classes and Resource Room periods. I also conversed with him during his lunch periods and at other times of the day. Often, we were interrupted by individual staff members and students, thus setting up additional occasions for me to gain a sense of Mr. James's presence in the school. His evident steadiness, perseverance, and advocacy of students do not go unnoticed. His departmental colleagues often defer to him. For example, one morning in January students in the program met in an assembly room to take a standardized test. When a hall monitor came in to complain about students wandering out of the room, the departmental chair promptly replied, "See Mr. James, he's the head honcho here!" Two colleagues seated nearby smiled and nodded their agreement. Mr. James went out to resolve the matter.

As part of a facultywide in-service day in October, Mr. James, his chairperson, and two of the other eight Special Education faculty each led a separate discussion with a quarter of the school's teachers. This hour-long session came on the heels of talks to the entire staff given earlier that day by the principal and by a specialist from the board of education. They emphasized the importance of Special Education services and of working cooperatively as a faculty. Mr. James began his group discussion by distributing a handout with a cartoon depicting a teacher asking a solitary student seated at his desk, "Where's the rest of the class?" The student's reply is, "You sent them all to Special Education!" Below the cartoon is a statement urging teachers to realize that the term "learning disability" should not be employed as an "easy out" for ignoring or looking down on poor-achieving students. Teachers are asked to consider "personal and extrapersonal" factors that may be causing or contributing to classroom problems. After discussing the handout, Mr. James spoke at some length about what he called the "humanity" of his students, about their varied needs and difficulties as young people. He urged teachers not to lose sight of how valuable an influence they can have on them. "It's good for them to be with you," he contended, "to have your regular curriculum." He described a typical Resource Room session, the kinds of advising he provides students, and the mathematics classes he had set up.

Mr. James's principal scheduled the in-service day in order to address perceptions of mistrust and miscommunication between the school's Special Education and academic departments. Some Special Education faculty suspected their colleagues of "dumping" students on them, while some academic faculty regarded their Special Education colleagues as "babysitters" who do not provide enough substantive help to students. As mentioned previously, it is not hard to find evidence in support of both viewpoints. However, during the in-service session Mr. James's peers gave him their attention and posed questions and concerns of their own. Perhaps one reason they listened to him in the first place is that they knew he backed up with deeds what he was stating in words. For example, Mr. James regularly prepares reports on students placed in his care, and he ensures that teachers receive them in a timely manner. He talks individually to teachers in positive terms about students and encourages them to consult with him if they encounter problems. I heard evidence of the impact of these efforts earlier that year during a meeting of the English Department faculty. The faculty were complaining about what they regarded as the Special Education department's laxity in sharing information with them. One teacher said she did not realize until well into the quarter that a student she had was hard of hearing; another said he had only recently discovered that one of his students had reading problems. However, several teachers qualified their complaints by stating "Mr. James is different . . ." To judge from these and similar comments, Mr. James is perceived by many of his peers and students as a person who takes their concerns seriously.

WHY TEACH?

Mr. James was not destined for the work he does. "There wasn't ever any grand plan that resulted in my being a Special Ed teacher," he explains. He felt no altruistic call to help struggling young people, although he says that as an adolescent he did harbor images of becoming a social worker. On graduating from college he obtained a Master of Arts in Teaching in English. He entered a tight job market and was unable to find a position. However, there were opportunities available at the high school level in the nascent field of Special Education, and he accepted one of them. "It was just another aspect of making myself up as I go along," he avers. "I just knew you had to pay the rent and I wasn't going to be a mechanic!"

Mr. James never pursued teaching English again, and he does not regret that decision. When asked about the impact that fourteen years in Special Education has had on him, as contrasted with who he thinks he would be if he had become an English teacher, he responds:

> I guess [what I've learned is] to accept the good, *find* the good in all the students I work with. I don't think my concentration would be on them if I'd been an English teacher. I would say I would be more academic and less sensitive, less tolerant. . . . There's more of a personal relationship [in Special Education], because it's part of your position to form a personal relationship with the student. . . . I'm not trying to pass myself off as the goody-goody of the year, but to be a Special Ed teacher, that's what you have to do. You're

dealing with a person who is handicapped and it's not just a physical handicap. It's a very personal psychological and emotional type of handicap. And I think the first thing you have to do is try to give that person some support. And in order to do that you have to like them and find something to like in them.

Mr. James's account reflects his judgment of the treatment his students receive from some regular classroom teachers. "Other teachers sometimes come down on my kids," he complains. "Some are pretty hard on them, quite sarcastic and impatient. That really bothers me, when they single them out for a hard time." It is not the rough handling per se to which Mr. James objects. He knows that his students often misbehave and do not concentrate on their studies; repeatedly, he himself urges his students to attend to the tasks in front of them. What disturbs Mr. James is when his students are "singled out" for sarcastic treatment, as if they were somehow abnormal and not entitled to "normal" human respect and care. One of his students once said to him, in talking about her English teacher: "She gives me no respect, and she's teaching me that when I grow up *I* can talk down to the young myself, and this is bad! I think I can't respect her either!" Mr. James's protective, proprietary tone—note his reference to "my kids"—may resonate with teachers at all levels of education. The closer one becomes to students, the more one wants to see them do well and to be recognized favorably by others. Because that does not always happen, one can become angry, defensive, and an advocate.

Mr. James acknowledges how hard it can be to reach some students. However, he seeks both to remind himself and to make clear to colleagues a lesson he has learned over the years. "It's a given," he explains, that "there will be misbehavior" from the students he works with:

> They will be acting out, expressing their problems. To do my job I can't respond with nastiness everytime somebody misbehaves. . . . [Their behavioral problems are] the natural thing. That's the way they are, they're working out whatever their problem is. . . . [When confronted with bad behavior], I have to stop and say to myself, "Well, it's not your job to reject it. Your job is to try to help that student toward the point where he can make a good-faith attempt. If he shows up it's your job to try to deal constructively with whatever he comes up with."

A second-grade teacher in a nearby independent school, Mr. Jordan, sheds light on Mr. James's orientation toward students. According to his self-description, Mr. Jordan treats his second graders as though they have entered his classroom with a clean slate, unburdened by perceptions and expectations brought from outside the school. "I expect these children all to be normal," he says. "I know some of them have problematic home lives, and I know some of them have specific problems, whether it be learning disabilities or emotional problems. But if I set up a situation where they come and can feel normal, and perhaps for the first time in their lives some of them are treated as just another kid, then . . . they're going to be more relaxed and relieved. Their checkered past hasn't followed them into this room" (Hansen, Boostrom, & Jackson, 1994, p. 26).

Although the "checkered pasts" of Mr. James's students are much harder to ignore, he does appear to insist on treating them as "normal" in Mr. Jordan's sense of that term. From the perspective of a long-term observer, Mr. James often talks with them as a regular classroom teacher might talk with his or her favorite students. In addition, he often talks to them as the people they might *become* rather than as the troubled, confused youths many of them presently are. That posture of assuming the best in one's students—of assuming a hopeful future—is central to the idea of vocation and I return to it in Chapter 7.

English teachers would undoubtedly object to Mr. James's assumptions about what teaching English "does" to its practitioners—namely, it seems, make them less personal, less tolerant, less concerned with their students. Moreover, some critics might ask how a teacher can genuinely care about students without placing at the core of his or her work students' intellectual development. They might point out that teaching is distinct from other practices, such as parenting, in part because of its pedagogical focus on the student's growth in knowledge and in intellectual ability. As we have seen, Mr. James's academic success with students is often quite limited. It appears to be true that, as he contends, "with Special Ed students, showing that you're tuned into them and listening to their problems is number one. Because if they don't feel that you're gonna do that, then they won't learn anything from you either." Granting that premise, one still wants to ask when the "tuning" in stops and the academic learning begins. Some students seem to demand incessant tuning in, and Mr. James and his colleagues appear to comply uncritically with that demand.

Mr. James is aware of such criticisms. He wonders aloud about the adequacy of his work with students—doubts that found expression, for example, in his spontaneous headshaking about what an observer could find of interest in his teaching. From one point of view, he reveals a sense of vocation similar to what we witnessed previously with Ms. Payton and Mr. Peters. For example, he devoted after-school hours for several years to completing a certification program in secondary education mathematics. Then, he created three math classes for students assigned to Special Education.

"I have a feeling for kids with problems with mathematics," he explains. "I was always helping kids with their math and I thought, 'Well, why don't I start my own math classes and teach my own Special Ed kids. I'll be their math teacher. Then I won't spend all my time helping them with their math classes which they might fail anyway. And it would just be a more efficient way to do things.'" His plan was approved by both the administration and the Mathematics Department. It so impressed a colleague that she constructed similar classes for low achievers in English.

However, as we have seen, the conduct of these classes is problematic. Students continue to act out and Mr. James and his colleagues respond promptly and at length to them. They find it difficult to break the habit of one-on-one interaction as contrasted with working as a group. Mr. James reports feeling pulled in several directions while teaching his self-designed courses. On the one hand, as he emphasized above, "with Special Ed students showing that you're tuned into them and listening to their problems is number one." On the other, "to teach the math class, you have to be orderly, be prepared, to a certain degree I think you have to suppress a student's personal responses so they can get along with the task." In practice, he admits to having much to learn about how to juggle these responsibilities. Meantime, the classes proceed unevenly and sometimes with significant loss of instructional time.

Mr. James's self-doubts make him speculate that he "should be burning up the midnight oil thinking up something specific for each kid, each day." Time and again, however, he returns to the personal dimensions of his work with students. He talks about the distinctiveness of each of his students. He says that he derives considerable satisfaction from developing ways to "connect" with them. He underscores the importance of "finding something to like" in each of them. He claims that doing so is indispensable if one is to have a positive rather than a negative influence as a teacher. In short, rather than condemning English teachers—which is what he himself might well have become—Mr. James seems to be saying to all who teach subject matter: Beware of assuming that your students will like your subject as much as you do. To draw them into an interest in it, or, even more, into a passion for it, you may want to make sure you're paying enough individualized attention so that they sense you like teaching *them* as much as you like teaching your subject.

Mr. James admits that he does not find it easy or natural to like every student. "I do find it hard sometimes," he states. "There are always some that you—my colleagues and I talk about that sometimes. There are some people, some students, that you really don't like." He goes on to say, however, that "the funny thing is, that part is, with more experience, it's getting easier. I can't explain that." He suggests that one reason for this change is simply his familiarity with the students assigned to him over the years. He also mentions his experience as a parent, and implies that it has deepened his sympathy for his students' needs and concerns. Although he continues to be taken aback, even shocked, by some of the things students say and do (more on this below), he appears quick to forgive and quick to respond.

Matters were different when he first began teaching. At that time, he explains, the task was close to overwhelming. "At first it was kind of tormenting to me to work with students who had heavy problems." In words that recall Mr. Peters's testimony, he says: "I was just twenty-three, twenty-four years old. You really don't feel so good at the end of the day. I remember back at that time it was hard to reflect. It was more a case of survival than being able to reflect too much. I was only six or seven years older than my students." Like teachers at all levels of education, Mr. James can still recall vividly many of his early frustrations and setbacks. The most dramatic instance he described concerned a boy he worked with a decade before. The student was known as a troublemaker. One day, Mr. James angrily threw him out of class. The boy went down to the front office, as required, and once there promptly got into a fight with the school principal, literally exchanging blows with him. The boy was sent to a reformatory shortly thereafter, and eventually landed in jail for armed robbery. "For a long, long time," Mr. James says,

> I was burdened with this guilt feeling. If I had just said, "All right, Mitchell, just relax!" Or if I'd been able to stand it for another fifteen minutes, then all the rest wouldn't have happened. . . . I was completely fed up with the student's behavior. I was fed up for the whole school with his behavior because he'd been a problem in a lot of different places. But I didn't really give him too much of a warning at that time. You could say he'd had a lot of warnings but, you know, it was how I handled being at my limit that made me feel guilty.

Mr. James implies that one should not make decisions about students when one is at one's emotional "limit," a hard-won truth surely familiar to many teachers. "Maybe I should have gone a little further," he concludes.

However, based in part on what has been reported in this chapter, it seems evident that Mr. James has taken his own lesson to heart. Not once in two years did I observe him send a student out of his room for punishment. He handled every instance of misbehavior himself. Moreover, his orientation toward his work appears to have moved well beyond the "survival" stage. As he has grown in experience and confidence, he appears to have discovered sources of satisfaction. He appreciates that external rewards will not be forthcoming: lucrative pay, public recognition and honors, increased prestige. Those forms of compensation are simply not available given the lowly status of Special Education in his school. But Mr. James earns the respect of peers and of many of his students. He enjoys getting to know students, warts and all. The fact that he finds it "easier" to like them appears to go hand-in-hand with liking his work—its ambiguities and all. "Here I'm approaching forty," he says, "and I'm still, I feel like a young person, new to the world, not set in my ways, still making myself up, each day being new. . . . I don't know how I'm going to act and how I'm going to respond to each situation that comes up." He appears to relish that very uncertainty. In effect, Mr. James acts as if he sets himself a challenge before walking through the school door each morning: In the face of all the unpredictable and thorny events that are guaranteed to happen today, how will I go about maintaining a respectful and encouraging posture?

Mr. James takes advantage of the discretion he perceives in his role—what might be viewed, ironically, as another positive aspect of that role's ambiguity. Technically, he explains, a Special Education teacher's services "are to be appropriate" in light of how a student's needs are assessed and described. Mr. James endeavors to provide those services. In practice, however, he also interprets that charge to mean he should be a "supporter" of the students placed in his care. "Students as much as anything need support. . . . [So] I react to what students bring to the situation. If they seem to call out for counseling, for emotional support, I try to respond. . . . You deal with that [first] rather than force the schedule on him." However, Mr. James distinguishes "support" from becoming intimately familiar with students' personal lives. He does not seek, as he puts it, to be "really personal" with students. Over the years he has abandoned what he calls psychoanalytic and Freudian approaches to working with students. "I really feel now that it's not constructive for me to know all of the Freudian explanations for why these students [act as they do]," he says. "I don't go into that social work/quasi-psychoanalysis business too much any more. In the context of teaching my class, if somebody's having 'support problems' I try to deal with what they are saying, even if it's disruptive." To judge from his testimony, Mr. James endeavors to teach students to perceive their conduct from a social perspective, to see themselves as acting in relation to other people.

Mr. James capitalizes on the otherwise lowly status he and his department have in the school. "You know, in some ways I feel free, maybe, by my marginality. I feel free to tune in to the students as opposed to having to maintain some particular authoritarian figure." He can offer students what he calls "a type of sanctuary" from what he regards as the bureaucratic and "petty" interference they experience elsewhere. He supports his school's emphasis on order and on rule-following, mindful that it reflects, in part, the worries of school staff and parents alike about students' harming themselves or others. But he downplays rules when he perceives them as interfering with his determination to treat his students respectfully and to help them learn to treat others that way. For example, he dislikes calling boys' attention to the fact they are not supposed to wear earrings in the school. "It's not that I feel hostile toward the policy," he explains. "I just feel like I'm after bigger game, like somebody's being disruptive or walking in the halls causing trouble." He does not operate outside the rules. "I have no qualms," he says, "about bringing in the guns of the administration for punishment if I feel students cross over a line of behavior." He has supported many administrative decisions to discipline his students, including strong sanctions such as suspension from school.

However, he appears to support the spirit of the law more than the letter. He displays a higher allegiance to his personal relationship with students. In fourteen years of teaching he has yet to jettison that stance despite the fact that students sometimes take advantage of it. Some complain and gripe incessantly, tapping into Mr. James's sympathy and, in effect, sabotaging his desire to teach. Some resort to all manner of petty and obnoxious tricks to avoid working. For example, they ask to go to the bathroom in the midst of a lesson. Mr. James routinely complies with the request, believing it "unfair" to treat his young adults as if they were still in elementary school. However, some individuals end up wandering the halls, looking for trouble and getting into it. As usual, Mr. James is the one who must put out the fires. Consequently, he must sacrifice even more instructional time to deal with such problems—again a cost he appears willing to accept, and have his students accept, so long as he can maintain a respectful relationship with them.

His relaxed posture on some school rules occasions conflict with colleagues, which again leads to a loss of instructional time, not to mention embarrassment and hurt feelings. Moreover, what Mr. James views as respectfulness—that is, treating his students like responsible adults—fuels the suspicions of other staff that his department is anything but responsible. One afternoon a teacher serving hall duty brought two students to Mr. James, saying coldly in full hearing of his class, "Next time, make sure they have a hall pass"—as if Mr. James were a novice who had never heard of the rule. On another occasion, as per his custom, Mr. James gave a student permission to go to the bathroom. The boy, Rick, lingered in the hallways and disrupted another class. A teacher serving hall duty appeared on the scene, and within moments was engaged in a shouting match with Rick, largely because the boy refused to give his name (he was also not wearing his required student ID). Hearing the commotion, Mr. James sped out to the hall. As he did so, a boy named William cried out to his peers, "He goin' to report him!" "Naw, man," replied another student, Robert. "Don't worry about Mr. James! He's too cool for that! He ain't gonna crack him!"

Shortly thereafter, Rick and Mr. James returned to class. They wore tense expressions on their faces, in part because neither had given the boy's name to the hall monitor. As he explained later, Mr. James had pleaded with the teacher to be lenient with Rick, arguing that the boy was making good progress as a student and deserved this break. His pleas went for naught. The hall monitor had gone down to the front office to report the incident and to secure administrative support to force Mr. James to cooperate. At the end of the period, she walked into Mr. James's classroom to explain that she had filed a report and that the front office insisted on knowing the student's name. As she and Mr. James conversed, several boys hovered around them (Rick had sprinted from the room at the bell). "No, Mr. James, don't do it, man!" urged Robert. "Put her off, man!" The hall monitor coolly ignored the boy. Mr. James turned to him and asked quietly, "What do you want me to do, Robert, lie or make up a name?" Robert hesitated, as if weighing the matter. Seeing no recourse, he turned to leave the room, sputtering "Aw, man! Man, yeah, just make it up!" Once the boys were gone Mr. James yielded Rick's name, but with great reluctance, as if he were betraying something sacred.

The incident reveals Mr. James's strong fellow-feeling for his students, which he reports has grown over the years. It illuminates the trust his students place in him—students who, in some cases, perceive other adults in the school as "against them." Though some individuals, like Rick, take willful advantage of him, they appear to appreciate his support. One might argue that Mr. James is unwise if not naive to adopt practices such as letting his students go to the bathroom on demand. One might regret the loss of instructional time he tolerates in the name of maintaining personal bonds with each student. But Mr. James's tradeoff appears understandable in light of the point emphasized earlier, that he is perceived in the school culture as an ambiguous mix of teacher and counselor. Those perceptions "free" him, as he puts it, to focus on what matters to him most: his everyday treatment of students and how they are treating themselves and others. Nor are these overriding concerns difficult to comprehend. Mr. James does not have the luxury of working with students dedicated to schooling. He does not have students who get along easily and comfortably with others. Mr. James's search for rapport with the students placed in his charge does not blind him, he says, to the need to work hard with them on improving their conduct. Rather, it can be seen as a consequence of that need.

Mr. James states that some students are downright cruel and unforgiving of others. He has a store of episodes to illustrate his claim. For example, another of his many efforts to provide beneficial experiences for his students is organizing a basketball session the last period of the day on Fridays. He arranges the activity through the Physical Education department. Mr. James says that the boys (girls rarely participate) greatly appreciate the opportunity to "blow off steam" after what often feels to them, or so they report, like a long week in school. Mr. James usually rolls up his sleeves and joins them in play. One Friday in November, two members of the school's football team showed up and promptly crashed the game. Mr. James was unable to persuade them to leave. The two large fellows bullied and banged around his students, creating an environment of extreme hostility marked by verbal abuse and near fighting—Mr. James's students do not back down from challenges from peers, even if the latter happen to be physically much stronger. Eventually, Mr. James coaxed the two marauders to leave them alone. But the incident left him shaken and emotionally drained. The last thing he wanted for his troubled students was to have the last period of the last school day of the week wrecked by such a stressful experience. It so upset and angered his students that Mr. James feared they would get into trouble and possibly injure others and themselves over the weekend (every weekend is something of a moral gauntlet for his students, Mr. James said; some are often left on their own without any adult supervision or care).

The incident also left him wondering how the two varsity athletes could have acted so brutishly. He was struck by the fact that they apparently had no idea that what they were doing was wrong, that their action was, as he emphasized, "a *bad* thing." Mr. James believes that some students he encounters literally do not know right from wrong. In words that recall his statement about a "battleground of values" that opened this chapter, he suggests that students often have no moral bearings, no sense of what it means to act well and in a spirit of cooperation with others. The incident and his response to it recall the pattern of student behavior he works hard to break. That pattern features a short attention span, a quick emotional fuse, and an often relentless game of verbal one-upmanship and competition.

As we have seen, Mr. James struggles against that pattern not with aggressive tactics of his own but with a persistent reasonableness, as if he would provide his own model of how to conduct oneself. He comes to school well dressed every day, with pressed slacks, polished street shoes, and a sports coat over a dress shirt. His demeanor symbolizes respect at several levels: for himself, for his role in the school, and for his students. Every class and Resource Room period he conducts is saturated with comments intended, he explained, to teach students to respect others and their own efforts. "What you're doing, Andrew, is breaking the concentration Sean and I had. . . . Terrell, Jackie and I can't work out the problem *you're* supposed to be working on if you keep that up. . . . You're breaking up my class, Andrew. . . . You lost concentration when you got up to sharpen your pencil right in the middle of doing the problem." He persists with this reasoned and patient form of "moral commentary" (Jackson et al., 1993) despite the sarcastic responses it occasionally elicits. "I tell kids sometimes," he explains, "that if somebody does something that bothers them, say that. Say: 'You did such and such and I didn't like that.' Because, [even] if 'bother' isn't the word they like, there's a way of saying that, standing up for your rights, without being name-calling and insulting about it in return. Sometimes I can get that across." When students begin to complain about other students or teachers, he always interjects "No names!" He attempts to lead them to think through their concerns rather than just to castigate individuals they dislike. He seeks to replace their anger or resentment with reflection on the causes of those feelings. He tries to build responsibility. I mentioned previously that his habit of making paper and pens readily available does not support that aim. From another perspective, however, the fact that he unhesitantly gives students his keys to go to his office for papers or other materials demonstrates to them that he trusts them, even if they often fall short of that confidence. For some students, Mr. James is one of the very few adults who treat them as respectable persons.

CONCLUSION: PERCEPTION AND CIRCUMSTANCE IN TEACHING

Mr. James knows that actions such as giving students permission to go to the bathroom during classtime will lead some of them, and himself, into trouble. He knows he fulfills not the letter but what he prefers to see as the spirit of the school's rules and regulations. It seems evident that he does not take his occupational bearings from that institutional frame of reference, which is not to say he disapproves of his school or of schooling in general. Rather, in practice he appears to fulfill more the spirit and the letter of his own sense of vocation. In an almost literal way, Mr. James lives and works in a different world from that which meets the eye of a casual onlooker. To such a person, as I have documented throughout this chapter, his working environment appears bleak and sad, a backwater of the public school system. *But Mr. James does not inhabit that world.* He inhabits a world in which he sees young men and women with a host of strikes against them, with much to learn about life and about getting along with others. He acts as if his efforts are significant, that it is worth the trouble to enunciate repeatedly, "You're breaking the concentration we had," that it is meaningful to maintain his self-control, and that he should act day after day in a reasoned, respectful way with each student.

Mr. James's posture implies that the question heading the previous section of this chapter—why teach?—is an example of a "bad Socratic question" (Stout, 1988, p. 301). Stout's term refers to questions that, while perhaps well meant, call for answers or explanations that persons are unable to provide, and this for sound ethical and moral reasons. For example, an interviewer might ask a young person why he or she values the quality of thoughtfulness toward other people. The person might be so surprised by the question that the initial response might be, "I really don't know" (or it could be silence, as witnessed in Chapter 3 when Mr. Peters was asked if he would teach differently if he did not hold his religious beliefs). If pressed about the answer, the young person might reply, "I guess I just think we can't live without being thoughtful toward one another." "But why can't we live without doing so?" the interviewer persists. At this point, the person might feel utterly bewildered, and perhaps resort to providing an example or story of what thoughtfulness means in practice. This confusion would be understandable. The young person can provide the interviewer no justification for valuing thoughtfulness because there is nothing of which he or she is more certain than the value of it. There is nothing more plain to which he or she could appeal. There is no principle underlying the value of thoughtfulness; it is its own principle. Without knowing it, the interviewer has found the person's moral bedrock.

To press Mr. James about why he continues to work with the difficult students that come his way would be like asking him a comparable set of questions. This is not to say that his efforts are heroic or worthy of uncritical emulation by other teachers. Mr. James would be the first to repudiate that claim. Rather, his work reflects the fact that, sometimes, there may be no "reasons" a person can cite in defense of a viewpoint beyond the example of the very way of life that viewpoint makes possible. Italo Calvino sheds light on this idea. In a study of the values of literature, Calvino quotes from a rendition of Socrates' last hours before his execution. "While they were preparing the hemlock, Socrates was learning a tune on the flute. 'What good will it do you, [Socrates' friends asked,] to know this tune before you die?'" (Calvino, 1986, p. 19). Socrates' friends were asking him a bad Socratic question. His way of life embodied the belief—surely an educator's creed if there ever was one—that self-improvement and the improvement of human affairs is always worthwhile, right up to the end of one's days. There is no "reason" for seeking such improvement beyond the lived conviction that doing so creates a better world for all. Socrates' flute-learning in the last hours of his life implies the counter-question: What would it be like to live in a world that lacked such conviction?

Williams (1985) writes that "a practice [like teaching] may be so directly related to our experience that the reason it provides will simply count as stronger than any reason that might be advanced for it" (p. 114). There may be no reason for Mr. James to perform the often thankless and fruitless work he does outside the belief that it is better to do so than not. Until such time as society changes so that all students are supported in learning, it is better to try to attend to Rick, Jackie, and Chris than it is to give up on them. Mr. James's efforts affirm a central theme of the previous two chapters: that a teacher's sense of personal agency has a decisive impact on the quality of his or her work. Teachers' perceptions of their role and of their students constitute more than casual, individualized points of view. Those perceptions reside at the heart of what a teacher is about. Teachers can let their perceptions be informed, or possibly even determined, by others. Or, they can influence them through reflection and through their own actions, as Mr. James has so obviously done. One may still want to ask him that bad Socratic question—how he could teach year after year, in good faith, in such difficult conditions. But herein resides the power of a sense of vocation in teaching, of a sense that one has something to contribute, that one can make a difference, and that one can shape the world and not just be shaped by it.

Mr. James's work also reveals that the sense of vocation is not a "lens" that one can take on and off at will. It is not an arbitrary way of regarding things. Mr. James could no more abandon his hopeful way of looking at students than he could abandon his character or identity. Character and identity result not from arbitrary choice but from lengthy experience. That is one reason why changing one's perception of students or of teaching takes considerable time and reflection, as we have seen to be the case with Ms. Payton, Mr. Peters, and Mr. James.

None of these points imply that teachers can either ignore or easily overcome inhospitable working conditions. "There is no creature whose inward being is so strong," Eliot reminds us, "that it is not greatly determined by what lies outside it" (Eliot, 1871–1872/1985, p. 896). As we have seen, Mr. James's circumstances do not lend themselves to realizing vocation. They militate against educational success and against the enactment of a calling on his part. That Mr. James maintains a sense of purpose reveals just how central perception is in teaching. But so are supportive conditions, no matter what point of view one takes.

5

Connecting Students and Curriculum

Ms. Smith teaches sixth-grade social studies in an independent school where she has worked the last four years. Prior to joining its faculty, she taught middle grades for ten years in a public school. Ms. Smith enjoys her work and invests it with a great deal of meaning. She regards it as an "adventure." She perceives it as an opportunity to promote learning in children and in herself. Moreover, she appears to hold these views *because* of her years as teacher rather than *despite* them. I put the matter in those terms because previous studies suggest that the practice of teaching narrows and hardens some teachers' thinking and spirit (Lortie, 1975; Waller, 1932; Yee, 1990). It wears down their enthusiasm, their creativity, and their dedication. According to these studies, it reduces some teachers into functionaries who "deliver" the curriculum to students but who do not invest their work with personal conviction. In contrast, Ms. Smith's years of teaching appear to have broadened her outlook on education and on life.

Judging from her testimony as well as from her spontaneous responses to students in the classroom, her work remains full of surprises—both big and small. Most of these are welcome to her and sustain her hopeful belief in teaching. Others frustrate and dispirit her, the way that bad news reported in the press can cast a cloud over all one's doings. In Ms. Smith's classroom, surprises and unanticipated doings often occur within minutes, even seconds, of one another. As routine as some appear, at least at first glance, they add substance to her view that teaching is an "adventure."

For example, during a lesson one afternoon in February, Ms. Smith was sitting at the podium at the front of class asking students a series of questions on the short story they had read the night before. Her twenty-four students were seated around five separate tables, with books and materials spread out before them. Most students raised their hands at one point or another to answer her questions, some of which were factual, others interpretive and requiring both an opinion and evidence in support of it.

Suddenly, in the very midst of the discussion, Ms. Smith walked over to one of the tables, while continuing to listen to a student reply to a question. Without a word or sign of annoyance, she took a magazine on sports cars from Michael, who, in turn, said nothing. She placed the magazine on a stack of papers, all the while attending to the student giving her opinion. Returning to the podium, Ms. Smith then called on Ben to paraphrase what his classmate had just said. But Ben shrugged his shoulders. "Were you listening, Ben?" Ms. Smith asked. "No," the boy admitted. "Ben," sighed Ms. Smith, "what am I going to do to get you to listen?" The boy shrugged again, with a look that seemed to say that he knows he goofs around but also knows that his teacher will forgive the transgression. Simultaneously, Ms. Smith noticed Larissa's hand in the air. She called on this normally quiet and reserved child. Larissa offered a new and provocative response to the original question on the floor, and the discussion took off on a whole new course.

These minor dramas occupied less than a minute of classtime. Yet they illustrate in microcosm the everyday ups and downs of teaching that Ms. Smith confronts. She must be alert to students who are engaged and to those who are not. She must be ready to draw in daydreaming or misbehaving students without breaking her concentration or that of the class. She must be ready to recognize when a shy or quiet student wants to contribute, and she must have the knowledge and the skill to build on such contributions. This ebb and flow between daily events that confirm the value of teaching and those that call it into question is certainly not unique to Ms. Smith. It characterizes teaching everywhere, at all levels of formal education. What the events reveal, however, is how intertwined that ebb and flow is with the most ordinary of classroom affairs. The unpredictable and the uncertain accompany teachers the moment they walk through the classroom door, and often before and after class as well.

To judge from Ms. Smith's testimony and from that of her colleagues in the practice we met in previous chapters, these vicissitudes need not undermine the desire to teach. They come with the territory, as the familiar adage has it. They are not a problem to be eliminated or overcome, but are a basic condition of teaching. They are the ups and downs that derive squarely from taking one's work and oneself as teacher seriously. To adopt that posture is to guarantee that a measure of disappointment and failure will accompany the success one attains.

In this chapter I focus on Ms. Smith's primary goal as teacher, which according to her is engaging students with social studies and history. She wants to tap into her students' interests and to connect them to the record of the human past and to the prospects of the human present. She wants students to learn the tools of reading, writing, and public speaking so that they can articulate what they know and believe. She wants them to enjoy these activities. She employs a variety of methods to spark their curiosity and to get them to work together cooperatively. At the same time, Ms. Smith also hopes her students will become better persons as a result of taking her classes; she hopes they will learn valuable things about themselves and about other people. That aim, in conjunction with her more purely academic purposes, gives rise to an ambitious agenda as teacher. Moreover, her ambitions appear to have grown rather than narrowed over the course of her fourteen years in the classroom. As the three previous chapters suggest, that fact appears to be true of many teachers who remain committed to the practice.

CONDITIONS FOR VOCATION

Ms. Smith moved to her present school in part because she wanted to teach in a more academically demanding environment. She wanted to work with dedicated and imaginative colleagues. She wanted to teach children whose parents supported their schooling, not just financially but with hands-on time and involvement. In her previous school, she explained, she found herself more and more falling into the role of a "surrogate parent," a trend that she found uncomfortable. She disliked having to act as a psychologist, and over the years has increasingly sought to distance herself from what she calls "therapeutic" approaches to working with children. Echoing Mr. James's shift in perspective, Ms. Smith states that she has abandoned her earlier "psychoanalytic framework." According to that standard, she explains, "if kids were not behaving . . . then the problem was some sickness and was pathological, and if they had the proper therapist they [could obtain] treatment. You could fix them; they're broken and you can fix them."

However, she no longer relies on what she calls a "cookbook" to tell her what to do. "I don't think one exists. But I see the possibility in working toward another approach, another way to think about these things." That approach has emerged in response to her changing views of students and of teaching. Rather than turning to "therapeutic" techniques, or to sending her students automatically to the school counselors, she now reasons directly with individuals having academic or behavioral problems. To recall the terms of the previous chapter, she begins with the assumption all her students are "normal." She resorts to social solutions to rectify problems, for example, having weaker students work in small groups with stronger ones. She has maintained her long-standing habit of building personal relationships with students and, as we will see, regards doing so as an obligation. But her vision of teaching is centered squarely around the notion that the intellectual and moral development of her young adolescents best takes place in the context of a classroom community.

Still another reason for her switch of schools was that she had wearied of the materialism she felt was rampant in her former setting. "Whereas here," Ms. Smith reports, "the greed shows up in knowledge. 'I know more than you do.' . . . I'm somewhat more comfortable with that, for whatever reason, than I am, you know, with 'I have a bigger house.'" Somewhat tongue-in-cheek, she says that both forms of "greed" are "equally bad," but adds that "if you have to choose poison, I'd rather have somebody who knows more than me!"

An ethos of academic commitment and competitiveness is palpable in many of the school's classrooms, including Ms. Smith's. Teachers assign considerable amounts of homework and in-class work, all of which is expected. Most administrators, teachers, and students act as if the value of academics is understood. Students who perform poorly or who routinely misbehave are "counseled out" of the school. Faculty meet regularly to discuss the progress of individual students. Many parents are actively involved in their children's learning and encourage teachers to challenge them.

In brief, along many objective yardsticks, Ms. Smith's working conditions are more attractive than those of the three teachers met previously. Ms. Payton and Mr. James work in a large public high school marked by many of the difficulties that accompany schooling in the urban setting today: uneven resources, low morale among some faculty and staff, students distracted and injured by neighborhood violence, and more. (Ms. Smith's school is located but a mile or so away and does not entirely escape these predicaments.) Mr. James, and Ms. Payton to a lesser extent, must work with students whose records are so poor that they would not be considered for admission to Ms. Smith's school. Mr. Peters works in a Catholic school two miles distant, in an economically depressed environment. His school is repeatedly strapped for funds and is in a more or less permanent search for dedicated staff, given its low salaries and challenging working conditions. Its physical resources, like those of the nearby public school, do not compare with what is available to Ms. Smith's students. Nor do its human resources considered *in toto*. Ms. Smith can reap the benefits of working on a comparatively stable and strong faculty.

However, a central premise of this book is that the vocation of teaching invites one to adopt high expectations and standards regardless of what colleagues near or far might be doing, and regardless of what kind of external support one might receive. Teaching depends far more on what a person brings to it than on what it affords her or him by way of resources. Clearly, some teachers face more strenuous burdens and external constraints than do others. They must struggle that much harder to realize their aims and goals. Sometimes, as we witnessed with Mr. James, conditions render it almost impossible for them to do so. But even their peers in more advantaged settings have to work within limits. Successful teaching never happens by itself. It presupposes a pattern of persistent engagement and effort. No teacher can make learning take place. No teacher can reach inside students' heads and implant knowledge or values. Teaching remains a challenge and its outcomes remain uncertain regardless of where it occurs.

Moreover, previous chapters illustrate that what one can do within the constraints of a given setting has no limit that should be set in advance. Imagination and energy have a value that is not determined by external resources and support. Taken in themselves, those resources are meaningless. One must know what to do with them, a fact that puts a spotlight once again on the teacher's agency. That agency resides at the core of vocation and its enactment in practice. To repeat, this is not to downplay the impact of circumstances on teachers, a point to which I return again in Chapters 6 and 7. But it is to underscore the centrality of the person in the work of teaching.

One quality that makes Ms. Smith's faculty dynamic in the first place is its sheer hard work, and this for lower salaries and benefits than those received by nearby public school colleagues. Ms. Smith and some of her peers regularly clock six- and seven-day work weeks throughout the school year. They are often bombarded with calls after school and in the evening from parents and students about the latters' academic and behavioral progress.

Ms. Smith confronts other challenges as well that will be familiar to her counterparts in both public and religious schools. For example, her teaching and advising load is not light. In my first year of observation in her school, she taught four sixth-grade social studies classes, each with about 25 students. She was academic counselor to a varying number of students, with whom she met daily for an "advisory" period during which she discussed their progress in keeping up with assignments and the like. The school placed considerable pressure on her to work hard with her students. As Ms. Smith puts it, to "be there" for students academically "[means] I have to know them fairly intimately. I have to know what questions they may or may not be interested in and what level they can [work at] because that does vary from individual to individual." Not only were her 100 students individually distinct, but all four of her classes moved at different paces. This was not the result of an institutional tracking system, but rather reflected the individualized way she worked with each group. From time to time, as she pointed out, she found herself forgetting in the midst of a busy workday what each class had already covered. By her fourth class of the day, she admitted, she occasionally discovered she had forgotten to supply certain information or instructions she could take for granted in earlier periods. She described her fear that attempting to get to know 100 students well was literally wearing down her concentration. She was distressed by the feeling she sometimes had of being "blurry-eyed" by the last period of the day, a state she regards as unfair to students who have no option about being assigned to her at that time. In addition, she found that she did not always have the focus to attend properly to hallway discipline (for which all teachers are responsible) and especially to individual counseling outside of class, to which she devotes considerable time. Finally, having to teach 100 students a day discouraged her from assigning as many essays and open-book tests as she would have liked. However, she continued to do so, which meant that her late afternoons, evenings, and weekends were often devoted to evaluation. "It takes me a long time to read their stuff," she explained. "You really have to read in-between the lines and try to figure out what it was they were trying to say in the first place."

One of her crowning achievements during the nearly three years I visited her school was implementing, with her administration's approval, a combined English and social studies core curriculum. As a result, she was able to switch from teaching four 45-minute classes with a total of 100 students to two 90-minute periods with a total of 50 pupils. According to her own testimony and my own observations, this change created conditions for instituting a much more varied and sophisticated academic program. She could become more familiar with students' academic interests and abilities; she could investigate topics in much greater depth; she could involve students in tasks that gave them more responsibility for their own learning; she could put a dent in what she regards as the "silly [academic] compartmentalization" of middle schools "that doesn't bear any resemblance necessarily to the way kids learn." The ninety-minute periods every day provided fertile ground for developing a classroom community centered around learning (see Hansen, 1992, for an extended discussion of this point; also see Noddings, 1992, for an argument in favor of creating longer periods of contact between teachers and students so that they can work together more fulfillingly).

Ms. Smith continues to encounter other barriers to her goals. Some are minor but nonetheless nagging, like a toothache one cannot shake. For example, in her previous school she had a "wonderful departmental secretary who ran off things, typed up stuff, who was tremendous. It really freed me up to teach. . . . Whereas here," she observes, "we have a departmental secretary, but the politics of getting her to do anything for me is so negative that I do it myself. Those are the institutional things that get in the way because ordering a film can't take me two or three hours!"

She feels other constraints more deeply. For example, she believes strongly in the value of academic learning, and respects her school's focus on that goal. Yet that very conviction obliges her to be more strict with students than she would like to be. For example, she remains conflicted about how to assess and evaluate students' progress. After the first quarter of the year, she has students who fail their quizzes take them home to be signed by parents or guardians. She enforces this policy in spite of her awareness that it will create tension and anxiety for some students, particularly those who have problematic relationships with adults at home. "But what can I do?" she wonders aloud. "I don't grade homework strictly because I don't know who's helping [the students] on that." Yet she is also troubled about grading quizzes in the first place, because she knows students sometimes cheat on them. Moreover, she appreciates the dilemma in which her tests place students. On the one hand, Ms. Smith wants to teach students to be cooperative learners and good classroom citizens. On the other hand, as she puts it, "you have this artificial thing where 'this is a quiz, guys, now you *can't* help each other.'" According to her testimony, she has not resolved the question of evaluation. In previous years, she experimented with group grades for projects and even for quizzes. "But they don't spend enough time together [on a topic] to make that right," she believes. She also continues to value strongly individual initiative, responsibility, and recognition, such that the idea of a group grade just "doesn't feel right." As a result, she experiments with a variety of evaluative measures, including soliciting student input on each other's work.

PERSONAL INFLUENCE

Ms. Smith's career-long wrestling match with the issue of evaluation mirrors her recurring effort to reconcile high academic expectations with her students' need for adult guidance on conduct. She believes her students are seeking more from her than knowledge of subject matter. "The role that I can play in a kid's life is maybe more important now than it was twenty years ago," she argues. "They perceive that I am an adult who has confidence and that is really important to them. . . . I do feel they need more." Her students, she argues, "are definitely looking at what it means to be good, and how to be a good person. . . . They want to be good. They want to know what is good behavior, and they're willing to think about it." While leery of becoming a "surrogate parent," she believes she owes it to her students to help them learn how to conduct themselves confidently and knowingly. In terms that recall Mr. James's view, she says that students need her guidance because "a lot of times they don't know something's wrong. That's been the biggest change for me, realizing that I just yelled at a kid for something that he honestly didn't know was wrong." She contends that her students often need "help, respect, and nurture," but don't know how to ask for it. Students "need somebody to turn to," she concludes, "and if you're not there for them, then I think that it's a betrayal somehow. Then that's being a bad person maybe."

Ms. Smith wants to be a person students can turn to. That aim surfaces repeatedly in her conversation. For example, she states that a teacher can make a "huge difference," and she sees herself as responsible for "everything" that occurs in her classroom. "There is an awful lot that goes on that I am not aware of. [But] the fact that I am there and it's happening means I am condoning it or encouraging it. And that worries me. . . . Something will hit me later on as I am walking home and I will think, 'Oh my God, he did that to her and it was so forceful, and I didn't pay attention to it and it is already gone.'" She considers her sense of vigilance an "expectation that goes along with the classroom." "I don't feel like that [elsewhere] in life," she adds. "[But] I should be aware of what is going on around me, and I should be a positive influence rather than a negative influence."

Evidence of her students' worries about conduct is not hard to find in Ms. Smith's classroom. For example, after class one day in May, Nancy came up and asked earnestly: "Was Charlemagne a *nice* person? He liked scholars and musicians, but he also killed those who wouldn't become Christians. So was he nice?" Ms. Smith listened attentively, and recommended that the girl write out a dialogue in which she posed questions and had Charlemagne respond. She told the girl she would be glad to read and talk about the dialogue. Nancy persisted: "But did the people Charlemagne convert stay Christian? I mean, how did he keep them that way? Wouldn't they just fake it to save their lives? How can you get people to change like that, to go from things they've believed in for years?" With several other students waiting their turn, Ms. Smith urged the girl to explore her queries in her dialogue and to keep her posted.

Nancy's questions are the kind teachers encounter everywhere. From the first grader worried about how to care for the pet rabbit in the classroom, to the twelfth grader troubled about a classmate's treatment of other people, teachers are called on to be sources of moral counsel. They must routinely put their integrity and their sense of judgment on public display. Moreover, there is no escape from this requirement. Even a teacher who refuses to offer a response is sending a signal—namely, that he or she has no intellectual or moral stance on such subjects and would rather "pass the buck." As many teachers could attest, helping students resolve thorny issues can be unsettling. While students look on—and students at every level of education seem to tune in closely at such moments—the teacher wonders, if not in so many words, "How should I react? What is the right thing to say?" In the midst of class, teachers can usually fashion a response, or engage students in a discussion. Just as often, however, teachers must create the time to talk with students outside of class. That is not always easy to do. As Ms. Smith says, in the helter-skelter of schooling things sometimes rush by and are "already gone" before one can address them.

Nancy's question about Charlemagne's character is one thing. But like the teachers met in previous chapters, Ms. Smith is also called to deal with more drastic issues. For example, in the middle of the school year a sixth-grade child attempted suicide, an action that threw the entire school off its stride. Many of the child's peers were deeply troubled. To help them regain their composure and confidence, Ms. Smith began to invite individual students to sit with her during her otherwise free lunch period. Eventually, the lunch group ballooned to some twenty-five students, and began to take on the feeling of a formal occasion. "If I have to raise my hand *here*," one student said at one point, "I'm not interested anymore!" By that time, students' anxieties about their fully recovered peer had eased. Yet the fact that so many individuals took up Ms. Smith's offer attests not just to their worries (nor to their desire to mimic their friends, doubtless a motivation for some). They went to Ms. Smith not because they regarded her as a trained counselor with expertise to share. Rather, they did so because she is a person they appear to trust. That sense of trust helps account for the fact that students often crowd around her desk immediately after the end of a class, to ask a question, to comment on the lesson, to share an item of personal news, or just to listen in.

These facts illuminate Ms. Smith's possible moral influence on her students. Many of her students repeatedly look to her for advice, counsel, and guidance. They do so deliberately, as we have seen, and they do so unawares, almost despite themselves. For example, during class her students are sometimes unselfconsciously absorbed in watching her. One afternoon in November she cut short spontaneous reactions to a comment from a student by saying to the class, "SH! Quiet! I want to *understand* this." Leaning over the podium where she often sits, she looked intently at the speaker as the girl proceeded with her opinion. As Ms. Smith did so, several students regarded *her* wonderingly, almost as if impressed that she would be so interested in something one of them might say.

Ms. Smith was not seeking at that moment to demonstrate what it meant to attend respectfully to another person. Rather, she *was* attentive. As she points out, the fact that she often loses herself and becomes absorbed in a class discussion is "good" for her students. "They can see that I'm just as engaged as they are," she says, "that I want to know what they have to say just as much as they do. Their perceptions are just as important as anyone else's." Students might not know what to say if asked about the absorbed manner in which they regard the subtleties of her conduct. Such questions might make them self-conscious or even confuse them. However, as Aristotle emphasized, one of the ways in which persons learn what virtues such as respectfulness or attentiveness to others mean is by witnessing them in action and by having opportunities to practice them.

To judge from students' informal testimony as well as their daily actions, they appear aware of the fact that Ms. Smith likes teaching and wants her students to do well. Moreover, they appear to assume that she is interested in who they are as persons. For example, in the same lunch group mentioned previously several students complained about another teacher. One girl said, "He just doesn't show that he cares about us." The fact that the student could feel comfortable saying this in Ms. Smith's presence, and the fact that so many students took advantage of the opportunity to have lunch with her, seems to imply that as far as they are concerned Ms. Smith has made it clear that *she* cares about them.

However, in nearly three years of observational work in her classroom and school, I never once heard Ms. Smith say to her students in so many words that she "likes" them or "cares" about them. I have no record of the other three teachers described in this book declaring such things to their students either. Yet there is abundant evidence that all four teachers hold generally favorable views of students. Should anything be made of this observation? In principle, a teacher who tells students that he or she cares may have as positive an influence on them as a colleague who shows care rather than talks about it. But the possibility remains that one's sense of service as teacher may have its greatest impact on students when it is embodied in what one does rather than merely in what one says about oneself in their presence.

A GUIDE IN THE CLASSROOM

While Ms. Smith likes teaching, she corroborates Mr. James's and Ms. Payton's testimony that it is not always easy to like all students. She admits that some individuals drive her to distraction, and that she has to take great care not to lose her self-control with them. Moreover, she would also say that her liking extends to more than a purely personal feeling. According to her testimony, Ms. Smith's interest in her students derives from her fascination with how they learn and from her reflection on how she can best facilitate that process. She explains that when she first began to teach, she was so taken with what students said and did that she neglected her duty as a teacher:

> I didn't know anything about changing [students'] behavior,
> nothing! I knew how to observe things, so I would sit in the front
> of the room and just kind of look at this. "This is fascinating!" And
> it was chaos! I was so interested in what the kids were doing, and
> how they responded to one another, and I had no idea [what to
> do]!

She says that her posture at that time resulted, in part, from her having
recently completed a stint as an ethnographer in which she made use of
skills of observing and listening she had learned as an anthropology major
in college:

> I was so used to just opening myself to the experience altogether
> and then waiting for the pattern to hit me. Whereas, with teaching,
> I need to have an agenda. Otherwise I get overwhelmed with all this
> stuff. That is a real personality switch for me, just to say: "This is
> important and I'm screening out [that]."

Over her 14-year career, Ms. Smith explains, she has worked hard to
set priorities as teacher. She has endeavored to "tune in" as best as possible
to how students learn (a phrase she uses quite often). She has deliberately
"cultivated" that capacity, she says. "I've spent a long time working with
kids. I know them, and I've gotten better at it, at having a sense for kids."
Her greatest fear is forgetting these lessons. "I have this terror that one day
I am going to wake up and I'm not going to be able to listen. Something
is going to happen and I won't be able to hear what they are really saying."

For Ms. Smith, at the heart of what students are "really saying" is their
reaction to each other's ideas and to the curriculum. She strives to engage
them with her social studies curriculum. She feels successful, as teacher,
"when kids are somehow motivated by something that happened in my
classroom over which I had some control." She works persistently to encourage a sense of classroom community centered around the academic
material. She leads students in discussion virtually every period. She asks
them a barrage of questions of fact and interpretation about the texts and
stories they read. She asks them whether they agree or disagree with what
peers have said. She asks them to support their views with evidence and
argument. She asks them periodically to summarize what the group has been
saying, and to describe the purposes of the work in which they are engaged.
She asks for their advice on how they can all be more efficient and productive as a class.

Her students respond in their own exuberant if not always focused ways.
To students who wave their hands too frantically and call out her name in

an effort to obtain the floor ahead of others, she responds: "No, Dennis, not if you make all those noises . . . Megan, just relax, you'll get a chance . . . Mary, no! Just hold on!" To students who, in the early weeks of the year, make fun of a peer by laughing at an answer or by calling out such things as "That's dumb!" Ms. Smith reacts swiftly: "Hey! If you disagree raise your hand and give your own opinion!" By her own account, Ms. Smith works hard to teach students how to respect one another and how to respect differences of opinion. "I don't like the kids to have their hands up while somebody else is speaking," she explains. She tells students that raising their hands while another person has the floor "shows that you're waiting your turn [but] you're not listening to the other person. . . . I say, 'If you're fully present your hand is not up while somebody else talks. Your hand is down, because you listen to see if you do have something to say. It's not that you have an agenda the moment I have asked the question and you are [just] trying to meet that agenda.'" According to Ms. Smith, participating in the life of the classroom means more than securing one's own "air time."

Ms. Smith seeks to encourage respect for the subject matter. For example, during a discussion of a short story she calls on a boy who has been eagerly waving his hand. He gives an implausible account of the behavior of one of the characters. Cutting short some teasing by his peers, Ms. Smith asks him for evidence to support his view. At first nonplussed by this request, the boy picks up his book and begins thumbing through the story. Meanwhile, Ms. Smith commands "Hands down!" to the class and snaps "Sh!" to several students chorusing "Oh! Oh! Oh!" as they wave their arms. For a moment complete silence descends. Students search their own texts or watch their teacher. Finally, Ms. Smith says to the boy, "Okay, Andrew, so you see the difference between making up an answer and finding one in the story?" He nods his understanding, and Ms. Smith calls on another student.

As mentioned, she habitually attempts to keep her class focused on a single topic (at least when they are involved in whole-group activities). In so doing, she publicizes the values of concentration, of consistency, of persistence in thinking collectively. She routinely interjects into a discussion queries such as "What is the question we're dealing with now?" or "What is the topic we are discussing?" Through her questions, she provides students with repeated occasions on which to learn to reflect and to build on each other's ideas: "Burt, what did Mary add that we haven't heard before?" "Richard, what have we been saying thus far about their culture?" "Sarah, tell us in your own words what you think Dennis was saying. And then— Tom!—I'd like you to say if you agree with Sarah's summary." Ms. Smith also encourages students to call on one another if they get an answer wrong or are stuck. Her students adopt this practice quickly, calling out when someone needs help: "O Steven! I have an answer!" or "Here! I know!" And whenever a student who has been called on by a classmate starts explaining matters to *her*, Ms. Smith responds by saying, for instance, "No, Peter, explain your answer to *Mary.*"

Although she overlooks or is oblivious to some misbehavior, Ms. Smith tries to corral students who distract others or who in other ways disrupt the proceedings. She calls on them by name to answer questions or to summarize what another student has just said. She also asks direct questions such as "What are you supposed to be doing?" or "How can you improve your behavior?" Further, if a student responds to a question about what he should be doing by simply saying, for example, "listening," Ms. Smith does not stop there. "'Listening' to what?" she asks in one instance. "Listening to the discussion," the student replies. "No, that's too vague," retorts his teacher. "What's the *point* of this discussion?" The boy hesitates, then recalls, "Well, uh, we were talking about Roman roads." "*Right!*" confirms Ms. Smith, and promptly resumes the class discussion.

Ms. Smith also involves students in the process of disciplining disruptors, an approach that complements her habit of having students ask others for help when stuck or confused about academic matters. She asks such questions as "Mark, maybe you can call on someone for suggestions on how you can learn to pay attention" and "Who has some advice for Peter?" As the year advances, students learn to offer and to accept counsel on their conduct as if doing so were as natural as coming to class itself (which is not to say that such advice is always gladly received).

Considered in isolation from their context, the questions Ms. Smith poses might sound wooden and pedantic, the kind of generic queries one can find listed in textbooks on teaching. However, *in* context Ms. Smith's questioning style serves to focus attention and to help students develop a sense of how to investigate an intellectual issue. It enables students to perceive what it means to gain understanding and what it means to comprehend something they hitherto did not know—and, in some instances, did not know they did not know. With her assistance, students develop criteria for judging their own progress, and for appreciating what makes some ideas and arguments an improvement over others. Moreover, both her unhesitant admonishments of poor behavior and her persistent academic questioning invite students to become more self-disciplined and self-possessed. Her persistence encourages students to become more mindful of the reality of others—to become more aware of the self as standing in relation to others. Her repeated questions and comments help crystalize a sense of what it means *in practice* to focus both on learning and on respectful relations with others. Over the course of a school year, to judge from what Ms. Smith and her students say and do together, her classroom becomes less and less a setting in which each student, like an individual spoke of a wheel, has a formal relationship only with their teacher (or "hub"). Rather, through their daily actions students are made aware of the benefits of membership in a purposeful, educational endeavor.

For Ms. Smith, teaching means promoting not just this sense of purpose but also a sense of interest, even of wonder. She emphasizes the value of articulating "genuine" questions. To provide a background to her meaning, she talks about her previous teaching experience in English (also in the middle grades). She recalls how she became frustrated with the ways she felt obliged to teach grammar:

> I no longer had patience for the grammar that I was required to teach. I had gotten to a point where my resentment of the material was so great that I was blocking [students'] learning. . . . I realized that a computer could do what it was that I was teaching. And then I resented it more because I could be replaced by a machine, and if I can be replaced by a machine then I am no longer teaching.

Ms. Smith continues to teach students grammar, and she says she appreciates how essential it is for good communication. However, she emphasizes that when she and her students talk about a "genuine" question, "we are talking about a question that only a human being can grapple with. It is not something that a machine can feed back to you." She describes her continued delight in the questions students raise about the material they read and discuss, including texts she has taught many times previously.

For example, she has taught the story of Agammemnon and the Trojan War eight times—"I mean," she exclaims, with "eight different groups of kids! And every time one kid says, 'But why did Agammemnon do this [sacrifice his daughter]?' it sends a chill up my spine and I think that is really a very profound question. So maybe a good question is one you never get sick of." As another example, she recalls an incident when she was teaching grammar. "You had to divide the universe into concrete and abstract nouns," she says. "And the question came up, 'Is God an abstract noun?' If I wrote a book, that would be the title! I mean, that is why I teach. I said [to the student], you are going to have to answer that for yourself, because I don't know."

Ms. Smith's hope is that all her students will discover such questions in their studies. Part of her task in enabling this, she says, is to take what she regards as their "natural excitement about things" and provide them with "skills that allow them to pursue those in school." "Insofar as I can take what kids would be doing if they weren't in school," she explains, "just on their own—fun—take some of that energy and that excitement and then figure out a way that they can do it in school, I feel like I've succeeded." She recalls her own childhood joy when she would "leave school and go home and read and read and read. But it never occurred to me that my passions could be satisfied in school."

However, she strongly believes such passions can and should be met in school, despite the fact that that setting is often perceived as artificial. To illuminate her point, she draws an analogy with a visit to an art museum:

> Yesterday, when I was at the Georgia O'Keeffe [exhibit], I thought: Every time I look at one of these paintings, there's some real deep part of me that resonates with the painting, and that's the experience I'm looking for in my classroom—where I'm providing kids with a stimulus. And, you know, I'm looking at this whole [museum] room of people who are all crowded together, and there are all these paintings, and I think everybody wants to just take one home and put it in their living room and look at it for days. I mean, nobody wants to be *there* looking at it. [But] it's a compromise you have to make. That's what I'm looking for . . .

Ms. Smith implies that both schools and museums require "compromise." To enjoy Georgia O'Keeffe paintings in person, one must go to a museum crowded with other admirers. To enjoy subject matter, at least in some of its forms, one must go to a school crowded with other learners. Both settings, while in some respects less than ideal, provide persons the opportunity to focus systematically on the products of human imagination, experience, and effort. While some of those products are located in museums, far more are embodied in the curriculum of school—for example, the achievements of mathematics, science, language, culture, and history. Schools and museums *are* artificial, but they are so in the nonpejorative, root sense of that term meaning created or constructed by human beings rather than by natural forces. According to Ms. Smith's viewpoint, both a school and a museum can and should promote individual growth and appreciation for human accomplishments.

Ms. Smith tries to create conditions for such involvement in her classroom. She wants to engage "the kid who's never been there, [who] doesn't really have a sense of how to make that happen [in the classroom] for himself." In brief, Ms. Smith seeks to help her students learn how to use school effectively, to learn how to take advantage of the particular learning opportunities it affords. She hopes that students will learn to take themselves and their school setting seriously enough to make this effort. As she implies repeatedly, she does not believe students are born with a capacity to do so. As with every artificial setting—that is, every humanly constructed setting—

newcomers must be apprised of the *purposes* behind the artifice, of what it is there to help them learn or to do. This truism holds with schools, museums, law courts, churches, and more.

Ms. Smith wants students to leave her classroom "talking about what we did" and feeling that it was "fun," as she regards learning itself to be. As she says, she hopes her students will "resonate" with the curriculum. In seeking to construct a classroom environment supportive of such aims, she not only barrages students with the kinds of questions described previously, but also urges them to develop a healthy respect for "time on task." She describes that familiar pedagogical maxim as "an important idea" she derived years before from her teacher preparation program. She wants her students to learn to "spend time with some degree of awareness." She wants to see them "participating at a high level, so that when they come into my classroom, they are there, which means that their focus is there, that 'who' they are is somehow engaged in learning." She believes students intuitively understand this aim. "They know what it feels like to be involved," she contends. "They know what it feels like to be present. . . . They know that feeling. And they know when they're not."

Ms. Smith clarifies further her sense of teaching by explaining that she wants students to focus not on their relationship with her per se but on their connection with the historical material they discuss. She says that students cannot have "direct experience" of history, as they can, in her view, of art or of physical education in classes in those disciplines. History is "already gone," to recall one of her tropes. Consequently, she seeks to help students "enter" the subject by sparking their imagination. In many classroom lessons, she has them pretend they are living in the past. "What would it be like if you were placed in a different time period?" she will ask. "What kind of appearance would you have? What technology would be available for you? How does using technology affect whether or not you enjoyed your life? . . . Pretend you're an archaeologist and you've found these objects, what can you make of this civilization? . . . Pretend you're the cartographer and Rand McNally needs this map, what would you include? . . . Pull together what you've learned about Etruscan culture and put it together in a travel brochure."

When questioned about the presentism embodied in this approach— the fact that "tourism," for example, did not exist as an experiential category in Etruscan times—Ms. Smith replies that she is mindful of the point. She does endeavor to discuss with students the fact that ways of thinking differed in the past, just as did ways of building homes or engaging in trade. However, she claims that "it's hard enough to get [students] to dig one another's points of view! It's hard enough to get them to imagine the people they know [now], what they might be thinking." For Ms. Smith, history lessons become not only opportunities for students to understand aspects of the human record. Ideally, they help them to better understand themselves and the people they know. Ms. Smith hopes that by spurring students to think about history, she is influencing the persons they are becoming. At one point she described her curriculum in these terms:

> [It's] thinking about what kind of people [students] want to be, and how to be that kind of person. I mean, that's what I think the curriculum is about. It's looking at what does it mean to be human, and the difference between a good human and a not so good human—how to think about being human.

Her lessons often culminate in discussion of how to judge a particular historical or fictional character, both in terms of the character's point of view and students' own.

As we have seen, Ms. Smith wants her students to wrestle intellectually and imaginatively with history. She describes an instance of how this can happen—and what it can lead to—in talking about a lesson she implements that involves studying Greek vases, both in textbooks and in one of the city's museums. "There was [one] kid," she recounts, "who looked at a vase, figured it out, [then] put it together with another vase, figured out what the words meant, started thinking about where language comes from, thinking about how to use words more precisely, thinking about other words he might know. That's part of what I'm talking about." As another instance, consider a not untypical interchange between her students. One afternoon in November they had just completed a unit on life in ancient Sumer. Ms. Smith asked them to compare what they had learned about culture back then with their lives today.

Robert began the discussion. "People back then were smarter than we are today," he offered. "Because today we have so many gadgets to protect us, we just don't have to think so much. But they did, they had to be real careful."

"Yeah," added Barbara, "we've been pulled so far from nature with our technology, we couldn't defend ourselves any more like maybe they could back then."

"We're taking credit for being so smart today," said Liza, "but really it's all from the past. We owe them for what we know today."

"Yeah, pretty soon people are going to forget the important things," opined Marie. "Like, we have TV and videos now, you can go down a street and find five video stores but no bookstores! We can't survive now without machines, we are forgetting so much."

"But wait," objected Rachel. She argued that "we" do know more than people did in Sumer. As an example she described how impressed she was with the construction people working in her family's house at that time. She talked about their careful planning and their use of modern tools. "They know a lot about what to do," she concluded.

"Yeah," injected Marie, "but I mean something like the shell of the house, why *this* kind of house. I mean—" The end of the period cut her off, but she and some of her classmates left the room hotly debating the issue.

Their discussion illuminates why Ms. Smith treats her curriculum as a crucible. She seeks to draw her students into a different and what she regards as a larger world, one based on a feeling for the past and its relation to the present. In her classroom, this becomes a process quite distinct from passively ingesting material. Her approach to teaching is not "mimetic" (Jackson, 1986), in which teacher delivers subject matter and student regurgitates it back. That process leaves *both* subject matter and learner substantively unchanged. In contrast, Ms. Smith's classroom appears to invite change in both the child and the curriculum. She affords students the opportunity not just to learn facts but also how to think about their meaning. In so doing, she creates conditions in which students' thinking can shed new light on those facts. For example, in principle an individual student's view of the causes of the Crusades, a topic Ms. Smith examines as part of a study of Medieval culture, will be unique to that child. That is, the *particular* way in which the child conceives those causes and events could be a rendering never heard before in any classroom anywhere. Moreover, it could be a seed of change, however microscopic it appears at first glance, in the way the child's culture itself comes to regard and make sense of that historical event. This presumes that the student becomes engaged with the material to the extent that he or she takes it into his or her other interactions with people. It also presumes that one does not just make up facts or draw unsubstantiated interpretations. Rather, it recalls Dewey's argument (1902/1990, 1916/1966) that learners are dynamic, meaning they can grow and change, and that the curriculum is dynamic, meaning it can grow and change through new discoveries and through new ways of seeing familiar phenomena.

TENSIONS IN TEACHING

As with the other teachers we have met, Ms. Smith's educational hopes are not always realized. Though she wants her students to encounter the curriculum in an imaginative and dynamic way, there are times throughout the year when it appears to take on a prescriptive momentum of its own.

"Covering" the material takes precedence over engaging with it. For example, it is not uncommon to hear Ms. Smith suddenly cut off students as they struggle to articulate their ideas: "Look, we're getting near to the break. This is dangerous. You've got to go fast. Hurry, Marie!"; "Now, *swiftly*, because we don't have a lot of time!"; "Okay, that's enough, we've got to move on now or else you won't cover all the material"; "Let's move on now or we won't be where we need to be by next Tuesday [the day a test is scheduled]"; "Your point is good, Robert, but we need to move on"; "Now, in your [small] groups choose the person who is the fastest writer!" In her occasional haste to cover material, Ms. Smith sometimes forgets her goal of leading students to think and reason for themselves. "Was this guy Thales for real?" asks Richard in the midst of a discussion of what philosophers and mathematicians did in Ancient Greece. "Yeah, he's in the history books," Ms. Smith casually replies, promptly moving on to the question of what a philosopher does. Marie raises her hand. "It says in the book, it gives a definition." "Yes?" "'A philosopher,'" reads Marie, "'looks for the truth.'" "Very good, okay," replies Ms. Smith hastily, neglecting to ask the child what it means to "look for the truth"—something they themselves are presumably intended to do as students of history.

At times, instead of asking a student to come to grips with a question he or she has just posed, Ms. Smith will move on by replying "That might make a great test question!" Inadvertently, she thereby contributes to an impression that personal understanding is less important than knowledge suitable for tests. In other instances, Ms. Smith conveys the view that "good" answers are those that allow her to cover her day's lesson. For example, one day in January she replied "Very good!" to Ben, who, in the midst of several students talking excitedly about their opinions, answered Ms. Smith's prior factual question. The other students immediately quieted down and looked at Ben—something they did not do during his comment but only after hearing it graced with the approving "very good" from the teacher. The message emitted by this incident, however brief, is that what constitutes "very good" is not genuine queries and reflections students generate but rather answers that "move them along."

Ms. Smith is aware of her occasional tendency to treat student input instrumentally—that is, to twist it into the service of her curriculum rather than the other way around. She knows she sometimes rushes headlong through material, as if fulfilling a rote duty rather than teaching. She also is mindful of falling into what she calls "bad habits." In her initial years as a teacher, she explains, she was sometimes "tyrannized" by her curricular plans, in effect forcing them on students without checking on how they were responding to them. One reason she did so, she explains, was her lack of experience and confidence:

> I remember being very cautious that this was a sort of game called "school," and I didn't want anyone to discover that I didn't know what I was doing. Because I felt like a fake, just a complete and total fake! Every time someone came into my classroom I thought, well, this is the moment they are going to discover that I am a fake. All I wanted to do was basically to cover the material I was supposed to cover and feel like I was a teacher, whatever that meant.

Her account recalls Mr. James's remarks about "surviving" the initial plunge into teaching. Because of unfamiliarity with being a teacher, as contrasted with years and years of watching teachers as a student, one often resorts to the safest course of action, namely, the narrowest and most conservative. One key to successful teaching, Ms. Smith and the other teachers we have met imply, is not to let bad habits harden. Rather, practitioners should experiment until they realize what it is they *can* accomplish as teachers. A central claim of this book is that a sense of vocation can sustain a person through these difficult and uncertain times in the classroom. That sense can help keep one's eyes on the larger picture rather than simply on how to get through the next period of the day, although circumstances can sometimes reduce even the most veteran teacher to thinking about the latter aim alone.

With the confidence and understanding gained from over a dozen years in the practice, Ms. Smith says that "I'm more willing to put down the curriculum that I wrote and deal with the curriculum that's present." She means that if conditions warrant, she will take up students' spontaneous questions and comments even if doing so absorbs time she would otherwise devote to her instructional plan. She regards this act as central to good teaching, as an aspect of what was previously described as her interest in "genuine" questions. She believes that taking seriously student questions is a major vehicle for learning, a dramatic opportunity to connect learner and curriculum.

Nonetheless, she continues to wrestle with the issue of how and when to respond to students' personal reactions to the material. Nor is she averse to employing carrots to persuade students to do her bidding. One morning in January, she told her students they could prepare for the skit they had been discussing in recent days if they first completed their review of their assigned textbook chapter. Students clapped enthusiastically, eager to get on to the role-playing they so enjoy. "But we *won't* do it unless we get through this chapter!" repeated Ms. Smith. After class, she volunteered the following observation: "Boy, talk about destroying my own lesson! It was like telling them chapter 2 was not worth anything!"

During another class in April, she resorted to calling only on students she knew to be reliably prepared and more able academically than others. Here is what she had to say about the class: "If you wanted to see all my rules broken in one lesson, that was it. And I really reflected on that because it was such a repulsive difference. I thought what happened is: 'I want to get through the material. I'm not thinking about what people are writing. It's hot and I want to get this over with.'" She describes her posture that afternoon as a "throwback to a much earlier state" in her teaching career. It was a "horrible class," she says, because "I kept calling on the people who knew the answers. I didn't stick with anybody who didn't know the answer because I wanted to get done. So I wanted the right answers to be heard, and [I thought]: 'Let's not monkey around with where [students] come from, or with [their] own incomplete understanding, let it be' . . . I mean, it was a perfect example of how not to teach." "I forgot the fundamental principles," she concludes. "This is a cooperative enterprise. You can't just go through the material, you can't learn by just hearing the right answers. I know all that stuff . . . I broke all the rules."

Ms. Smith's self-reported failure as teacher will doubtless strike a chord with others who have taught in schools. There are days and times when one is simply not prepared to meet the demands of teaching: to be attentive, flexible, patient, courteous, energetic. One wants to get through the period or through the day. For Ms. Smith, such moments stand out as a source of frustration and even sadness. As we have seen, she typically enacts high expectations of herself and her students. She monitors what she calls the "rhythm" of a classroom, and even her own tones of voice, as signs of whether she is "with it"—a phrase that echoes Kounin's (1968) disarming description of experienced teachers as having a certain "withitness" while in the act of teaching. "I have a sense for the classroom being in synchrony or out of synchrony," Ms. Smith explains, "and that shows up in peculiar ways. I can feel when kids are basically working together, and I can feel when I don't have them, when we're not, not a 'corporate body,' an integrated group of people." And she can sense when students do not "have" *her*. "There are a lot of clues to remind me that I'm not with it," she says. She describes her sudden awareness of a brittleness, even a harshness, in her voice. "There's a voice that doesn't sound like my voice, that will come in when I'm strained and I'm not being honest any more. I'm not comfortable in the situation. I'm fighting back, I'm fighting with myself. And all of a sudden I'll hear that [tone] and I know that I've got to change the activity, that I'm out of sync."

Student demands can push any teacher "out of sync" from time to time. Classrooms are crowded environments, as Jackson (1968) called to our attention in his pioneering study of schooling. They are filled with individuals with diverse needs, moods, and capabilities, all of which can change rapidly. Students bring into classrooms their personal worries, hopes, joys, and fears. Experience has taught Ms. Smith a great deal about these facts. She strives to make herself available before and after class, during free periods, lunch, advisory periods, and the like. Usually, she reports, "the kids who really seem to need some warm attention have managed to get it from me by the time class begins," thereby allowing her to focus on academic work.

Ms. Smith also believes she has to be cautious about investing too much energy in her students' personal predicaments and worries. She tries to remember that other adults are there in the school and beyond to be of help. She keeps in view her self-warning: "If I burn myself out, then I can't be there when [students] need me." Her testimony underscores the fact that while students bring to bear a host of personal concerns, so do teachers (Lightfoot, 1983). Yet in the presence of their students, the burden is on teachers to bracket their own needs, moods, and anxieties. Their obligation is to teach—that is, to serve. They owe students a good deal more than students owe them. These moral obligations render teaching a permanently demanding task, and it comes as no surprise that every teacher will periodically fall short of his or her own expectations, as well as those of society. The wonder is how often some teachers are able to meet them.

CONCLUSION: TEACHING AND PERSONAL INSIGHT

This chapter began with the claim that Ms. Smith's 14-year career in the classroom has broadened her outlook on education and on life—an outcome, incidentally, that could be ascribed to the three teachers we met previously. Ms. Smith's experience has not narrowed her vision, as a number of reports from researchers and ex-teachers cited earlier suggest is the consequence of teaching. Rather, teaching seems to have deepened her enthusiasm for working with the young, and for learning how to prepare and teach an educative social studies curriculum. To judge from her testimony, her years of work have had this effect in part because of her increased sense of confidence, efficacy, and understanding. Throughout the course of her career she has enrolled regularly in university classes in history, literature, drama, and so forth. She has taught and mentored groups of teachers on aspects of middle-school and social studies teaching. She has earned public recognition from her school and beyond for her efforts.

However, teaching seems also to have shed more and more light for her on what she does *not* know: about her subject, about young people, and about herself. She sometimes feels disquieted by what she regards as her ignorance. "The greatest single obstacle" she confronts in her work, she reports, "[is] my own limitations as a person. . . . [There are] all kinds of things that I find lacking in myself for as seriously as I take my profession." She lists both qualities of character, such as being more patient and attentive, and qualities of intellect, such as being more steeped in conceptions of history and social studies. "I don't want to make that sound like, you know, really prissy or moralistic or saccharine," she adds. But "I do feel teachers can make a huge difference." The irony she describes is that the more she is in fact able to make a difference as a teacher, the more she realizes what she does not know or understand.

That state of affairs should come as no surprise. It accompanies a discovery made by Socrates and countless other teachers: With experience comes increasing awareness of how much more there is to learn. Moreover, no teacher can master completely his or her subject or the ways and means of how the young learn. Every academic discipline continues to change as new studies are completed and new perspectives are articulated. The same holds regarding views of how to teach each discipline. In addition, every generation of children differs from those that came before, for many socioeconomic, cultural, and political reasons. And every student differs from every other: The variety of human character and disposition far exceeds what any individual teacher can ever fathom. Finally, these observations hold for the self. As Eldridge (1989) writes, "Failure in self-understanding is a permanent possibility, and failure of perfect self-understanding and perfect self-realization a permanent fact" (p. 14). No teacher will ever know everything he or she would like to know. Yet as tempting as it might be to have that Olympian knowledge, at least when one is tired or frustrated with teaching, one suspects that Ms. Smith and the other three teachers we have met would not accept it were it offered.

6

The Senses of a Vocation

In previous chapters I have shown how four teachers talk about and enact a sense of vocation in their work. In this chapter I return to the idea of teaching as a vocation and describe its value for how we conceive the practice today. However, before doing so I want to reemphasize the point that my intent has not been to cast the teachers as "heroic." They are serious-minded educators, but tags like "hero" have no place in this analysis of teaching. For one thing, the teachers would be the first to acknowledge that other people might hold views of teaching that differ from theirs. For another, they would be uncomfortable with notions like "hero." While they do perceive themselves as role models—as adults who seek to act their best when working with students—"role model" and "hero" are not synonyms. To judge from these four teachers' efforts, to be a role model implies, among other qualities, paying attention to students, being consistently prepared, and being conscientious. In contrast, to be a hero conjures up images of bold deeds and of plaudits from the crowd that are ill-suited to what the teachers and countless others like them do.

Another reason I recall this point is that the language of vocation is all too easily romanticized. Employed uncritically, the concept can trigger images of self-sacrifice and devotion that may be appropriate for the likes of Mother Teresa but not for teachers like those met here. To romanticize and sentimentalize teaching is analytically sterile. It inflicts on teaching and teachers the same disservice as accounts that reduce the practice to a by-the-numbers recipe. The previous chapters underscore how complex and challenging classroom teaching always is, regardless of the settings in which it takes place, and regardless of the kind of support teachers and their students receive.

Yet the very complexity and difficulty of the work make it natural for teachers to employ terms that border on the romantic to describe what they do. The emotions the job triggers, the involvement in students' lives, the daily successes and failures, seem to call forth such terms. The language of "occupation" or "job" by itself will not suffice. That occupational language cannot capture the deeply personal aspects of the work to which these teachers so abundantly attest. Nor can it satisfactorily convey the importance of the person who occupies the role of teacher, a point illustrated time and again in the previous analysis.

The title of this chapter—"The Senses of a Vocation"—highlights the fact that teaching is a highly individualized endeavor. The four practitioners we have met differ from one another, as teachers, in more ways than could be enumerated here. They employ their own unique terms to describe their work. Each has particular hopes, and each is troubled by particular concerns and doubts. Each has a distinctive style of working that conveys its own set of messages about the meaning and value of education. Moving from one of their classrooms to the next has the feel of journeying through a succession of different worlds.

But while their example does not yield a blueprint for how to enact a sense of service in teaching, it does illuminate what I have described as the vocation of teaching. In Chapter 1 I spelled out the basic terms of that conception. In this chapter I revisit that framework, equipped now with considerable testimony and observational data from the classrooms of the four teachers. I argue that the practice of teaching and the sense of vocation many bring to it are symbiotic. The practice provides teachers a recognized social medium in which to serve; but without dedicated persons to take it up, the practice itself would wither. I distinguish both the practice of teaching and the idea of vocation from the institutions, namely schools, in which most teaching occurs. These contrasts set the stage for the final chapter of the book, which focuses on whether teachers should regard their work as a vocation.

REVIEWING THE DIMENSIONS OF VOCATION

Public Service and Personal Fulfillment

I argued in Chapter 1 that vocation emerges at the crossroads of public service and personal fulfillment. Vocation describes work that is of service to others, and that at the same time provides the person with a sense of identity and meaning. Ms. Payton, Mr. Peters, Mr. James, and Ms. Smith all conceive their work in terms of service. To judge from their testimony and their classroom work, they are committed to their students' intellectual and moral well-being. Moreover, they also seek to be of service in their schools. They work on committees, develop curricula, supervise school events, address colleagues in formal circumstances, and more. They perform this work despite the extensive time they already invest in their teaching, and despite the conflicts of personality and philosophy that invariably arise among any school faculty and that can tax the energy of all concerned.

At the same time, all four teachers derive personal satisfaction and meaning from what they do. As the cliché has it, teaching for them is more than a job. When they step through the doorways to their respective schools, they act as if teaching is more a way of life than a task that calls on only minimal aspects of the persons they are. They bring into play in their work their knowledge of subject matter, of pedagogy, and of human development. They repeatedly make intellectual and moral judgments of their students' effort and conduct. They express their emotions. They reveal the values they "embrace," as Mr. James claims all teachers do. Their personal character infuses their everyday treatment of students. To recall Ms. Smith's terms, they act as if they bear responsibility for all that takes place in their classrooms, regardless of whether they in fact do so or not. The personal fulfillment they derive from teaching may be a direct consequence of the very fact that they do bring so much of themselves to bear while on the job.

Being an Architect

This last point recalls another feature of vocation identified in Chapter 1. A person with a vocational orientation toward his or her work treats it as an architect would, rather than merely as a laborer. A good architect not only has the skill and the imagination necessary for design, but also knows for whom he or she designs the work. As we have seen, all four teachers appear to be continually on the lookout for ways to improve their teaching and to enrich and augment their curricula. For example, Mr. James single-handedly designed mathematics courses for his students, while Ms. Smith took the lead in creating a core English and social studies sixth-grade curriculum. The teachers seek professional development, as Mr. Peters did through eventually matriculating in a Masters of Arts in Teaching program that also provided state certification to teach English. They enroll in university courses in their subject areas, as Ms. Payton has done annually since beginning her career fifteen years ago. They strive to develop expertise in new disciplines, as Mr. James did through securing state certification in secondary mathematics. They try to stimulate and renew their pedagogical imagination, as Ms. Smith does through taking courses in drama and the arts. When schedules and resources permit they attend outside seminars, summer enrichment programs, and the like. They reflect, they read, they talk with colleagues about their work. They *inhabit* the role of teacher to the extent that each gives it, as we have seen, a distinctive personal stamp.

Attention to Details

To shape the role of teacher as these four persons do implies devoting fine-grained attention to the details of practice. That disposition is another aspect of vocation described at the start of the book. I argued that discharging faithfully the often mundane chores that accompany teaching does not represent a distraction *from* the work. Rather, each of the seemingly minor acts and steps one takes adds up over time to the teacher one becomes and to the influence one might have on students. A person who neglects the everyday obligations built into teaching may become a person who neglects students. This is not to suggest that one must *like* tackling the routine requirements of the work. An artist may dislike having to mix paints before starting work. Yet how can he or she create art without doing so? A teacher may chafe at having to do the organizing, counting, sorting, photocopying, and more, that often go into creating a lesson. But how can he or she create a meaningful class without doing so?

The four teachers we met attend to teaching's everyday demands. For example, they devote a great deal of time and energy to student evaluation. They write comments on homework and often lengthy remarks on periodic reports. They talk repeatedly with colleagues, with parents, and with students themselves about the latters' progress. They devise mechanisms for drawing students into the process of evaluating one another. For example, Ms. Payton has a form she distributes in class for students to evaluate each other's oral reports. Ms. Smith coaches students on how to criticize intellectually—rather than personally—other students' poetry readings, stories, performances in class skits, and the like.

The details of teaching also encompass students' everyday worries and concerns, their daily academic efforts, and their typical conduct. The teachers appear to be habitually vigilant to these and related matters. From the perspective of a long-term observer, they appear alert to even the most subtle of their students' actions, while also acknowledging how much they fail to notice given the sheer number of young people they must teach.

Uncertainty and Doubt

The teachers' cognizance of how much they do *not* see attests to their awareness of the uncertainty that accompanies teaching. It is a truism that teachers often cannot know what their influence on students has been. That fact alone can make teaching a daunting prospect. It can render it intolerable to anyone who requires immediate and ongoing evidence of making a difference. As the four teachers affirm, it takes considerable time to become familiar enough with students to *recognize* their reactions to the subject matter and to how it is being taught. It takes time and experience to realize that change and growth in students emerge unevenly, unpredictably, often haltingly. It takes courage and faith to appreciate that those developments may not manifest themselves until after—perhaps well after—a student has moved on to another grade or level of formal education.

The teachers we have met are not comfortable with the doubts and uncertainties that accompany the vocation. For example, Ms. Payton worries a great deal about her relationship with her eleventh and twelfth graders. She fears she may not be having a positive influence on them, and she remains in doubt about what the most appropriate science curriculum for them might be. Mr. Peters struggles with his uncertainty about whether he is teaching or preaching. He reflects continually on his religious studies curricula and on how to make possible opportunities for students to question beliefs and values rather than to absorb them passively or uncritically. Mr. James is troubled by such questions as how much latitude to give his often unruly students, how to promote respectful and responsible attitudes, and how to fashion successful group lessons when he has spent virtually his entire career working with students individually. Ms. Smith worries about whether her students are finding social studies and history meaningful. She wrestles with how to make possible genuine connections between student and curriculum. She is disquieted about the recurrence of what she calls her "bad habits"—such as moving too fast through course material—that interfere with her larger goals.

All four teachers also admit to considerable uncertainty and concern about broader issues of education and society. Mr. James's talk of working on a "battleground of values" where his students' future is at stake comes to mind. All four teachers discuss the lack of adult guidance they believe some children suffer from. They speak of the economic pressures graduates face. They suggest that the materialism of contemporary culture (video games, MTV) renders students distracted and restless. Their testimony underscores the fact that teachers do work on a social "frontline," to employ one of Mr. James's terms. They encounter face-to-face many of the dilemmas and problems that arise in society. This reality will be familiar to teachers, but it does not always find a place in the perspectives of policymakers and curriculum-makers, much less in public talk about teacher accountability.

The teachers wonder about the extent to which they themselves might be contributing to societal problems. "We don't know what education is doing," Mr. Peters asserted at one point. "We could be just bringing about 'American machines.' We could be cogs in the system that's just maybe keeping people in order. Maybe that's all I'm doing, just kind of keeping control of the masses. . . . I really don't have proof that what I'm doing isn't unjust, that it isn't contributing to more evil." Ms. Smith echoes Mr. Peters's doubts, albeit in less dramatic terms. She "abhors" the thought that she may be simply "socializing" her students rather than teaching them to think for themselves. As we saw in Chapter 5, she wants schooling to be a meaningful experience for children. But she continues to question her success in making that possible.

In addition to these sources of doubt and uncertainty, all four teachers are regularly called on to make important decisions about curricula, about instructional method, and about students, all of which sometimes occasion considerable second-guessing on their part. Ms. Payton remembers acutely her shock and discomfort at how academically weak her upper-grade students turned out to be, this after she had been "piling it on" at the start in response to their apparent interest. She describes her discovery with embarrassment, as if she feels she should have known better. Mr. James recalls the student he ejected from a class years ago, who promptly initiated a fight with the school principal and eventually landed in jail. With distaste and sadness, Mr. James recounts how he handled—or failed to, as he puts it— being at "his limit" as teacher that day. Ms. Smith describes at length her year-long troubles with a student who, while good-natured as an individual, routinely disrupted class. "He's playing the clown," Ms. Smith suggested, "because he doesn't feel secure about his abilities. There are a lot of skills he missed along the line, and I don't think he's made up for them yet." She implemented every step she could think of to draw the boy into the classroom community: talking with him one-on-one about taking advantage of her class to learn; calling his mother; urging other students not to egg him on; making him leave the room for brief periods; having him sit in a corner away from peers or sit right by her desk; go to detention hall; and so forth. All of these strategies failed. The boy was expelled from school near the end of the academic year for trouble he caused elsewhere, a fact that only fueled Ms. Smith's doubts and wonder about what else she might have done.

This review of the teachers' concerns is not meant to suggest that they perceive teaching as a perilous journey into the unknown. As we observed, all four teachers accomplish many of their goals and derive substantial personal reward in doing so. According to their testimony, those rewards continually renew and invigorate their commitment to teaching. They motivate them to improve their ability to teach.

At the same time, however, their very engagement with the work heightens the stakes and the risks involved. Were the teachers to conduct themselves in a routinized, bureaucratic manner, they might be able to shield themselves from having to take responsibility for the basic terms of their role in the educational system. They might be able to ignore or to pass on to others the pedagogical tasks that confront them. Instead, the teachers appear to have accepted the notion that they are, in practice, "guides through difficulty" (Sockett, 1988)—that they have an obligation to help students chart the ever-challenging course of educational growth. As discussed previously, the teachers conduct themselves as architects of their learning environments rather than as passive functionaries carrying out the dictates of others. Their posture means they will have to deal with, rather than side-step, the problems and predicaments that accompany serious attempts to teach.

Mr. Peters's work on his Catholic school's Discipline Committee dramatizes the kinds of moral judgments the teachers are called on to make, as well as the doubts those judgments can trigger. By "moral judgments," I mean decisions and actions that reflect the view that some forms of conduct are *better* than others. Every educator the world over harbors some such view. Moreover, most would agree on a wide range of judgments, such as opposing the use of drugs and weapons in school, esteeming respectfulness rather than disrespect, valuing thoughtfulness rather than its opposite, and so forth. Without such judgments, teaching would be impossible because nobody could ever say, or even suggest, "let's do this rather than that." Teachers could neither approve nor disapprove, nor even criticize, anything students did. The analysis in previous chapters reveals that every educational endeavor embodies moral judgment, regardless of whether it is identified as such (Midgley, 1991).

The Discipline Committee on which Mr. Peters serves is chaired by the vice-principal and has three other teachers as members. It meets with boys with serious academic or behavioral problems, and recommends courses of action they must take in order to remain in the program. They convene after school in the library. I will describe in some detail a session with a ninth-grade boy, Raymond, one that is typical of the task Mr. Peters faces as a member of the committee. It is also a task all teachers confront—time and again—although usually in less formal circumstances.

Raymond had already been called before the committee some months before. He had a notorious reputation for acting out and disrupting classes. He had gotten into several fights with peers. He had also recently skipped detention hall and was caught writing grafitti on school property. The purpose of the present session was to determine whether he should be expelled immediately.

Raymond took his seat gingerly at the library table and seemed nonplussed to be surrounded by so many adults. He did not look anyone in the eye. His father sat on his right. His mother had refused to come to the session. The parents had separated five months earlier, and Raymond had moved in with his mother. According to what was said in the committee discussion afterward, the breakup of Raymond's family coincided with the period when he started to act out in school. His grades during the first quarter, in his major subjects, had been an A, four B's, and a D. In the second quarter—the period after his move—they were a C, four D's, and an F.

As per custom, each committee member posed questions and offered advice. Much of the hearing centered around whether Raymond could rein in his emotions and what kinds of specific actions he was prepared to take. One teacher asked him repeatedly why he tagged along with eleventh-grade boys known to be troublemakers in the school. "You know those boys are tough and are tryin' to be tough, don't you?" Raymond's father interjected, in a caustic tone of voice, "Yeah, you and those juniors who won't be back here next year, you can all have each other at Williams [the local public high school]. You'll be together there all right!"

They returned to the issue of the boy's explosive anger, which erupts in the classroom and in the school hallways. Two of the teachers initiated a mock boxing match, pushing each other and bopping each other on the arm. As they did so one of them barraged Raymond with questions: "What would you do if you were pushed in class like this? Or if somebody knocked you?" The boy remained taciturn, but said at one point, "Well, I wouldn't take that." The teacher pounced on this response. He told him he had to "take it," just like he and other teachers "take it all the time." "You don't *have* to respond to everything, Raymond, not *in* class!" He urged the boy to talk to his teachers, or to talk matters out with the students bugging him outside of classtime. He asked Raymond himself how he might acquire self-control.

Meanwhile, Raymond's father dropped complaints about the boy's mother, saying she did not discipline him and "couldn't care less" where he went or how late he stayed up. After the hearing had been going on for well over an hour, the vice-principal politely asked the father if he would excuse himself for a short time because the committee wanted to ask Raymond some "one-on-one questions." Those questions centered on how and whether Raymond thought he could get along with his parents. The committee suggested that he was falling into a dangerous pattern of not getting along with anyone. They reminded him that he had shown he could succeed in school, and pressed him to think of ways he might regain that attitude.

Mr. Peters took the lead, recalling the boy's good work in his class earlier in the year. He probed the boy's feelings about what he might do, until at one point, large tears started to roll down Raymond's face. He wept softly for a time, saying that he thought he could try. He received a strong word of encouragement: "Hey, you're *fourteen* now. Don't forget to enjoy this time! You'll be sixteen soon enough, and then you can be like a junior!"

The committee had a hard time deciding what to do about Raymond. While emphasizing how reluctant he was to make the recommendation, Mr. Peters said he did not think the boy could make it in the school. He acknowledged that Raymond had a difficult home situation, but also recalled how often he and other teachers had tried to help him. He reminded his colleagues of the many other students they are charged to help. "I know this isn't lightly done," Mr. Peters said, "but he just has too many problems for us." The others disagreed, although none of them wholeheartedly. They decided to give the boy one more chance, in part by requiring him to join one of the teachers for swimming after school on Fridays and another for gardening around the school on Saturdays. (These were but two out-of-school activities individual teachers had instituted, in part for the very reason of providing adult guidance for boys who needed it.) The vice-principal also volunteered to try to persuade Raymond and his parents to obtain family counseling. However, Raymond continued to disrupt classes, and also failed to show up for his required after-school activities. He was expelled a month after this two-hour-long hearing.

Mr. Peters's Catholic school has limited human and material resources. If it is to fulfill its educational and religious mission, it cannot accommodate—beyond a certain point—students who persist in disrupting its life. Mr. Peters believes the Discipline Committee's work is vital and he serves conscientiously. But he often leaves the sessions with unanswered questions about his own conduct, questions that nag him and often stay with him for a long time. He wonders about both the adequacy of and the warrant for his judgments, given the fact that they influence so directly the fate of individual students.

In varying degrees, the other three teachers must also make the kinds of decisions Mr. Peters confronts on his committee. They must do so because, like him, they treat their work in larger than bureaucratic terms. They accept responsibility for the terms of the practice. As a consequence, they are constantly called on to judge their students' capability, effort, and behavior. They are called on to offer their opinions, their recommendations, their advice, and their guidance. They do not always have time to weigh a course of action. Often, they must act immediately or else—to recall Ms. Smith's terms—the moment will "already be gone." Moreover, they must render their judgments in public circumstances, before the watchful eyes of students and fellow adults, thereby revealing their moral and educational standards. As Mr. James put it, teachers undergo the "ceaseless scrutiny" of their school communities. That reality accompanies the vocation of teaching.

The Intellectual and the Moral

Most teachers have few institutional opportunities to reflect on the many judgments they must make each day. They must find the time to do so in the interstices of a busy day or when they have returned home. Nor are courses on the ethical and moral aspects of teaching typically part of teacher education curricula (Soltis & Strike, 1992; Strike & Ternasky, 1993). Such curricula usually feature pedagogical and subject-matter knowledge. That focus is essential, otherwise teachers would have nothing to teach. But most teacher education programs appear to be premised on the assumption that good judgment about instructional methodology, lesson planning, and the like can be taught. That being so, why not assume that good ethical and moral judgment could be encouraged through being interwoven throughout a preparation program? The teachers' experience and testimony reported in this book reveal how repeatedly their work calls on their moral judgment and their moral strength. Time and again, it draws on the very core of their character as persons.

Moreover, these demands do not occur according to a schedule. They cannot be rigidly segregated from judgments about what to teach and how to do so. As previous chapters affirm, teaching is always and at once both an intellectual and a moral endeavor. The two aspects are thoroughly intertwined. One can argue, in the abstract, that the cardinal purpose of formal education is to teach the mind. But in the concrete circumstances of learning and living in schools, the mind becomes much more than a cognitive entity (or machine; see Searle, 1992, for a powerful critique of the idea of the mind as a "computer"). The mind becomes an evolving constellation of attitudes, dispositions, and capacities that takes shape through the process of education. A math teacher may claim to be teaching students only how to think well in their manipulation of numbers. However, "thinking well" involves qualities such as self-discipline, concentration, effort, imagination, and more, all of which extend well beyond addition and subtraction to how one addresses the questions and predicaments that constantly arise in life (Dewey, 1933). In addition, the claim that one is "only" teaching good thinking or good understanding of subject matter presumes a moral conviction in its own right, namely that a person's life will be *better* as a result of that teaching—else why engage in it? In brief, the issue is not either/or: that teaching is an intellectual act *or* a moral enterprise. To conceive teaching without encompassing both dimensions is to truncate it beyond recognition (Goodlad, Soder, & Sirotnik, 1990).

The language of vocation helps draw these dimensions together. I have reviewed in this section how that language captures some important features of the work of four successful practitioners. It calls attention to their sense of service and to the personal fulfillment they derive in rendering that service. It underscores their academic focus (more on this below) and their efforts to improve their subject-matter knowledge and their ability to teach. It reveals their attentiveness to students and to the details of teaching, a quality of carefulness that recalls the notion of teaching as a craft (Tom, 1984). And it highlights the ways in which they address the many uncertainties that accompany the work as well as the doubts and wonder those uncertainties can spark. That teaching is a complex act is a truism. But the language of vocation helps bring into sharper view that complexity as well as how teachers can succeed in responding to it.

THE CALLER AND THE CALLED

I argued in Chapter 1 that vocation implies more than an inner drive or desire to contribute to others. A social practice is the other and equally important side of the coin. For example, a person may want to be a doctor. But that desire would be meaningless without the practice of medicine in which to work. I do not mean without "a hospital" or "an infirmary" in which to perform. A practice is not the same thing as an institution. In principle, a doctor can work anywhere, for instance in a small town, on a battlefield, or at the site of an accident. The practice of medicine does not describe institutions like hospitals. Rather, it encompasses what it means to *be* a doctor as contrasted with being a cabdriver, an astrologer, a photographer, or a shipbuilder (MacIntyre, 1984).

The sense a person may have of being impelled from within to teach would remain lifeless were not the practice of teaching there to receive one. The practice *precedes* the individual. From this perspective, it "calls on" all who take it seriously to fulfill its requirements and responsibilities. It obliges teachers to manifest the willingness and the courage to confront the demands of the work that have been illustrated throughout this book. As we have seen, some of those demands are minor and mundane (what color paper is best for this poster?); others are major and dramatic (should I recommend this student be promoted to the next grade?). But teachers do not "invent" these situations. They emerge from the terms of the practice itself. It is the practice that calls one to act, not the individual per se. The practice is the "caller," inviting the person to meet its obligations.

At first glance, this argument appears to place the teacher with a sense of vocation in a passive posture. The verb itself can be rendered in passive voice: The teacher "is called" by the practice. This observation touches on a related dimension of vocation spelled out in Chapter 1. I claimed that many persons who want to teach do not conceive that desire as a "choice" among competing jobs. That is, the question they face is not whether to teach but rather when and under what circumstances. They may work in other lines of endeavor, sometimes for many years, until the right conditions materialize. Those conditions can include states of mind and heart. For instance, it may be years before a person feels ready or mature enough to enter the practice. All along, while working in business, law, the medical field, in parenting, or whatever, the person may feel prodded by a persistent whisper that seems to say: Try teaching. For persons with a vocational disposition, the desire to teach constitutes something more than casually selecting a job off the employment shelf.

However, to suggest that the desire to teach on the part of some practitioners is not a casual "choice" once more casts them in a passive role. It implies that something about teaching is larger than the person—something, to employ the familiar terms, that calls the person to it in the first place, that whets the appetite, that captures the imagination. The concrete source of that call may be one's own teachers, the influence of friends who are educators, one's experiences working with the young in an educational capacity. But notice that those sources reside not *within* the person but without, in the broader social world of education.

How can this apparent passivity—of being called—be reconciled with the contrasting claim emphasized in Chapter 1, and illustrated in subsequent chapters, that teachers with a vocational orientation are *active* and outward-looking, attentive to the terms of teaching, to students, to their obligations? Are these passive and active aspects of vocation like oil and water, or can they be blended?

One way to answer the question is to consider why a person might "hear" the call to teach in the first place. What is it within a person that picks up the call—that tunes into the vocational frequency, as it were? The testimony of the four teachers we have met offers a clue. Each describes classes, teachers, books, and other educational experiences they had when young that remain memorable. Significantly, their memories attest to their being active persons, *doing* things such as reading, writing, numerating, imagining, role-playing. I would suggest that the reason they heard the call to teach has to do with their active lives up to that point. Without any prior or deliberate intent, all that they have done has fashioned them into people capable of hearing the call *and* of responding to it—a point worth underscoring because some may hear it but lack the courage or circumstances to act. It would be misleading to say that the teachers or others like them were "born" to teach. Persons who give that impression were more than likely active when younger—they were curious and interested in things—such that their doings then and their efforts today add up to their appearing "natural" at the work. But what appears natural to a person is often the result of years of activity.

The idea of vocation does not privilege the practice over the person. The passive dimension I have identified—of being called—is dependent on persons who can *heed* it and who will actively and willingly take on its obligations. Person and practice are symbiotic, just as are the core vocational themes of public service and personal fulfillment. Teachers would literally be powerless without the practice of teaching. They would have no recognized, acknowledged social medium in which to act. Yet the practice itself would disappear without persons who invest themselves in it, persons who find meaning and identity within it. From this perspective, the practice takes on its own passive aspect. It must "wait" and depend on serious-minded individuals to take it up. Were nobody to do so, the future of the society in which the practice is embedded would be in peril.

VOCATION AND SCHOOLS

Some readers might have wondered whether the accounts in previous chapters conflate teaching with working in schools or in other educational institutions. Many educators would reject that association, pointing out that teaching can take place without classrooms, without schools, without all the other familiar institutional apparatus (Huebner, 1987; Illich, 1970; Neill, 1962). The argument in this book presupposes that teaching is not coterminous with schooling. Moreover, as I make clear in this section, I am not equating teaching with terms such as "schoolteaching" (Little, 1990) or "schoolteacher" (Lortie, 1975). Both of those compound terms grant the school a certain priority over the act of teaching. In contrast, to speak of the vocation of teaching is to center the work on sources beyond the confines of any particular institution. Those sources are the practice of teaching and the hopes and capabilities of individuals. The experience of the four teachers described in this book suggests that teachers may be well served to root their identity not solely in their particular institutions but rather in a larger vision of teaching.

This notion is not as remarkable as it might appear. After all, most persons who aspire to teach do not have in mind working in a *particular* school. Rather, they want to teach and to have a beneficial impact on the young. To perceive themselves as members of a practice—one, incidentally, with a history as old as civilization itself—can guide them through difficult times. It can help them appreciate that their perspectives and actions need not be determined solely by their specific circumstances. To encounter a series of rough classes; to fail to reach a student; to feel let down by colleagues, administrators, or parents—none of these troubling events so familiar to teachers need demoralize them or lead them to abandon teaching. If they perceive the work in terms larger than their own immediate situation, they might discover unexpected resources.

The Importance of Perception

The analysis in previous chapters features several examples of this claim. As we observed, for instance, Mr. Peters had a difficult time as a beginning teacher. He had problems defining and implementing his curriculum, and his relations with students were often strained. Yet one reason he stayed the course and eventually began to flourish was his sense that teaching promised something more than his present lot. Thinking back to his own experience as a student, he says, "I knew there was a way of reaching these students because I [had seen] it happen. I knew it was possible; not in my room, at that point, but it was possible." We observed a comparable distinction between personal vision and immediate context in Mr. James's work. As we saw, he does not perceive his students in the negative light many colleagues appear to. I suggested that in an important respect he does not inhabit the same world as those colleagues. He sees possibilities in his students where others do not. But that is precisely because his sense of teaching and of working with the young is not rooted solely in an institutional or occupational framework. Both he and Mr. Peters appear to find strength and motivation in a larger vision, one that I have argued can be understood through the language of vocation. Both teachers act as if teaching has its own integrity and is not defined by the immediate context of the school. The same can be said of Ms. Payton and Ms. Smith, both of whom treat their classrooms as distinctive communities in which to engage students in learning. All four teachers appear to believe in the idea of teaching. They do not pin that belief on any particular success, nor do they call it into question on the basis of any particular failure. Their testimony suggests that their perceptions of teaching and of themselves figure more prominently in how and why they teach than do the specific circumstances in which they work.

Their shared stance recalls a tenet common to many philosophies of life from around the world. This conviction says that a person's perception helps, in effect, to determine the world in which he or she will live. How one sees oneself and one's circumstances makes all the difference. As the saying goes, one can see the cup as half-full or as half-empty, and that viewpoint will shape the meaning and the possibilities one finds in life. Moreover, the issue of *which* way to see the cup resides, at least in part, in one's own hands.

Leo Tolstoy captured the power of this idea in his fable "The King and the Shirt" (in Dunnigan, 1962), which is his rendition of an old and timeless human story. A king who is ill offers half his kingdom in exchange for a cure. His wise men say that if he can find a happy man and put on that man's shirt, he will be well. The king sends his emmissaries out far and wide. After scouring the kingdom in vain for somebody who is happy, one day the king's son overhears a peasant inside his hut say: "Now, God be praised, I have finished my work, I have eaten my fill, and I can lie down and sleep! What more could I want?" Overjoyed, the son orders the man's shirt be taken—but the happy man is so poor that he has no shirt. The fable's message appears to be that the man with no shirt is not nearly as poor as everyone else in the kingdom, and that happiness is more a consequence of how one perceives things than of one's actual material conditions.

This familiar lesson does not imply that one can simply invent one's own reality. As understood here, "perception" differs from fantasy and invention. Ms. Payton can perceive her upper-grade students as unteachable and can act accordingly, perhaps by offering them time-killing worksheets. Or, she can see them as persons to whom she has a pedagogical obligation—to whom she owes a good-faith effort. *Both sets of facts are equally real.* Some of her students have virtually given up on classroom education and pine for the day when they are done with school. At the same time, because she has willingly taken on the role of teacher, Ms. Payton has an obligation to try to reach them. The question is which set of facts she will focus on and take as the guide to her actions. To pretend that either set did not exist would be an act of fantasy (not to mention of irresponsibility). But to assume that Ms. Payton's perception did not matter in the outcome would be an act of blindness.

To emphasize the centrality of individual perception in teaching, as I do throughout this and the next chapter, does not downplay the importance of conditions. Tolstoy's man with no shirt may be happy, but were *he* to fall ill he would have no royal emmissaries to send out for a cure. Circumstances and resources make a considerable difference in any teacher's life. Moreover, as we have seen in previous chapters, every school setting constrains what teachers can do. No teacher can create a classroom that is completely self-contained and shut off from the larger social environments of the school and beyond. Previous research has shown that the conditions in which teachers work influence, for both good and ill, their perceptions of what they can do (Huberman et al., 1993; Johnson, 1990; McLaughlin, Talbert, Bascia, 1990; Sikes et al., 1985).

How and to what extent this influence takes place remain complicated questions that call for continued inquiry and reflection. These questions are part of a larger concern that remains in considerable doubt today. Over a century of research across the social sciences has not settled the issue of how individual identity and perception are formed. Metaphorically, we do not know where society's influence stops and the individual begins. Assertions that the human person or self is a cultural or social construction beg the question, as do assertions that the person has an identity that stands apart from the social world in which he or she lives. We do not know in any final sense how or to what extent individuals' beliefs, values, perceptions, and actions are shaped by their culture and society, nor, in contrast, to what extent they reflect their own unique dispositions and moral sensibilities. We find it useful for many purposes to speak in global terms about specific cultures, societies, and groups. But when brought to the level of the individual, those terms suddenly become wooden, stiff, unable to capture the distinctiveness of persons. They are like listing colors: red, green, yellow, blue, orange. But a particular painting, for instance, is much more than the sum of the colors used in its construction. Similarly, an individual person is much more than the sum of the social, cultural, and economic forces at work in his or her environment.

Although the experience of four practitioners is hardly a basis for generalization, their testimony and actions affirm how complex is the question of what "forms" a teacher. Clearly, the teachers have been influenced by their upbringing, by their education, and by their present working conditions. They are influenced by their colleagues, their students, their administrators, their friends, their families. I have also argued that they are influenced by the practice of teaching itself, which "calls" on their knowledge, their judgment, and their character. Just as clearly, however, one cannot conclude that their perceptions and actions are determined by these factors. Each comes across as much more than a mere "product" of the forces at work in his or her respective environment. Each strikes one as a teacher distinct from all others, often in subtle ways, perhaps, but no less significant for that. Each is noninterchangeable with other practitioners, another dimension of vocation I touched on in Chapter 1 and that I clarify in the next chapter.

The teachers' testimony reveals their mixed views of schools. On the one hand, all four believe in the formal process of education represented by school. They are supportive of the schools in which they work. They suggest that their respective institutions are, on balance, forces for good rather than for evil. They speak sympathetically about their administrators, their colleagues, their school settings, and they warmly acknowledge the support they receive.

On the other hand, their testimony suggests that the structure and the functioning of their schools sometimes interfere with their efforts rather than complement them. The teachers speak of tensions generated by their schools' rules and regulations. They talk about the challenges of getting to know all of their students well enough to appreciate their learning styles and capabilities. With the exception of Mr. James, their classes average about twenty-five students—low in numbers in comparison with some teachers, but large enough to render personalized teaching difficult. Mr. James's classes average about seven students, but as we have seen these are individuals with special needs; moreover, he acts as consultant and counselor to faculty and other students. The teachers also refer to the limited time they have to teach each group of students. Ms. Payton and Mr. James have 40-minute periods in their public school; Mr. Peters, 50 minutes in his Catholic school; and Ms. Smith, 45 minutes in her independent school (until she fashioned a combined core curriculum that provided her 90 minutes a day with each class). Hargreaves (1994) employs the sociological term "intensification" to highlight the pressures teachers face in hectic, busy schools in which they have limited time to work with many students. These circumstances render it difficult for teachers to enact the terms of vocation that I have described and illustrated in this book.

If my argument thus far is sound, however, the tensions between institution and vocation should come as no surprise. The idea of teaching as a vocation is not identical with the occupational description "working in a school." I have shown that the four teachers' views of their work transcend their particular settings. That point does not mean, it bears repeating, that they disapprove of their schools, or that they do not derive meaning and professional identity from teaching in them. Far from it. As we have seen, all four are active in their schools, working on committees, creating curricula, interacting with colleagues in many other ways—all of this on top of the time and energy they devote to teaching. To judge from extensive informal testimony from peers, administrators, parents, and students, all four are highly regarded members of their school communities.

Nonetheless, the decisive factor in the conduct of their work remains their perceptions of themselves, their students, and the practice of teaching. Their perceptions guide them through the maze of the particular, complex, and ambiguous circumstances in which they work. Those perceptions influence which instructional and curricular instruments they employ. The latter are indispensable to teaching, as I will affirm in a moment, but are as meaningless as windmills in a waterless desert without a teacher's vision behind them. It is Ms. Payton's perception of her role—a perception infused by much more than the particular institutional setting in which she works— that led her to move from one school to another where she would have greater challenges. It is her perception that determined whether she would merely use worksheets with her upper-grade students, or would instead develop (as she endeavored to do) other tools such as experiments and small-group activities to try to trigger their involvement.

Instructional Method and Subject-matter Knowledge

The idea of vocation as developed in this book highlights teachers' dispositions, attitudes, beliefs, and values more than it does methods of teaching. The teachers we have met emphasize that sound instructional methods are necessary in teaching. To teach without them, they imply, and without an understanding of what they are and what they can do, is like trying to paint without a brush and colors. But the danger in granting method priority in any conception of teaching is similar to the danger of giving a hammer to a small child, who, as the familiar image has it, might suddenly see everything around him or her as a nail. Previous research on teaching has amply demonstrated a corollary: If one teaches would-be practitioners instructional techniques without rooting them in a larger conception of what they are for, one should not be surprised if they promptly treat their classrooms and students like "nails"—like persons on whom to use those techniques willy-nilly.

This analogy does not imply that methods and techniques of teaching are low on the totem pole. They are important, but so are the personal characteristics of the people who take on the role of teacher. A more promising image than that of children and hammers is a growing plant. No plant can grow and prosper without good soil. Similarly, no teaching methodology can have its desired effect without a person disposed to employ it—a person who is active, interested, engaged, curious as much about the rationale behind a method as about the steps it contains. The sense of vocation described in this book is what brings methods of teaching to life—and renders them in the service of life as well, rather than, as Mr. Peters and Ms. Smith worry, in the service of merely socializing students, passing them along, keeping them under control, and so forth. In sum, vocation without skill is ineffectual, but skills without a sense of service informing their use may be damaging.

These points hold in relating the sense of vocation to subject-matter knowledge. All four teachers emphasize the importance of academic knowledge and understanding in their work. As we saw, all four continue to take university courses and to deepen their background in the subjects they teach. They work hard to render their curricula educative and interesting. As we also observed, some of their most frustrating difficulties in the classroom can be traced to gaps and inadequacies—which they describe themselves—in their subject-matter knowledge.

However, the fact that they *feel* these frustrations in the first place attests once more to the animating force their larger commitments and hopes play in their work. Without their sense of service, it is hard to imagine them caring enough to bother about either pedagogical self-improvement or the intellectual improvement of their students. Their testimony also suggests that a love for their academic subjects is not their primary reason for teaching, although it did help motivate them at the start of their careers and continues to do so today. This is not to downplay how seriously they treat their subjects. Nor is it to imply that teaching implies a "choice" between dedication to subject matter and dedication to students. Good teaching at any level takes place at the intersection of the two. For example, Ms. Smith waxes enthusiastic in talking both about students and about history and social studies. However, at the same time one of the major reasons she sought to work with fewer numbers of students was her conviction that they "need more" from her and that she wants to provide more in terms of personal influence:

> They need someone to recognize their uniqueness and specialness and respect it and nurture it. I need to be able to love them. . . . I can imagine someone else coming into my classroom and being a sharper teacher, a better storyteller, more capable of choosing the right selections, and [with] a better sense of history and all that. But I feel like in terms of loving kids, that there I can do as good a job as anybody.

Ms. Smith appreciates the danger that such remarks might be taken as "prissy" and "saccharine," to cite her own terms. She makes it clear that "loving kids" does not mean relaxing her standards with them or indulging whim or fancy. She states that she has no interest in taking on the role of a surrogate parent. But she underscores her strong interest not just in her students' academic learning but in the persons they might turn out to be. Put differently, she appears to care as much for the persons they might become as for the persons they are now. In brief, her commitment to her subject is centered in a broader vision of wanting to be a force for good in students' lives. That desire resides at the heart of the work all four teachers perform.

A SENSE OF TRADITION

I have argued that there are tensions between vocation and institution. The structure and goals of the latter can make it difficult for an individual teacher to enact his or her aspirations. Similarly, there will always be friction between specific institutions and the larger practice itself. The practice of teaching, with its core focus on the intellectual and moral development of students, is not identical with working in a specific setting. The practice is much older than and will outlast every school in existence today, just as the practices of medicine and of law are older and larger than their contemporary institutional settings.

This point needs elaborating, although doing so means moving beyond the testimony of the four teachers in this book. As has been shown, all four see past the immediate circumstances in which they work to larger hopes and goals as teachers. But they do not speak in the historical terms I have just mentioned. Nor, to judge from previous research on teachers' views and beliefs, do many other practitioners. However, just as a sense of vocation can guide one's efforts in the classroom—a point amply illustrated in previous chapters—so can a sense of history and of tradition. If one conceives of oneself as working in a practice whose origins reside far in the past, and whose value will persist long into the future, one can derive additional sources of strength and perhaps even of imagination as a teacher.

Those sources can be valuable when one has reached the end of one's tether, an experience described by all four teachers in this book and one that teachers everywhere are likely to encounter. In addition to the complexity and uncertainty in teaching discussed previously, many studies suggest that social pressures on teachers appear to have magnified in recent years (Beynon, 1985; Hargreaves, 1994; Powell, Farrar, & Cohen, 1985; Yee, 1990). Such changes bring with them the unnerving prospect of new forms of perceived failure as a teacher—failure to be a surrogate parent or counselor; failure to overcome the competition of a commerical and materialist culture; failure to single-handedly make up for a student's years of poor-quality education. However, analogues to these contemporary pressures have always accompanied teaching in schools. The difficulties faced by urban teachers in 1895, for example, in the rapidly changing economic, social, and cultural environment of the time, were in their own way as challenging as those faced by teachers today. Among other things, teachers in that era had to work with large class sizes, children from a myriad of cultural backgrounds, and inadequate material and professional support from the system (Altenbaugh, 1992; Cremin, 1988; Cuban, 1992; Hoffman, 1981; Tyack, 1974). In short, the shape and the terms of the difficulties facing teachers may have changed, but not the inherent challenges themselves.

These challenges can trigger questions sometimes detectable below the surface of the testimony we have heard in this book. Why bother to teach? What difference does it make what I do? What influence can I really have as a teacher, when I am but one among so many that children will encounter? Such questions are, in turn, the stepchildren of larger skeptical worries. Why bother to do anything for society? What difference can it make what I do? I am but one among millions. How could the world ever care for what I do? How can it matter? Why *not* abandon this talk of public service and concentrate instead on serving myself? At least that course of action seems easier, more certain, and more tangibly profitable.

A sense of history and of tradition in teaching can assist one in withstanding these doubts. As history reveals so abundantly, one of the things that differentiates human beings from other creatures is the need to *cultivate* ways of getting along together. Other creatures do not confront that challenge; they inherit and do not alter nature's plan for how to "get along." Because of that fact, categories like politics and morality and ethics, which all have to do with issues such as respect, justice, and caring, do not exist for them. They live in worlds without the categories of "good and bad" or "better and worse." The question whether their worlds are superior or not as a consequence of that state of affairs is one human beings will never be able to answer. That is, the question itself presupposes the differences being drawn here. Human beings, in part by virtue of their minds and their self-consciousness, must craft ways of living together. They do confront good and evil—or, in less dramatic terms, they face the prospect of living in better or worse worlds of their own making. People can act well or they can act badly. They can perform "good" in ways inconceivable to other creatures, just as they can perform "bad." Consequently, it is worth taking a stand on which kind of world one would like to live in—good or bad—and to contribute to the coming-into-being of that world. As many political and religious leaders have sought to remind us, every individual person can make a difference in the balance. This is particularly so for teachers, who are positioned more than most others to have an influence on a large number of young people.

In Chapter 2 I quoted Henry Adams's remark that "a teacher affects eternity. He can never tell where his influence stops" (quoted in Jackson, 1986, p. 53). That thought may be heartening to those who teach. But it may also appear abstract. What kind of influence is Adams talking about? How might one exert such an influence? One way to answer the questions is to recall the testimony of the four teachers met here. For example, Ms. Payton's colleagues tell her that they are grateful that she has taught students to think of science as a process of inquiry rather than as a mere store of facts. Ms. Payton has probably not had this kind of influence on all of her students, of course, and we do not know how many actually do conceive science as a process or in what sense they do. Still, the fact remains that some students are evidently able to accomplish things in subsequent classes as a result of her work. In turn, that fact implies that these students may influence their peers who did *not* have Ms. Payton as a teacher. They may teach them, as much through personal example as through precept, to see science as a journey of discovery—and perhaps to perceive learning itself in those terms.

Imagine for a moment Ms. Payton's students' never having had her as a teacher. Although this proposition borders on the sentimental—one thinks of James Stewart in the film *It's a Wonderful Life*—it remains conceivable that without knowing her some students would never have learned that science is more than a body of facts. Even more tellingly, some might never have come to appreciate the excitement of inquiry that resides at the heart of science. Many teachers can construct a comparable scenario about their own work. To ponder how things might be had one never taught should trigger a rush of faces, scenes, events, that attest to the ways in which young people have heeded what one has tried to teach. That influence constitutes a kind of web, with the teacher at the center, and with strands linking him or her with students as well as linking students one with the other. Thinner strands (but strands nonetheless) connect students with the people they know outside the classroom, who may themselves be influenced by what the students have learned and absorbed as a result of the teacher's work. As we have seen, that learning can encompass new attitudes and dispositions as well as academic knowledge.

This extended web of connections, materialized through time, constitutes a world that would never have existed without the person at its center, the teacher. *It would never have existed.* The fact that the teacher will never see the totality of that world—if Adams is correct, he or she will be aware of but a small portion of it—does not call its existence into question. Moreover, this argument features only a single teacher. If one ponders for a moment the number of persons who have taught and who are teaching today, the vastness of the intellectual, social, and moral influence of teachers becomes striking. The importance of the practice of teaching in societies the world over comes to the fore.

This sense of history and tradition in teaching can help teachers place their immediate circumstances against a larger backdrop, one that adds significance to what they perform. They work in a practice whose origins reside long in the past and whose present effect is felt everywhere. Rather than attempt to "remake the world"—an idealistic aim that appears to animate many new teachers—they might strive to remake their classroom environments over and over again to render them as educative as possible. As the teachers we have met imply, the greatest influence a teacher can have is right under his or her nose, such that a central task of good teaching is to learn to pay attention to what is right in front of one.

Yet this argument may not address deeper fears, such as the prospect of being forgotten once one has left the ranks of teaching. After all, who remembers the village teacher from the nineteenth century? In a literal sense, no one does of course. Does that mean the influence of that teacher has dissipated, finally spent itself, like the ripple caused by a tossed stone reaching the far shore? If what has been said up to now is valid, the influence of that teacher is as present today—albeit in different form—as it was when he or she stood in front of the wooden rows of seats, chalk and dog-eared reader in hand. It has found expression in the buildings, the tools, the arts, and so much more, constructed by people who as children passed through that classroom and who, perhaps unaware, picked up an idea, a way of looking, a skill, that became a part of their working orientation as adults, and that they have in turn passed on. The web that teacher began to spin the first day he or she walked into the school produced strands that continue to find extension.

Webs can entrap and entangle, of course, rather than buoy and support. Consequently, it behooves teachers to take whatever steps they can to ensure that what radiates from the center of their work is something enabling rather than damaging. In the next and final chapter, I show how taking the idea of vocation seriously can enhance the likelihood of such an outcome.

7

Must Teaching Be a Vocation?

During the 1950s and 1960s there was considerable doubt about the efficacy of schools (just as there continues to be in some quarters today). The much-publicized report written by Coleman (1966) on educational equality that was released at that time appeared to show that forces beyond the walls of the school played a decisive role in whether students succeeded academically. That report and others like it seemed to imply that educators were painfully limited in what they could do to influence the young. Moreover, in addition to public doubts about the impact of schools, there was widespread suspicion that teachers were in any case not up to the task. Under the influence of behaviorism, considerable talk emerged at the time about "teaching machines"—literally, technology that could replace persons and yield more efficient, more predictable, and more assured educational outcomes in settings such as schools.

Times have changed, and the idea of replacing people with machines in the classroom doubtless strikes readers as bizarre. In addition, research undertaken since the 1960s shows that schools and teachers *can* influence students' learning (Jackson, 1992; Wittrock, 1986). The analysis in previous chapters supports that conclusion. It has also clarified what teachers themselves have long felt and known—namely, that the practice is complex, demanding, and often ambiguous in its terms and in its impact. Ironically, the challenges teachers face may make *them* wish from time to time for machines to assist them—machines that might identify the right instructional method and techniques at just the right time; that might provide mastery of one's subject and help determine what to teach at what time; that might help one gain awareness of how the young develop intellectually and emotionally so that one knows just what to do with a particular learner.

Of course such machines will never be forthcoming. Who could program them? Who could wire them to perform the nuanced, sensitive interpretations teachers strive to make of students' capacities, abilities, emotions, and hopes? Would not the ability to program a machine in such a way mean that the programmers were themselves masters of those gifts? What group of programmers possesses that qualification? What group of persons has ever had such Olympian understanding? Technology will always be a useful resource for teachers, and increasingly so as it develops in sophistication and "user-friendliness." But it is hard to imagine a machine accomplishing what teachers do, namely, recognizing and responding to the interests, difficulties, frustrations, and joys of students as they learn and grow.

A critic might teasingly reply: What if the programmers were the likes of Mother Teresa and Dr. Martin Luther King, Jr.? or Albert Einstein and Mahatma Gandhi? Might we not be tempted to return to the idea of teaching machines if those machines contained the wisdom, compassion, knowledge, and vision of such figures? Wouldn't even a mechanical Einstein- or King-surrogate be vastly better than your average, ordinary classroom teacher? King and other like-minded notables would themselves repudiate the idea of replacing a teacher with a machine. They would reject such a proposal precisely because of their understanding of human life. They would say: Nobody wants to live in such a world, where machines and not persons are the ultimate teachers. Education is and will always be a challenging enterprise, but turning to the nonhuman is not a solution to the problems and ambiguities of being human. Nobody who thinks the matter through to its logical outcome would exchange the morally frustrating but also redeeming unpredictability of human beings for the smooth-running, errorless, and therefore nonhuman world of machines. Better human beings with their foibles and gifts than machines with their inanimate perfection.

However, other critics might point out that the foibles sometimes outweigh the gifts, with unfortunate results for children. They might recall the fact that some teachers, at all levels of the system, are neither particularly sensitive to students nor knowledgeable about the subjects they teach (Goodlad, 1984; McLaughlin et al., 1990; Sirotnik, 1983). They might argue that while the idea of teaching machines is absurd, the commitment behind it to public accountability and to standards of quality is not. The four teachers met in this book would have no quarrel with that claim. Their example illuminates not only the importance of personal dedication in teaching, but also how that sense of service can promote both an active and an imaginative commitment to public accountability. These are not practitioners who follow their own idiosyncratic path, sidestepping or ignoring society's expectations regarding their work with the young. Rather, they accept the responsibilities that accompany the role. To judge from their testimony and actions, they successfully fuse these public responsibilities with their own aims as teachers. That fact helps account for why each appears as such a distinctive teacher, noninterchangeable with any other—unlike machines, to return once more to that contrast, which are constructed to be predictable, identical, and replaceable.

One purpose of this final chapter is to consider whether the vocational dispositions the four teachers manifest ought to constitute criteria for admitting teachers to the practice. Posed as a question, the chapter asks: Must teachers see their work as a vocation? To anticipate my own response, I will show that to regard teaching as a vocation does not require teachers to "drop everything" and become selfless servants of the public. Far from it. Ms. Payton, Mr. Peters, Mr. James, and Ms. Smith all have extended family and friendship circles from which they obtain the lifelong meaning most persons derive from those sources. They are friends, spouses, parents, neighbors, and more; for instance, three are married and have children. At the same time, however, they *treat* their teaching in ways that are best understood through the language of vocation. Because they conduct themselves this way, their time and their effort *while on the job*—which means while thinking about it as well as while doing it—yield considerable personal rewards as well as opportunities for influencing students and colleagues alike.

I will argue that professing vocation should not become a criterion for admission to teaching. Rather, the idea of vocation serves as a mirror into which all prospective and practicing teachers might look. It is a mirror that invites teachers to self-scrutiny and self-reflection. It asks teachers to ponder the extent to which they are meeting the responsibilities that accompany the role. It calls on them to be at their best when in the presence of their students. It urges them to act, at a minimum, as if their work were a vocation, regardless of whether they in fact view it as such. I show that adopting this stance renders teaching a much more interesting and fulfilling activity than it may otherwise appear to be. It enables teachers to have the kinds of positive influence on students society hopes for, and that they themselves perhaps imagined when they first considered entering the classroom.

I begin the chapter by illuminating how the sense of vocation goes hand-in-hand with respecting the public obligations built into the practice of teaching. This discussion sets the stage for addressing how the idea of vocation—an idea centered on the call to be of service—can itself be of service to teachers, to those who aspire to teach, and to those who wish to better understand teachers and their work. I conclude the chapter, and the book, with some comments on why teaching as a vocation is a realistic aim despite the educational, social, and political difficulties teachers face in our time.

VOCATION AND PUBLIC ACCOUNTABILITY

In previous chapters, I have distinguished the vocation of teaching and the practice in which it is embedded from the institutions—namely, schools—in which it usually takes place. I have sought to emphasize that those differences do not mean that teachers must choose to serve either their vocation or their schools. There will always be tensions between the allegiance teachers have to the terms of their practice and to their respective institutions. Those tensions come with working in schools, and do not in themselves call into question the validity of either the practice or schools. As the four teachers attest, schools always constrain what teachers can do. Yet they also offer valued forms of community and of professional support. In this light, the challenge teachers must address is how to balance their personal aims and judgment with the public obligations embodied in the life of their institution.

Teachers teach not to serve themselves but rather to serve others: students first and foremost, but by extension the communities and the society in which they live. Moreover, teaching implies serving learners in ways that are distinct from those of other practices. To want to "help" young people is not identical with teaching. One can be helpful as a parent, as a counselor, as a priest, as a doctor, and so forth. But those practices differ from the practice of teaching. None place both intellectual and moral development at their center in the formal and public ways that teaching does. In addition, because one may have success in one social endeavor—for example, as a parent—does not imply one will necessarily be a successful teacher, any more than achieving as a sculptor means one will automatically be accomplished at painting, poetry, or any other art. Social practices like teaching and medicine are distinct. Each calls on practitioners to accept the particular responsibilities and obligations that accompany it, rather than either to ignore them or to impose their own.

Though teaching as a practice evolves with social change, it remains a public act that bears directly on the shaping of society. Consequently, the constituents of that society have a right to offer input into what is taught and into how teaching is judged. What kind of input and how much are thorny questions that educators and philosophers continue to debate (Barber, 1992; Goodlad et al., 1990; Gutmann, 1987; Strike, 1991). However, all but the most intransigent individualists would agree that teachers are accountable to others. Teachers do not "own" their work lock, stock, and barrel. They must do more, as Rosenholtz (1989) put it, than seek "to enhance their own self-esteem by selecting only those goals [of teaching] that suit them best" (p. 15). The intellectual and moral purposes of teaching—which the four practitioners we met amply describe—are not "selected" by teachers, much less invented out of whole cloth. As I suggested in Chapter 6 in discussing the "caller" and the "called," the practice itself shapes those purposes. Moreover, both vocations and practices are embedded within a particular society, one without which there would be no rationale for them in the first place. In short, to the extent that teachers control their curricula and their approaches to instruction, they must be prepared to defend them to larger publics.

They will have to do so in local circumstances, which brings us back to institutions. Schools, and the publics that support them, provide teachers a salary and accompanying benefits. They also provide nonpecuniary rewards, such as membership in a community, opportunities for intellectual and pedagogical development, and more. In practical terms, teachers must be accountable to their particular schools and to the communities they serve. They must acknowledge the interests and goals of those actors and fashion a response to them. In addition to students, that will mean paying attention to colleagues, departmental chairs, principals, and parents. It bears emphasizing that responding in respectful terms to these persons does not imply ceding to them control over what is taught and how it is taught. Such control is actually impossible because every practitioner will interpret and teach content in unique ways—no matter who defines it—the desires of outside parties notwithstanding (Jennings, 1992). But the argument does mean one cannot cavalierly go one's own way as if one had a private practice based on private wisdom. As I suggested at the start, to look into the mirror of what vocation implies can remind all who teach of this central fact.

To define how much and what kind of voice society ought to have in shaping the terms of teaching is beyond the scope of this book. Gutmann (1987) argues that in a democratic society, teachers merit firm protection from undue social demands. They should be responsive to parents and other public interests, but should not be obliged to kowtow to them. According to Gutmann, teachers should be granted an authoritative position—not to be confused with an authoritarian one—because by virtue of working on the very front lines of public education, they are well positioned to engage the young in both academic learning and in qualities of democratic citizenship (for criticism of Gutmann's viewpoint, see Bilow, 1988; Hansen, 1991; and Strike, 1991).

Acknowledging the place of vocation in teaching substantiates this perspective. The term highlights the fact that there *are* limits to society's role in influencing and judging what teachers do. Appreciating the idea of vocation might assist others in the educational system to realize that while teachers have obligations to schools and their constituencies, those who govern schools have obligations to teachers. This point acquires urgency when one recalls that an individual's sense of vocation can be taken advantage of or even manipulated by those in positions of authority. Gustafson (1982) warns that a person with a calling may inadvertently allow himself or herself to "have justifiable self-interests denied, even justice denied, because of a deep sense of vocation" (p. 505). Ellul (1972) argues that vocation has been used as "a pretext to give lower salaries (and sometimes no salary at all) to nurses, social workers, pastors, teachers" (p. 12). Emmet (1958) writes that "too often in the past people like nurses have been exploited . . . because they were supposed to have a vocation" (p. 255). They were "supposed" to be persons who sacrifice for the common good and who therefore require little institutional support (Chambers-Schiller, 1979; Hoffman, 1981).

As Douglas (1986) shows, institutions often appear to have a mind of their own. They often appear to run according to their own logic, which may or may not be in harmony with the needs of the individuals who work in them. Those who structure and govern institutions face the constant danger of overlooking conditions that may make it hard for people to enact their sense of service—or that may exhaust it without fostering opportunities for personal renewal (Bolin & Falk, 1987; Hargreaves & Fullan, 1992). Such conditions can make it difficult for persons to do what they believe is right for those whom they want to serve. Emmet (1958) argues for institutional structures that provide and support autonomy for individual practitioners. She makes her point by distinguishing social from personal or vocational ethics. "Social ethics," she writes, "should be concerned with matters of function and status." This claim recalls the argument above about teachers' obligation to be responsive to the needs and hopes of their schools and communities. Teaching does embody such a social ethic. But "'vocation,'" continues Emmet, "takes us into a sphere of personal ethics for which society cannot covenant" (p. 255). Emmet also calls this "sphere" of personal ethics one of "vocational ethics." It encompasses an individual's aims, motives, and standards of moral and intellectual judgment. It calls attention to how these are played out in the person's work with others. Vocational ethics, as Emmet puts it, address the "relationships of persons whose [individual strengths and] powers drive them to find their own ways of working from incentives internal to themselves" (p. 253).

The analysis in previous chapters suggests that what Emmet (1958) calls the "inner incentive" characteristic of vocation—an incentive that "prevents a person from treating his work as a routine job" (p. 255)—warrants respect and support. The four teachers we have met and their like-spirited colleagues everywhere are clearly motivated by more than considerations of salary and material benefit alone. They perform tasks that few others in the educational system are positioned to do. Few spend this kind of time and energy in developing students' minds and character. To accomplish their work, teachers require conditions in which to enact their vocational ethic—that is, to reach their own judgments about individual students' needs and problems and how best to address them. They should be prepared to defend their judgments, given the public significance of the work, and to alter them if they prove wrong. But they ought not to be forced to accept solutions and strategies without their own input. They ought not to be forced to shelve their personal judgment and motivation strictly in the name of bureaucratic need. They merit this support because they are hired, at least in principle, to make many important decisions about students' capabilities and futures. To take away this autonomy would be to undermine the basic terms of the practice. It would curtail teachers' ability to act independently, creatively, and imaginatively, and, of crucial social importance, to help the next generation develop those qualities themselves.

In short, the idea of vocation not only calls attention to teachers' obligations to their practice, but also highlights the question of how and whether the system of formal education can support individual endeavor and creativity. It invites those who govern the system to consider, among other things, their own sense of vocation, and to ask whether they are themselves acting in a spirit of service to those whom they are best positioned to support: teachers and, through them, students. "This is where wisdom and imagination are called for from administrators," urges Emmet (1958), "and where indeed administration itself calls for vocational qualities" (p. 256).

Teachers will always have to balance public obligations with their personal beliefs and purposes in teaching. There have always been—as there will continue to be—tensions between individual creativity and originality, such as that embodied in the enactment of vocation, and the maintenance of practices in institutions like schools. Teachers such as the four we have met will always face the task of being "true" to their vocational ethic. They will have to come to grips with their convictions about their role, and to have the courage to make the intellectual and moral judgments that comprise teaching. But they will also have to be mindful of the social ethic—their public duties and obligations—embodied in the practice of teaching as it is played out in institutions. The analysis in previous chapters has shown how the sense of vocation can buoy an individual as he or she strives to integrate these public and personal dimensions of the work. It can keep at bay both a despairing and a resigned response to the very real difficulties involved in successfully shaping the role of teacher.

THE MIRROR OF VOCATION

Fueling Interest in Teaching

An aim that teachers everywhere profess is to spark their students' interest in learning. They want to introduce their students to the marvels and joys of discovery. They hope to draw students into the worlds of experience and accomplishment embodied in their academic subjects.

Analogously, to see teaching as a vocation can render *it* more interesting to its own practitioners. This perception can expand one's horizons by positioning one to see more in the work than might initially meet the eye or that can be captured in a purely functional description of the job. It can shed light on just how much room there can be in teaching for individual creativity and imagination, notwithstanding less than ideal institutional conditions. As the testimony of the four teachers suggests, the idea of vocation turns the focus of perception in such a way that the challenges and the complexity in teaching become *sources of interest* in the work, rather than barriers or frustrating obstacles to be overcome. Teaching becomes not a string of annoying "problems" to be dealt with—having to create lessons, develop sound instructional methods, evaluate students' work, and more— but rather an open-ended series of new opportunities and possibilities.

I employ "interest" in the sense in which Dewey (1897/1973) develops the term. Interest constitutes more than "preference," argues Dewey, say for one brand of soft drink over another. It has a much more substantive relation to who the person is. The interest one shows in some larger concern or issue helps to shape the person's beliefs, convictions, and attitudes. Interest draws out the person's mind and imagination. It fuels greater curiosity, fascination, and even wonder. It implies not a detached stance toward the object but an involved one, such that one's interest influences how one sees that object and orients oneself to it. The four teachers we have met reveal an interest in a shared object: teaching. Their engagement with it, seen in both their classroom work and in their reflections on it, makes possible their having a positive influence on students—much more so than would a detached stance, in which one fulfills the terms of teaching in a strictly bureaucratic manner. The teachers' testimony reveals a reciprocal relation between interest and success in the classroom. On the one hand, their active interest in the work provokes them to take students that much more seriously and to try new and better ways of working with them. On the other hand, the very act of developing these improved approaches deepens and animates their interest in teaching.

Personal Agency and Noninterchangeability

I argued in Chapter 1 that to regard teaching as a vocation is to entertain the possibility that one has something to offer to it that nobody else can provide. It implies that one has a potentially unique and valuable contribution to make. Of course to perceive oneself as noninterchangeable with others, or as irreplaceable, could breed arrogance. Such an attitude is ill-suited to the work of teaching. However, understood through the concept of vocation, the perception that one has something distinctive to bring means appreciating that the webs of meaning one can trigger as teacher cannot be replicated by another. In the previous chapter I argued that those webs can extend well beyond the purview of the teacher—even beyond the teacher's lifetime. To presume, as teacher, that one is noninterchangeable with other practitioners can lead not to an overweening sense of self-importance, but rather to a conviction that one can make a difference in the classroom and that endeavoring to make that difference is worth the trouble.

However, a critic might reply that this thesis is more appropriate for describing parents or friends. Everyone can quickly agree that one set of parents is noninterchangeable with another. Most persons would probably say the same thing about their friends. But teachers? Are Ms. Payton, Mr. Peters, Mr. James, and Ms. Smith really no more interchangeable than are our parents and friends? Doesn't that presume that teachers play as large a role in students' lives as these persons? That is too strong a claim, the critic might charge. He or she might ask us to consider the work of professionals. Professionals who are well educated and well trained and who adhere to the code of conduct of the profession are interchangeable in a very important sense. The profession does not stand or fall based on the conduct of any one member but on the collective conduct of all. In theory, each professional should be able to take over the tasks of his or her peers if given advance notice and preparation. The critic might insist that from the perspective of the broader public service and functions they fulfill, good doctors, good nurses, good lawyers, *and* good teachers are quite interchangeable. Moreover, the critic might add, the argument in this book itself seems to imply that the practice of teaching has a larger significance than the efforts of any single practitioner. That being so, one can conclude that teachers are interchangeable so long as the practice itself flourishes along with the society in which it is embedded.

This argument has the ring of common sense. It appears obvious that in the functional and professional language the critic employs, teachers are interchangeable. With proper preparation and time, Ms. Smith could take over Ms. Payton's duties and vice versa. Furthermore, the analysis of vocation in this book shows that the four teachers share certain qualities as persons and as teachers that enable them to achieve success. For example, as we have seen they bring to bear patience, attentiveness, energy, and, at important moments, courage. They reveal an ability to reflect on what they do and a capacity to grow and improve as teachers. One might conclude that the important lesson of this book is not that each teacher is unique but that all teachers should have these dispositions and the appropriate preparation for the work. Thus, one might join the critic and ask: What is gained by suggesting teachers are noninterchangeable?

That question can be turned around by replying, What would it imply *not* to adopt this posture? What would it mean to perceive teachers as replaceable or as interchangeable with one another? For one thing, that stance might mean abandoning the language of vocation developed in this book— but not by replacing it with the language of profession. Rather, it could lead back to the popular understanding of "vocational education," in which one prepares for the discrete tasks of a wage-based job. In Chapter 1, I characterized a "job" as an activity comprising repetitive doings whose content is not shaped by those performing it. To describe teaching in these terms would be to equate it with labor on an assembly line, wherein one laborer is easily interchangeable with another because the requirements are all predefined and there is little need for personal judgment or reflection. However, as documented in this book, the practice of teaching cannot be reduced in such a fashion without desiccating it of its larger intellectual and moral meaning. A number of educators have argued that institutional imperatives in the educational system threaten to convert teaching into a "deskilled" form of labor (Apple, 1979; Callahan, 1962).

The critic might reply that this scenario is precisely why we need to focus on the ideal of a profession. That ideal, the critic might argue, implies neither the deskilling of teachers nor, in contrast, the claim that they are noninterchangeable. Rather, it sparks a recognition that one is part of a larger endeavor, a perspective that can in turn fuel professional conduct. I argued a similar point in the previous chapter. I suggested that vocation and practice are symbiotic and that neither is the same thing as "working in a school." Teachers would have no medium in which to work without the practice. Yet the practice would itself disappear without imaginative, active individuals to carry it forward into the next generation.

But vocation and profession are not symbiotic. A profession such as law or medicine can carry on without its practitioners' conceiving their work in vocational terms. Professionals can discharge their duties without entertaining the possibility that their work might form a part of their identity as persons. Some critics of contemporary law, medicine, and other professions argue that this state of affairs is precisely what has gone wrong with the professions, rendering them, so the argument goes, aloof from genuine social need. Such critics allege that the professions have erected bureaucratic and political barriers between their practitioners and the public (Gotz, 1988; Labaree, 1992). They claim that the professions concern themselves in an unbalanced way with issues of status, prestige, and reward. Defenders of the idea of profession counter that because professions are susceptible to corruption does not mean we ought to abandon what they stand for or slight their achievements. Rather, it means they should be continually reformed and renewed, and that the profession's own members should take the lead in the political task of articulating and defending their work publicly (Brown, 1994). Such critics might point out that the idea of vocation can be corrupted too, if, for example, it becomes equated with a sentimental and purely idiosyncratic conception of teaching. They might claim that teachers are weak politically, and that the sense of vocation may prove ineffectual unless and until teachers fashion themselves into a socially recognized organization with the power and prestige of other professions.

It is beyond the scope of this book to enter the debate about whether teaching should be seen as a profession, a debate being carried on vigorously today (Burbules & Densmore, 1991a, 1991b; Goodlad et al., 1990; Gotz, 1988; Herbst, 1989; Labaree, 1992; Sockett, 1993; Sykes, 1991). My point is that the concepts "profession" and "vocation" are neither identical nor dependent on each other. Terms like vocation or calling are rarely listed at all in the indices of important books on the nature of the professions (Abbott, 1988; Freidson, 1994; Kimball, 1992). That fact alone attests to the distinctive concerns the two ideas highlight. "Profession" sheds light on the functions an organized occupation serves in a given society as well as the purposes and aims that undergird those functions (Emmet, 1958). The concept takes one's vision away from what individuals do and spotlights the broad economic and political tapestry of a society against which the social division of work takes place (Abbott, 1988; Freidson, 1994). In contrast, vocation is by its nature a personalized notion, although I have shown how it articulates with public service. In practice, persons with vocational orientations need not and often do not worry about professional interests such as higher compensation, public recognition, political power and prestige, and so forth. Such issues are almost completely absent in the testimony of the four teachers described in this book. Their talk and their actions are focused on their students and on what they are trying to teach them. Their rewards and their motivation derive from considerations "internal to the practice of teaching. In brief, as the analysis in previous chapters shows, their language is that of vocation—an idiom that takes us *into*, not away from, their experience as individuals. In this respect the idea of vocation operates like others that help capture the motivation and ethos of persons who serve other people (cf. Colby & Damon, 1992; Coles, 1993; Wuthnow, 1991). The terminologies of job, occupation, and profession are of limited assistance here. A language is needed that recognizes and calls attention to the aims, the vision, and the actions of teachers who bring a sense of service to what they do. I have sought to help provide that language in this book.

The premise that teachers are noninterchangeable takes on importance when one grants that many teachers do more than simply fill a role in the system. In varying ways, all four teachers we have met began their careers with a functional orientation toward teaching—"how do I get the job done (and survive the difficulties of getting used to it)?" Over the years, however, that orientation has evolved to take into account larger relationships between themselves, their subject matter, and their students. As they gained experience, they increasingly came to shape the role of teacher rather than merely to occupy it. They began to understand students, and teaching, in richer and broader terms. These changes did not make their work easier or lighter to bear. On the contrary, they rendered it more complex, more demanding, and, at times, more confusing and frustrating. Ms. Payton elected to do more than simply distribute worksheets to her upper-grade students. But that very act, in itself, created whole new difficulties for her. She struggled to find effective ways to connect with the students and to construct an appropriate curriculum for them. Mr. James believed his students might prosper if provided the opportunity to study mathematics in a classroom setting. But that attempt to extend his teaching repertoire landed him in new problems. Now, he suddenly had to learn and implement whole-group teaching strategies when he had spent his entire career working individually with students. The changes the four teachers report undergoing reveal the ongoing challenge of balancing the familiar with the new, as well as of maintaining confidence and a sense of efficacy while taking such chances.

As the four teachers report, the personal fulfillment one can derive from taking risks is great. But the unanticipated frustrations and difficulties are equally real, as their testimony also affirms. Yet the teachers describe an increased rather than a diminished sense of commitment to teaching. The analysis in previous chapters suggests that as they recognized what teaching could mean—as they perceived larger possibilities in it for being a force for good—they grew that much more engaged with it. One might say that as their vocational orientation toward the work took shape, so too did their awareness that they could push themselves further, that they had neither exhausted nor even discovered fully their capacity to teach.

Tolstoy's story "The Three Questions," which is a well-known version of an old fable, sheds light on the emergence—or the recognition, depending on the angle of vision—of vocation in teaching. One day a king decides that, henceforth, he would never fail at anything if only he could get an answer to three questions: What are the most important things to do in life? When is the right time to undertake them? and Who are the right (and wrong) people to deal with in so doing? He promised a large reward to any person who could provide him answers. But the learned people who came to him from far and wide offered conflicting advice, which confused and annoyed the king and so he heeded none of it. Instead, he disguised himself as a peasant and went into the woods to visit an old hermit renowned for his insight. He found the hermit digging a garden. Noticing the man's frailty and fatigue, the king took over the digging. He dug for hours. All the while the hermit said nothing in reply to his questions.

Suddenly, just as the sun was setting, an injured man staggered out of the forest. He had been stabbed in the stomach. The king tended his wound and carried him into the hermit's hut. After settling him in, the tired king fell deep asleep. The next morning he awoke to find the now healing stranger gazing at him intently. The man confessed he had been lying in ambush to kill the king for injuries to his family the king's men had inflicted years before. The man had waited and waited in the woods, but the king never returned from the hermit. When he went looking for him, he stumbled on the king's soldiers, who recognized him and wounded him before he got away. The man begged for reconciliation, which the king was happy to grant. Finally, before taking his leave, the king once more asked the hermit his three questions. The hermit, bent over while sowing seeds, looked up at him. "You have already been answered," he said calmly. The king was dumbfounded. The hermit continued:

> Had you not taken pity on my weakness yesterday and dug these beds for me, instead of turning back alone, that fellow would have assaulted you, and you would have regretted not staying with me. Therefore, the most important time was when you were digging the beds; I was the most important man; and the most important pursuit was to do good to me. And later when the man came running to us, the most important time was when you were taking care of him, for if you had not bound up his wound, he would have died without having made peace with you; therefore he was the most important man, and what you did for him was the most important deed. Remember then: there is only one important time—*Now*. And it is important because it is the only time we have dominion over ourselves; and the most important man is *he with whom you are*, for no one can know whether or not he will ever have dealings with any other man; and the most important pursuit is *to do good to him*, since it is for that purpose alone that man was sent into this life. (Dunnigan, 1962, pp. 87–88)

Tolstoy's story reveals the educational value of holding one's experience up to the light of self-reflection and questioning. The king may not have had formal answers to his three questions. But when it came time to act, he knew what to do, even though he was not aware that he knew what to do. He sought a blueprint from elsewhere when the "answers" were in front of his own nose. He stayed to assist the hermit when another person, put in his place, might have simply walked away on receiving no reply. At the same time, someone else put into the shoes of the hermit might have been only too quick to offer advice, thereby eliminating an invaluable learning experience for the king—giving rise to the thought that perhaps kings and hermits are no more interchangeable than are teachers.

The four teachers we met have asked questions of themselves since they first began to teach. Over time, as their testimony attests, they not only realized what teaching entails in practice as contrasted with theory. They also discovered how they could be successful, in light of their strengths and aims, in helping students learn and grow. They had no formula to guide their teaching, no equivalent of answers to "the three questions." However, like the king, they cared about such questions. They came to care about teaching. That disposition alone seems to have provided them solid ground to stand on when dealing with the difficulties of the job. It suggests that the willingness to ask questions often signals that solutions already lie within one's grasp.

Every teacher will feel compelled from time to time to ask questions like the king's. As pointed out at the start of this chapter, one may occasionally long for a machine to tell one what to do: for example, how to reach *this* student *now* and with *what* curricular content and *which* instructional approach. As I argued, no machine could possibly provide meaningful answers to such questions. In the absence of a wise hermit next door, teachers must rely on their peers, their administrators and other school colleagues, parents, students themselves, and their own best judgment. They cannot simply mimic what another person has done. No other teacher or adult has the kind of understanding *this* teacher has of *this* student at *this* time. That understanding may be defective or inadequate. It will certainly never be complete, and so can always be improved. But it is a condition for communication between teacher and student and, consequently, is a prerequisite to successful teaching. No other person can simply "take over" a teacher's understandings of and relations with students. Those who have performed substitute teaching in schools can quickly affirm this point.

Teachers are not interchangeable because nobody can assume another person's character. As granted earlier, with proper time and preparation Ms. Smith could perform Ms. Payton's tasks and duties. But Ms. Smith cannot become Ms. Payton, nor vice versa—an obvious point, perhaps, yet one that the idea of vocation illuminates. All four teachers reveal that to them, the practice constitutes more than completing a predefined or imposed list of tasks and duties. All four infuse their everyday work with qualities that are distinctive to them and that define them as individuals. Virtually every remark they make and every act they undertake in the classroom is expressive of the persons they are. Their work embodies their vision of teaching, their beliefs about students and what they need, and their moral character as individuals. Their conduct shows how thoroughly interlaced their intellectual and moral judgments are in the act of teaching.

The teachers' example underscores the irreducible fact that the person who occupies the role of teacher makes all the difference. Were teachers to perceive their work as if it were a vocation—a notion I take up in the next section—they might find it easier to hold on to this truth and to make it work for them. To see oneself as noninterchangeable with others is to enrich what one does as teacher with that much more significance. In turn, as we have seen in previous chapters, the more aware one is of what one is doing and its possible meanings, the more attentive and prepared one will become as teacher. Just as the hermit mirrored back to the king his own actions, so the idea of vocation and all that has been said about it in this book can be a mirror for teachers, especially when they face hard questions about how and whether to carry on.

TREATING THE PRACTICE AS A VOCATION

Previous research has shown that many persons enter teaching for idealistic purposes (Cohen, 1991; Cohn & Kottkamp, 1993; Lortie, 1975; Serow, Eaker, & Forrest, 1994). They want to work with young people, to have a positive influence on them, and to pass on what they know and care for. Previous research also suggests that successful teachers conceive their work in broader than purely functional terms (Bullough et al., 1991; Dollase, 1992; Macrorie, 1984). The analysis undertaken in this book implies that without an inner motivation to serve, it will be that much more difficult for teachers to avoid the temptations all practitioners confront: to just "cover" the material in a mechanical fashion (Ms. Smith worries about this "trap"); to accept low expectations of one's students (Ms. Payton in particular struggles against this); to abandon public expectations and do what one pleases (for example, in the notorious manner of a Miss Jean Brodie [Spark, 1961]). To fall prey to such temptations is to jettison one's obligations to the practice of teaching. As we have seen, the practice calls on teachers to be active, imaginative, and responsive to the complex demands of the work.

An initial sense of vocation is more vital with respect to "hearing" that call than is a theoretical understanding of what the concept entails. This means, for example, that prospective teachers need not articulate in precise terms a vocational philosophy prior to entering the classroom. To insist on that would be like expecting a beginning teacher to appreciate the nuances of teaching in as sophisticated a manner as do the experienced practitioners we have met. Such a demand would be as peculiar as asking prospective parents to describe what raising a family is like before they have actually done so. If they themselves grew up in a family, they may be able to say quite a bit about it—just as any would-be teacher who has been to school can describe teaching at length. However, as Mr. Peters emphasizes, such talk will be quite unlike talk based on actual practice. "You're in a classroom with teachers your whole life," he contends, "but teaching doesn't just 'rub off.'" It takes the crucible of experience to test and give shape to one's sense of calling.

Consequently, rather than insisting on evidence of a vocational philosophy, it would seem more appropriate to seek evidence of intelligent, practical resourcefulness—the kind that makes it possible to realize vocation *in practice* as contrasted with in theory. Does the prospective teacher know what she will say and do the first five minutes of her first class? Does she know where the public library nearest to her school is? Does he know where to obtain inexpensive supplies? What would he say if students asked him why he wanted to teach his particular subject rather than another? The enactment of vocation does presuppose a certain "creative potential" on the part of the individual (Emmet, 1958). With respect to teaching, however, that potential may make its first appearance in how one responds to these familiar and practical questions. For most teachers, it is through the everyday aspects of teaching that they first forge educational connections with their students, which in turn can bring to life in a concrete way their sense of vocation.

At this point a reader might demur: If teachers need not profess vocation, why talk about the idea at all? A central premise of this book is that contemplating what vocation implies—"looking in its mirror," as I have put it—can better position teachers to perceive what the work involves. It can enable them to begin the task of balancing the obligations built into the practice with their own hopes and aims. It can assist them in anticipating the moral, the personal, and the intellectual aspects of the vocation that have been addressed at length in previous chapters. Such reflection can be valuable, not as a blueprint for what to expect or for what to do, but to sensitize and alert one to what is taking place, in oneself as well as in the classroom. In short, it can be useful from the very start to develop the habit of critical reflection, so that that habit rather than, say, one of uncritical acceptance of the tried and known guides one's efforts.

Moreover, the fact remains that until a teacher has come to grips with his or her convictions and capacities, there will be difficult times of uncertainty in the classroom. As the teachers we have met so openly attest, every practitioner is bound to stumble and fall, perhaps many times. In this light teachers are like characters in a timeless play whose script was written long before they took the classroom stage. Neither they, nor teacher educators, nor the best school principals in the world, can prevent their learning numerous lessons the hard way. Previous research has shown that many beginning teachers do not remain in the classroom longer than a few years (Carnegie Forum on Education, 1986; Lanier & Little, 1986; Yee, 1990). Metaphorically, they do not appear to get out of "Act I." Many leave for understandable reasons. Some realize their calling is elsewhere; some find they do not care for the work; others discover that practical considerations outweigh their commitment to teaching. However, one reason for exiting cited time and again is the difficulty teachers have of reconciling their hopes with the reality of having to work with large numbers of students who bring to the classroom varying degrees of interest and readiness to learn, and this in schools that sometimes cannot or do not offer much backing (or whose practices actually interfere with teachers' aims). In brief, some persons leave teaching because of their experience of being overwhelmed by students and of receiving little institutional and system support (Johnson, 1990; McLaughlin et al., 1990; Yee, 1990).

As I highlighted in the previous chapter, a sense of service by itself can rarely see one through challenging conditions. One needs at least some degree of institutional backing, just as one needs sound preparation to perform the work itself. Lacking either, one may face the predicament of Mr. James, who from one point of view is forced to become a finger in the dike—hardly a position from which to make a perceptible difference in the world. His difficulties attest to the inadequacy of a sense of service considered in isolation from one's preparation to teach and one's institutional context.

However, Mr. James's efforts reveal the importance of that sensibility, a point I also underscored in Chapter 6. Mr. James's conduct suggests that there are at least two ways to perceive his situation. One is as a holding action until the problem passes by—until, in blunt terms, his unruly and disabled students simply leave the system. The other is to regard what he does not as a reaction to hopeless circumstances but rather as an *active* response to certain possibilities. Mr. James acts as if he can and will make a difference in his students' lives. That conviction enables him to work patiently and persistently with young people whom many other teachers find unbearable. That Mr. James finds success with some of his students attests to the direct, practical value of his desire to serve. Of course not just anyone could perform as he does. My purpose in recalling his experience is not to hold up as a model for others to follow his willingness to work with students with special needs. To advocate that course of action would distort the idea of vocation. That idea does not imply self-abnegation or self-sacrifice, much less the notion that teaching is a cloistered act. Neither Mr. James nor the other three practitioners we met see themselves in those terms.

The point is that by acting *as if* one had a vocation, one will test in a more adequate way one's suitability and fit with teaching. One may leave the practice, perhaps sooner rather than later. But by entertaining seriously what vocation implies, one will at least leave on one's own terms rather than having been pushed out by external forces or pressures generated by the built-in difficulties of the work. Better to leave teaching having learned from it than to leave with a feeling of bitterness or defeat—or, in contrast, with a feeling that the work is boring or mundane. As I have argued, looking into the mirror of vocation can reveal the complexity and the fascination of teaching in a way no purely occupational language can. Whether one stays or goes, the ideal is to gain from teaching—as from any practice, for that matter—an enlarged sense of human possibility rather than a diminished one. The analysis in this book suggests that one's self-perception and one's sense of service will strongly influence that outcome. Many persons do leave teaching with a powerful belief in its value to society and an equally strong affection for what it has provided them personally. Many such persons take on new positions such as counselor, principal, district administrator, curriculum specialist, researcher, or teacher educator (Ducharme, 1993).

Assuming for the moment that one is uncertain of one's commitment to teaching, what does it mean, in practice, to act "as if" one had a sense of vocation? Ms. Smith sheds light on an answer. More than once in her career she has urged her students, as she puts it, to "fake it until you make it." She has encouraged students to feign attention and not distract others so that classroom lessons can proceed. She explains that what often happens is that such students will then "make it." They will become engaged and interested in the academic topics on the floor. She implies that if one is willing to adopt such a posture—in the purely behavioral sense of the term—one positions oneself to learn in the classroom.

Ms. Smith's viewpoint is widely shared by teachers, not to mention parents, coaches, counselors, and others who interact with young people. Teachers at all levels of education believe that in order to learn, students must adopt a physical posture that makes it possible for them to listen to others and to participate. This does not mean that such behavior has importance in and of itself. Rather, the behavior carries meaning in light of the educational purposes of classrooms. Ms. Smith urges her students to listen to one another not because she wishes to show off her power, but because she believes in the value of what they can learn from her, from the curriculum, and from each other. Her stance recalls the distinction often drawn in discussions of human conduct between behavior and action (MacIntyre, 1984; Polkinghorne, 1983; Taylor, 1985a, 1985b). Behavior describes easily observable physical movement: raising hands, shifting around in one's seat, walking to the blackboard, and so forth. Action takes into account the possible intentions that underlie what may otherwise appear to be mere behavior. Action describes the event of a student raising a hand in order to *contribute* to discussion; it describes the event of shifting in one's seat because one wants to *listen* to a classmate; it describes going to the blackboard to *share* one's answer with the class. In brief, Ms. Smith's colloquialism, to fake it until you make it, underscores the fact that behavior can often evolve into action. Accepting the teacher's request to listen to others can turn into purposive, intentional involvement in the activity rather than merely a passive tolerance or active dislike of it.

As teachers would be the first to attest, not all student actions embody desirable intentions. Students may shift in their seats to tease or distract one another. They may raise their hands simply to get attention rather than to contribute something meaningful to the class. Neither behavior nor action is inherently good or bad in its own right. The issue depends on such things as personality, prior conduct, purpose, and context. In addition, while behavior can evolve into action, the opposite can occur as well. If a teacher is poorly prepared or does not care about students or the subject at hand, students may lose interest and their actions may evolve into behavior. In such circumstances, they may move from "making" it to "faking" it. That result can happen to teachers themselves. They may begin their careers engaged with the practice, but lose interest and involvement over time.

However, my concern here is with those who want to teach but who may harbor doubts about doing so. As the testimony of the four teachers underscores, that feeling appears to be widespread in the field. The analysis in previous chapters affirms the fact that uncertainty and doubt accompany teaching, even for many veterans. Ms. Payton and her colleagues suggest that the more successful and dedicated one becomes as teacher, the more one's doubts may actually grow. One may overcome and dissolve some concerns and fears (e.g., "Will I survive") only to see those replaced by a new set of uncertainties.

To act *as if* one has a vocation positions one to "make it" as teacher. To act as if one were enthusiastic, interested, committed, can make it possible for those very qualities to take seed and grow. To act as if there were nothing more important in the world, at that very moment in the classroom, than working with students can motivate a level of teaching one might otherwise never realize one could perform. To accept this call—of acting as if one had a call—can override belief itself, especially if one's beliefs about teaching are governed by anxiety and uncertainty about one's ability and about whether teaching is the right thing to be doing. Treating the work as a calling can help one gain a purchase over those unknowns and doubts, rather than having them control one.

Ms. Smith sheds light on what can result from not treating teaching in larger than functional terms. She describes how disastrously class transpired one day when she substituted for a colleague who was home ill. "[It] was a terrible lesson," Ms. Smith says about her own performance, "because kids were engaged in all these really terrible behaviors and I wasn't calling them on anything. I wasn't present." By not being "present," Ms. Smith means that she acted as if she were a mere hired hand, obligated to walk in, deliver the curriculum, and, as she says, "that's it." She explains that when one adopts this stance, one "gets it bad." One feels alienated and frustrated, she says, squandering one's time and energy and that of students. "And I don't even know," she concludes, "to what extent my disregard for their bad behavior brought on their bad behavior. I'm sure there was a huge interaction going on there." Ms. Smith's experience, which each of the other three teachers could corroborate, illuminates how forbidding classroom teaching can become if one keeps oneself at a distance from the role—if one permits a gap to grow between what one does and the very convictions, hopes, and curiosity that may have led one to consider the practice in the first place.

I have responded to the question of whether teaching must be a vocation by arguing that a sense of service, however inchoate it may be, is more crucial than a full-blown theory or philosophy of it. Particularly for those unsure of themselves and of their commitment, I have advanced the idea of regarding oneself and the work as if one had a calling. I have described some benefits of conceiving teaching in those terms. I have suggested that doing so will enable teachers to realize more fully than would otherwise be possible the values inherent in the work. This argument complements the conclusions of Chapter 6, which suggested that teachers may benefit from thinking of themselves as connected not simply to a particular institution but to a larger practice with a rich history and tradition.

However, there is another response to the question that heads this chapter, one that has a ring more uncompromising than invitational to it. According to this viewpoint, teachers make an enormous difference in what the next generation will know and believe. Teachers influence the kind of persons the next generation will become. Consequently, the argument might go, it does not really matter whether a teacher sees the work as a job or as a calling. What matters is that teachers owe their students the dedication implied by the idea of vocation. That allegiance comes with the role. To act otherwise is to render a disservice to the practice, to students, to society, and, one might add, to oneself.

If one thinks of one's own children or children one knows and cares for, this argument becomes dramatically compelling. How could it not? Of course one wants the most talented and most dedicated people possible to take on the role of teacher. Moreover, to accept narrow rather than broad goals as teacher seems to imply shortchanging oneself unnecessarily—indeed, attenuating the very meaning of one's life. Why settle for that sad prospect? "Nothing is more tragic," wrote Dewey (1916/1966), "than failure to discover one's true business in life, or to find that one has drifted or been forced by circumstance into an uncongenial calling" (p. 308). In light of these perspectives, one might not hesitate to declare: Yes, teaching *must* be a vocation. For their own sake as well as for the sake of those they educate, teachers must commit themselves to their work in vocational terms, or else they should go elsewhere for employment.

Two rejoinders argue against these otherwise appealing claims. One is that vocation, as I have shown in this book, typically materializes and takes shape over time. It cannot be forced by others, or invented out of thin air, or "chosen" as one would select one consumer brand over another. Nobody can wake up in the morning and declare, "I think I'll make teaching my vocation today." Vocation comes to life as one comes to grips with the work, as one meets its challenges and realizes the personal fulfillment that comes from doing so. For many teachers, the quality and timing of that outcome— should it happen at all—cannot be predicted in advance. Consequently, to insist that would-be teachers conceive teaching as a vocation may be to ask them to imagine what they cannot yet know.

A second and related problem is that to demand that teachers have a vocational orientation from the start comes perilously close to the idea of administering a "vocational oath" to all who would enter the ranks. At the very least, such a prospect would be ironic. It would constitute an external imposition of what has been shown in this book to be in great part an internal motivation. Even if the suggestion could be defended, who would be equipped to assemble the oath? Who could conceive the appropriate language? Doesn't that notion return us to the impossibility of finding an all-knowing, all-wise programmer who could invent the perfect moral and intellectual teaching machine? The idea of an oath also raises discomforting images of fanaticism that contrast with the image conveyed in this book of teachers who are interested, open-minded, self-critical, and fallible, all qualities that illuminate the possibilities in treating teaching as a vocation.

Dewey's well-known tract "My Pedagogic Creed" (1897/1974) sheds light on why the practice of teaching is ill-suited to the administration of oaths. Dewey describes a powerful vision of the potential of education and of teaching. He states the beliefs and the values that comprise his vision, which center on lifelong growth as the aim of education. That Dewey did not employ the title "My Pedagogic Oath" attests to the fact that a term like "creed" comes much closer to what vocation implies than does the idea of an oath. A pedagogic creed is a set of convictions and hopes that undergird one's work as teacher (Jackson et al., 1993). Unlike an oath, which has a fixed aspect to it, a creed can evolve and become enlarged over time—just as can the sense of vocation. In this book, we have met four persons who have adopted a creedal posture as teachers, even though they do not employ that term. To judge from what they say and from what they do in the classroom, they believe in teaching, they believe in young people, and they are willing to learn. They have grown as teachers through the use of their own imagination and effort, and through accepting the responsibilities and obligations that accompany the work.

Their example suggests that what teachers *can* be asked to do is to look into the mirror of vocation and to ponder all that the term implies. Other things being equal, teachers need more than anything else an inner urge to serve and practical intelligence to bring that feeling to life—or, more to the point, to the lives of their students. It goes against the idea of vocation itself to set prior boundaries around the scope of this inner urge. As we have seen in such abundant detail, the sense of vocation differs widely from teacher to teacher in its nature and in its expression in the classroom. The conclusion to draw from these facts is that persons who aspire to teach and those who are now teaching need not profess vocation in order to be permitted entry to classrooms. They might instead be asked to reflect regularly on why they would want to profess anything at all—why they would want to teach or to keep teaching. The four teachers show that while those questions are never easy to answer—even for veterans—having at one's disposal a vocational language makes them less daunting than might first meet the eye.

PROSPECTS FOR VOCATION

This book has featured four teachers who put at the center of their vision of teaching the hope of having a positive influence on students. In pursuit of that ambition, they reach beyond the functional requirements of the job. They transform the occupation with personal imagination, and thereby position themselves both to be of public service and to realize personal fulfillment—the "crossroads" where vocation emerges, as described in Chapter 1.

However, as we have seen, the institutions in which they work place formidable obstacles and barriers in the way of vocation. In addition to having to work with large numbers of students—or unusually demanding ones, as in Mr. James's case—the teachers confront a maze of bureaucratic rules and conditions, encompassing everything from short class periods (which often spark the feeling one must hurry through a lesson) to extensive paperwork. On top of these institutional demands is the ever-present challenge of learning how to interact with peers and administrators who may have a different view of educational work. For example, recall Mr.

James's testimony about the disdainful way some colleagues perceive and treat his students. The fact that those teachers may have hit the mark to an extent—namely, that some of his students are not going to succeed in school—only intensifies Mr. James's predicament. Were he on a desert island with his students, he might be able to achieve greater results. But though teachers may be able to create those kinds of conditions for short periods of time, sooner or later they and their students must rejoin the public world of their school and beyond.

Throughout this book, I have identified these and other tensions between the idea of teaching as a vocation and the institutional realities of the educational system. I have argued that vocation and practice are not identical with being employed in a particular institution. The vocation of teaching is not the same thing as "working in a school"; and the practice of teaching is far older than and will long outlast any school in existence today. Nor are those concepts and what they embody interchangeable with other current frameworks for thinking about teaching—professional, bureaucratic, occupational, to name only a few. In light of this analysis, the question may have forced itself to the front for some readers: Can teaching realistically be a vocation? Given the institutional circumstances of education today, is it truly possible and viable to treat one's work in the classroom as a vocation?

Some critics doubt that possibility, save perhaps for unusually strong and talented individuals. "It is no longer possible in our society," asserts Ellul (1972), "to incarnate a vocation concretely" (p. 12). Ellul takes the somber view that bureaucratic and technological imperatives have overwhelmed social institutions, making it virtually impossible for a person to enact a calling. In his view, pressures of efficiency, predictability, and control undermine the potential for work within institutions to become a vocation. Moreover, Ellul implies, those pressures present a more disquieting problem than that described previously of having to reconcile social with vocational ethics—that is, of balancing public obligation with personal conviction. Rather, suggests Ellul, the naturally conservative tendencies of institutions make persons with a sense of vocation potentially threatening to them. Such persons may want to do something "different." They may want to be creative, and to break with or extend established ways of working. In the terms employed in this book, such persons may want to serve the practice of teaching and all that it represents rather than simply to ally themselves with the habits of a particular institution. As Ellul observes, that posture can be perceived as a threat to what is comfortable and familiar, rather than as a healthy and welcome challenge to what may be old and outworn.

According to Ellul (1972), "a calling no longer concerns what we had so long thought it did—an entry into an order (of life, of the world)" (p. 16).

By "order" of life, Ellul means something akin to the idea of a practice as that term has been employed in this book. Ellul implies, as does MacIntyre (1984) in his path-breaking discussion of the concept, that practices have been sundered in today's world by the rise of bureaucratically driven institutions. According to this view, doctors, nurses, lawyers, and teachers cannot fulfill the terms of vocation because the terms of their everyday work are determined by institutions and by regulations and rules prescribed through political processes in which practitioners often play little part. Given this perspective, Ellul believes it to be an illusion that vocation can be meaningfully enacted in institutions like schools. He advises persons to seek a calling outside of institutions and to pursue their life's meaning there. He describes his volunteer efforts with wayward youngsters in a neighborhood youth center undertaken outside his working hours in the university (he does not clarify why this youth center should not also be considered an institution).

The four teachers we have met attest to how bureaucratic rules and structures can inhibit their work. They describe moments of frustration with the system, and moments of doubt about being able to make a difference in their students' lives. However, they do not perceive their schools—or experience working in them—as the oppressive institutions Ellul describes. Quite the contrary. Their schools are places where they can seek out helpful colleagues, encouraging administrators, and engaged parents. These and other fellow adults help provide the friendship and the intellectual stimulus so necessary to sustaining one's dedication to the practice. Moreover, in purely practical terms their schools provide them jobs with salaries and other benefits that enable them to live. In brief, the teachers appreciate what their schools make possible even while struggling with the problems those very institutions create for them. Their testimony suggests that Ellul and other like-minded critics may harbor an overly romantic view of vocation and practice. The enactment of vocation, and the sustaining of a practice like teaching, has never been a simple or easy matter—neither in today's world nor in the past. The moment one steps into public life, as all teachers do when they walk through the doors of their schools and classrooms, one enters an unpredictable world that will require compromise and adaptation. To be with other people, and to engage in a purposive endeavor with them, automatically creates uncertain conditions.

The teachers we have met and others like them might reply to Ellul's viewpoint by saying that, however well-intentioned it may be, it merely adds to an ethos of pessimism or, worse, hopelessness. Teaching is bound to fail when conducted in a spirit of pessimism—and, certainly, of hopelessness. Teaching presupposes hope. However, hope does not mean the same thing as optimism (Havel, 1992). One may have troubling thoughts about the future and worried thoughts about one's capability to do anything about it. In short, one may not be particularly "optimistic." But being hopeful is another matter. It means that as a teacher, one can perceive one's work against a broader historical backdrop. One can keep the results of past human effort in view, and see that they were sometimes achieved in conditions far more difficult than those one faces today. One can see that teaching is an act that, when done well, fully occupies the present moment, but also always with an eye on the future.

The analysis in this book suggests that the prospects for enacting a sense of calling in teaching are as promising today as they have ever been. Are conditions for doing so ideal, or at least as supportive as they might be? Clearly not—nor have they ever been. The difficulties and problems that individual teachers face in an unwieldy system intended to serve millions of people remain formidable. One might wish that more teachers, more administrators, more policymakers, and, even, more hallway custodians (ask any school person) brought a sense of vocation to their work. One might wish that the spirit of vocation, of being of public service to others while also deriving personal fulfillment from it, permeated more of society itself. At the end of the day, however, hopeful thinking will be more productive than wishful thinking. The idea of teaching as a vocation does not provide a rose-colored lens through which to perceive education. Instead, it opens a window to the range of accomplishments accessible to any serious-minded teacher. It provides a hopeful perspective that can better position teachers to take advantage of the opportunities present circumstances afford them. As we have seen in this book, having a sense of vocation may enable teachers to identify those very opportunities in the first place.

References

Abbott, A. (1988). *The system of professions*. Chicago: University of Chicago Press.

Adams, H. (1918). *The education of Henry Adams*. Boston: Houghton Mifflin.

Altenbaugh, R. J. (Ed.). (1992). *The teacher's voice: A social history of teaching in twentieth century America*. London: Falmer.

Apple, M. (1979). *Ideology and curriculum*. London: Routledge & Kegan Paul.

Arcilla, R. V. (1994). *How can the misanthrope learn? Philosophy for education*. Paper presented at the 50th annual meeting of the Philosophy of Education Society, Charlotte, NC.

Arendt, H. (1958). *The human condition*. Chicago: University of Chicago Press.

Ashton, P. T., & Webb, R. B. (1986). *Making a difference: Teachers' sense of efficacy and student achievement*. New York: Longman.

Bailey, S. (1976). *The purposes of education*. Bloomington, IN: Phi Delta Kappa Educational Foundation.

Barber, B. R. (1992). *An aristocracy of everyone*. New York: Ballantine Books.

Beynon, J. (1985). Institutional change and career histories in a comprehensive school. In S. J. Ball & I. F. Goodson (Eds.), *Teachers' lives and careers* (pp. 158–179). London: Falmer.

Bilow, S. H. (1988). [Review of Democratic education]. *Educational Theory, 38*, 275–283.

Bolin, F. S., & Falk, J. M. (Eds.). (1987). *Teacher renewal: Professional issues, personal choices*. New York: Teachers College Press.

Boostrom, R. E., Hansen, D. T., & Jackson, P. W. (1993). Coming together and staying apart: How a group of teachers and researchers sought to bridge the "research/practice gap." *Teachers College Record, 95*, 35–44.

Booth, W. C. (1988). *The vocation of a teacher*. Chicago: University of Chicago Press.

Brann, E. T. H. (1979). *Paradoxes of education in a republic*. Chicago: University of Chicago Press.

Brown, A. (1994). *"What's in a name?": A response to "Revitalizing the idea of vocation in teaching."* Paper presented at the 50th annual meeting of the Philosophy of Education Society, Charlotte, NC.

Buchmann, M. (1989). The careful vision: How practical is contemplation in teaching? *American Journal of Education, 98*, 35–61.

Bullough, R. V., Jr., Knowles, J. G., & Crow, N. A. (1991). *Emerging as a teacher*. London: Routledge & Kegan Paul.

Burbules, N. C., & Densmore, K. (1991a). The limits of making teaching a profession. *Educational Policy, 5*, 44–63.

Burbules, N. C., & Densmore, K. (1991b). The persistence of professionalism: Breakin' up is hard to do. *Educational Policy, 5*, 150–157.

Callahan, R. E. (1962). *Education and the cult of efficiency.* Chicago: University of Chicago Press.

Calvino, I. (1986, October). Why read the classics? *New York Review of Books, 33*, 19–20.

Carnegie Forum on Education and the Economy. (1986). *A nation prepared: Teachers for the 21st century.* Washington, DC: Author.

Carpenter, P. G., & Foster, W. J. (1979). Deciding to teach. *Australian Journal of Education, 23*, 121–131.

Cedoline, A. J. (1982). *Job burnout in public education: Symptoms, causes, and survival skills.* New York: Teachers College Press.

Chambers-Schiller, L. (1979). The single woman: Family and vocation among nineteenth-century reformers. In M. Kelley (Ed.), *Woman's being, woman's place: Female identity and vocation in American history* (pp. 334–350). Boston: G. K. Hall.

Chubb, J. E., & Moe, T. M. (1990). *Politics, markets, and America's schools.* Washington, DC: The Brookings Institution.

Cohen, R. M. (1991). *A lifetime of teaching: Portraits of five veteran high school teachers.* New York: Teachers College Press.

Cohn, M. M., & Kottkamp, R. B. (1993). *Teachers: The missing voice in education.* Albany: State University of New York Press.

Colby, A., & Damon, W. (1992). *Some do care: Contemporary lives of moral commitment.* New York: The Free Press.

Coleman, J. S. (1966). *Equality of educational opportunity.* Washington, DC: U.S. Department of Health, Education, and Welfare.

Coles, R. (1993). *The call of service.* Boston: Houghton Mifflin.

Cremin, L. A. (1988). *American education: The metropolitan experience 1876–1980.* New York: Harper & Row.

Crow, G. M., Levine, L., & Nager, N. (1990). No more business as usual: Career changers who become teachers. *American Journal of Education, 98*, 197–223.

Cuban, L. (1992). *How teachers taught* (2d ed.). New York: Teachers College Press.

Cusick, P. (1973). *Inside high school: The student's world.* New York: Holt, Rinehart, & Winston.

Dewey, J. (1973). Interest in relation to the training of the will. In J. J. McDermott (Ed.), *The philosophy of John Dewey* (pp. 421–442). Chicago: University of Chicago Press. (Original work published 1897)

Dewey, J. (1974). My pedagogic creed. In R. D. Archambault (Ed.), *John Dewey on education* (pp. 427–439). Chicago: University of Chicago Press. (Original work published 1897)

Dewey, J. (1990). *The child and the curriculum.* Chicago: University of Chicago Press. (Original work published 1902)

Dewey, J. (1966). *Democracy and education.* New York: The Free Press. (Original work published 1916)

Dewey, J. (1933). *How we think.* New York: D. C. Heath and Company.

Dollase, R. H. (1992). *Voices of beginning teachers: Visions and realities.* New York: Teachers College Press.

Douglas, M. (1986). *How institutions think.* Syracuse, NY: Syracuse University Press.

Ducharme, E. R. (1993). *The lives of teacher educators.* New York: Teachers College Press.

Dunnigan, A. (Trans.). (1962). *Fables and fairy tales by Leo Tolstoy.* New York: New American Library of World Literature.

Dworkin, A. G. (1987). *Teacher burnout in the public schools.* Albany: State University of New York Press.

Eldridge, R. (1989). *On moral personhood.* Chicago: University of Chicago Press.

Eliot, G. (1985). *Middlemarch.* Harmondsworth, England: Penguin Books. (Original work published 1871–1872)

Ellul, J. (1972). Work and calling. *Katallagete, 4,* 8–16.

Emmet, D. (1958). *Function, purpose, and powers.* London: Macmillan.

Finkel, D. L., & Monk, G. S. (1983). Teachers and learning groups: Dissolution of the Atlas Complex. In C. Bouton & R. Y. Garth (Eds.), *Learning in groups* (pp. 83–97). San Francisco: Jossey-Bass.

Floden, R. E., & Clark, C. M. (1988). Preparing teachers for uncertainty. *Teachers College Record, 89,* 505–524.

Forman, M. B. (Ed.). (1935). *The letters of John Keats.* London: Oxford University Press.

Freidson, E. (1994). *Professionalism reborn.* Chicago: University of Chicago Press.

Gartner, A., & Lipsky, D. K. (1987). Beyond special education: Toward a quality system for all students. *Harvard Educational Review, 57,* 367–395.

Gilmore, P. (1983). Spelling "Mississippi": Recontextualizing a literacy-related speech event. *Anthropology and Education Quarterly, 14,* 235–255.

Goodlad, J. I. (1984). *A place called school.* New York: McGraw-Hill.

Goodlad, J. I., Soder, R., & Sirotnik, K. A. (Eds.). (1990). *The moral dimensions of teaching.* San Francisco: Jossey-Bass.

Gotz, I. L. (1988). *Zen and the art of teaching.* Westbury, NY: J. L. Wilkerson.

Green, T. F. (1964). *Work, leisure, and the American schools.* New York: Random House.

Gustafson, J. M. (1982). Professions as "callings." *Social Service Review, 56,* 501–515.

Gutmann, A. (1987). *Democratic education.* Princeton: Princeton University Press.

Hansen, D. T. (1991). Remembering what we know: The case for democratic education. *Journal of Curriculum Studies, 23,* 459–465.

Hansen, D. T. (1992). The emergence of a shared morality in a classroom. *Curriculum Inquiry, 22,* 345–361.

Hansen, D. T. (1993a). The moral importance of the teacher's style. *Journal of Curriculum Studies, 25,* 397–421.

Hansen, D. T. (1993b). From role to person: The moral layeredness of classroom teaching. *American Educational Research Journal, 30,* 651–674.

Hansen, D. T. (1994). *Shapes of the moral life in an inner-city boys' high school.*

Paper presented at the annual meeting of the American Educational Research Association, New Orleans, LA.

Hansen, D. T., Boostrom, R. E., & Jackson, P. W. (1994). The teacher as moral model. *Kappa Delta Pi Record, 31,* 24–29.

Hardy, L. (1990). *The fabric of this world.* Grand Rapids, MI: William B. Eerdmans.

Hargreaves, A. (1994). *Changing teachers, changing times: Teachers' work and culture in the postmodern age.* New York: Teachers College Press.

Hargreaves, A., & Fullan, M. G. (Eds.). (1992). *Understanding teacher development.* New York: Teachers College Press.

Havel, V. (1992). *Open letters: Selected writings 1965–1990.* New York: Vintage Books.

Hawthorne, R. K. (1992). *Curriculum in the making: Teacher choice and the classroom experience.* New York: Teachers College Press.

Heath, S. B. (1983). *Ways with words.* Cambridge: Cambridge University Press.

Henry, J. (1963). *Culture against man.* New York: Random House.

Herbst, J. (1989). *And sadly teach: Teacher education and professionalization in American culture.* Madison: University of Wisconsin Press.

Hoffman, N. (1981). *Woman's "true" profession.* New York: McGraw-Hill.

Holl, K. (1958). The history of the word vocation (Beruf). *Review and Expositor, 55,* 126–154.

Holland, J. L. (1973). *Making vocational choices: A theory of careers.* Englewood Cliffs, NJ: Prentice-Hall.

Howe, K. R., & Miramontes, O. B. (1992). *The ethics of special education.* New York: Teachers College Press.

Huberman, M., with Grounauer, M.-M., & Marti, J. (1993). *The lives of teachers.* New York: Teachers College Press.

Huebner, D. (1987). The vocation of teaching. In F. S. Bolin & J. M. Falk (Eds.), *Teacher renewal: Professional issues, personal choices* (pp. 17–29). New York: Teachers College Press.

Illich, I. (1970). *Deschooling society.* New York: Harper and Row.

Jackson, P. W. (1968). *Life in classrooms.* New York: Holt, Rinehart, & Winston.

Jackson, P. W. (1986). *The practice of teaching.* New York: Teachers College Press.

Jackson, P. W. (Ed.). (1992). *Handbook of research on curriculum.* New York: Macmillan.

Jackson, P. W., Boostrom, R. E., & Hansen, D. T. (1993). *The moral life of schools.* San Francisco: Jossey-Bass.

Jennings, N. E. (1992). *Teachers learning from policy: Cases from the Michigan reading reform.* Unpublished doctoral dissertation, Michigan State University, East Lansing, MI.

Johnson, S. M. (1990). *Teachers at work.* New York: Basic Books.

Jordan, E. (1949). *The good life.* Chicago: University of Chicago Press.

Kimball, B. A. (1992). *The "true professional ideal" in America.* Cambridge, MA: Blackwell.

Kounin, J. S. (1968). *Discipline and group management in classrooms.* New York: Holt, Rinehart, & Winston.

Labaree, D. F. (1992). Power, knowledge, and the rationalization of teaching: A genealogy of the movement to professionalize teaching. *Harvard Educational Review, 62*, 123–154.

Lanier, J. E., & Little, J. W. (1986). Research on teacher education. In M. C. Wittrock (Ed.), *Handbook of research on teaching* (3rd ed., pp. 527–569). New York: Macmillan.

Lesage, G. (1966). *Personalism and vocation.* Staten Island, NY: Alba House.

Lightfoot, S. L. (1983). The lives of teachers. In L. S. Shulman & G. Sykes (Eds.), *Handbook of teaching and policy* (pp. 241–260). New York: Longman.

Little, J. W. (1990). Conditions for professional development in secondary schools. In M. W. McLaughlin, J. E. Talbert, & N. Bascia (Eds.), *The contexts of teaching in secondary schools* (pp. 187–223). New York: Teachers College Press.

Lortie, D. C. (1975). *Schoolteacher.* Chicago: University of Chicago Press.

MacIntyre, A. (1984). *After virtue* (2nd ed.). Notre Dame: University of Notre Dame Press.

Macrorie, K. (1984). *Twenty teachers.* New York: Oxford University Press.

McDonald, J. P. (1992). *Teaching: Making sense of an uncertain craft.* New York: Teachers College Press.

McLaughlin, M. W., Talbert, J. E., & Bascia, N. (1990). *The contexts of teaching in secondary schools: Teachers' realities.* New York: Teachers College Press.

McNeil, L. M. (1986). *Contradictions of control: School structure and school knowledge.* New York: Routledge & Kegan Paul.

Midgley, M. (1991). *Can't we make moral judgements?* New York: St. Martin's Press.

Mintz, A. (1978). *George Eliot and the novel of vocation.* Cambridge: Harvard University Press.

Mitchell, D. E., Ortiz, F. I., & Mitchell, T. K. (1987). *Work orientation and job performance.* Albany: State University of New York Press.

Monk, R. (1990). *Ludwig Wittgenstein: The duty of genius.* New York: The Free Press.

Murdoch, I. (1970/1985). *The sovereignty of good.* London: Ark.

Neill, A. S. (1962). *Summerhill.* New York: Hart.

Nicholls, J. G., & Hazzard, S. P. (1993). *Education as adventure: Lessons from the second grade.* New York: Teachers College Press.

Noddings, N. (1992). *The challenge to care in schools.* New York: Teachers College Press.

Nyberg, D., & Farber, P. (1986). Authority in education. *Teachers College Record, 88*, 4–14.

Page, R. N. (1987). Lower-track classes at a college-preparatory school: A caricature of educational encounters. In G. Spindler & L. Spindler (Eds.), *Interpretive ethnography of schooling: At home and abroad* (pp. 447–472). Hillsdale, NJ: Erlbaum.

Page, R. N. (1991). *Lower-track classrooms.* New York: Teachers College Press.

Paris, C. (1993). *Teacher agency and curriculum making in classrooms.* New York: Teachers College Press.

Pavalko, R. M. (1970). Recruitment to teaching: Patterns of selection and retention. *Sociology of Education, 43*, 340–353.

Peebles, M. (1994). *Social alienation in the junior high school.* Unpublished doctoral dissertation, University of Illinois at Chicago.

Peshkin, A. (1990). *The color of strangers, the color of friends: The play of ethnicity in school and community.* Chicago: University of Chicago Press.

Pieper, J. (1952). *Leisure: The basis of culture.* New York: Pantheon Books.

Polkinghorne, D. (1983). *Methodology for the human sciences.* Albany: State University of New York Press.

Powell, A. G., Farrar, E., & Cohen, D. K. (1985). *The shopping mall high school.* Boston: Houghton Mifflin.

Rose, M. (1989). *Lives on the boundary.* New York: The Free Press.

Rosenholtz, S. J. (1989). *Teachers' workplace: The social organization of schools.* New York: Longman.

Searle, J. R. (1992). *The rediscovery of the mind.* Cambridge: MIT Press.

Sennett, R. (1980). *Authority.* New York: Alfred A. Knopf.

Serow, R. C., Eaker, D. J., & Forrest, K. D. (1994). "I want to see some kind of growth out of them": What the service ethic means to teacher-education students. *American Educational Research Journal, 31,* 27–48.

Sikes, P. J., Measor, L., & Woods, P. (1985). *Teacher careers.* London: Falmer Press.

Sirotnik, K. A. (1983). What you see is what you get: Consistency, persistency, and mediocrity in classrooms. *Harvard Educational Review, 53,* 16–31.

Smith, L. P. (1934). *All trivia.* New York: Harcourt, Brace & Company.

Sockett, H. (1988). Education and will: Aspects of personal capability. *American Journal of Education, 96,* 195–214.

Sockett, H. (1993). *The moral base for teacher professionalism.* New York: Teachers College Press.

Soltis, J. F., & Strike, K. A. (1992). *The ethics of teaching.* New York: Teachers College Press.

Spark, M. (1961). *The prime of Miss Jean Brodie.* New York: Harper and Row.

Stainback, W., & Stainback, S. (1992). *Controversial issues confronting special education.* Boston: Allyn and Bacon.

Stout, J. (1988). *Ethics after Babel.* Boston: Beacon Press.

Strike, K. A. (1991). The moral role of schooling in a liberal democratic society. *Review of Research in Education, 17,* 413–483.

Strike, K. A., & Ternasky, P. L. (Eds.). (1993). *Ethics for professionals in education.* New York: Teachers College Press.

Sykes, G. (1991). In defense of teacher professionalism as a policy choice. *Educational Policy, 5,* 137–149.

Taylor, C. (1985a). *Human agency and language.* Cambridge: Cambridge University Press.

Taylor, C. (1985b). *Philosophy and the human sciences.* Cambridge: Cambridge University Press.

Tom, A. (1984). *Teaching as a moral craft.* New York: Longman.

Tyack, D. B. (1974). *The one best system: A history of American urban education.* Cambridge: Harvard University Press.

Van Manen, M. (1991). *The tact of teaching: The meaning of pedagogical thoughtfulness.* Albany: State University of New York Press.

Waller, W. (1932). *The sociology of teaching.* New York: John Wiley and Sons.

Williams, B. (1985). *Ethics and the limits of philosophy.* Cambridge: Harvard University Press.

Wittrock, M. C. (Ed.). (1986). *Handbook of research on teaching* (3rd ed.). New York: Macmillan.

Wuthnow, R. (1991). *Acts of compassion.* Princeton: Princeton University Press.

Yee, S. M. (1990). *Careers in the classroom: When teaching is more than a job.* New York: Teachers College Press.

Index

AUTHORS

SUBJECTS

About the Author

DAVID T. HANSEN is on the faculty of the College of Education, University of Illinois at Chicago. He serves as Coordinator of the College's Secondary Education Program and is Co-Coordinator in the doctoral program in Curriculum and Instruction. He has taught at several levels including secondary school. He received his B.A. and Ph.D. degrees from the University of Chicago and his M.A. from Stanford University. Hansen is co-author (with Philip W. Jackson and Robert E. Boostrom) of *The Moral Life of Schools* (Jossey-Bass, 1993). He is Reviews Editor for the *Journal of Curriculum Studies* and was recently the recipient of a National Academy of Education Spencer Post-Doctoral Fellowship, which made possible the preparation of this book. Hansen's work focuses on the philosophy and practice of teaching.